Swami

Swami
Doug Boyd

Random House New York

Published in Association with Robert Briggs

LIBRARY OF CONGRESS CATALOGING IN PUBLICATION DATA

Boyd, Doug.   Swami.

1. Sadhus—India.   2. India—Religion.   3. Rama,
     Swami, 1925-   4. Boyd, Doug.   I. Title.
             BL2003.B6   181'.4   75-40566
                     ISBN 0-394-49603-5

Manufactured in the United States of America

9 8 7 6 5 4 3 2

First Edition

To Mike Martin

Introduction

"Swami means 'master of self,'" said Dr. Green. "Literally, the Sanskrit word means simply 'master,' I believe, but Swami Rama says that a real swami is one who has achieved self-mastery. What Swami does not mean is master of someone else. And that makes sense, doesn't it? The Hindu idea is that all of us are responsible for our own actions and their results. That's what karma is. And after all, mastery over others is only a matter of inducement or of force—some sort of temporary agreement of mutual agreement or of submission that may have nothing to do with skill or wisdom or growth. Any jerk can seem to be a master of others, but ultimately one can really master nothing other than one's own self."

It was late summer, 1970. We were sitting in Elmer Green's office at the Menninger Foundation in Topeka, Kansas, and we had just finished reading a letter to him from Swami Rama. Swami Rama had left his own ashram in northern India to offer himself as a research subject for Western scientists and medical doctors. In the spring of this year Swami Rama found the Greens—Elmer and Alyce—and performed a number of dramatic yogic demonstrations in their laboratory. Dr. Green was head of the Voluntary Controls Program at the Menninger Foundation's Research Department, and he, his wife, and their associate, Dale Walters, were pursuing their own research program on voluntary control of internal states. They were interested in mind-body relationships, in the mind's capacity to regulate physiological processes—even those bodily functions ordinarily labeled autonomic or involuntary—and the swami's demonstrations—including "stopping" his heart for seventeen seconds and producing a ten-degree temperature differential in the palm of his hand!—contributed beautifully to their investigations. The letter that we were now reading was dated April 16, 1970, and it was the swami's agreement and promise to return to the laboratory in the fall for further demonstrations. This time I would meet him and would be a part of the ongoing "Swami Rama Project"—not as a scientist, but as a personal assistant to the swami.

"Since you're adept at understanding and communicating with exotic cultures and people, you should be able to get along well with the swami," Elmer Green had told me at the outset of our meeting. "And since we're planning to provide the swami with his own office here and an official position as consultant to the project, your assistance will be greatly helpful."

The prospect of being involved in the Swami Rama Project fascinated me. Over the past several months I had been watching Eastern influence growing in the West, and I had come to see that the "New Age" that was now so often spoken of would be the concurrent result of Western growth in the East and Eastern growth in the West. For over ten years I had been working with Asians who were developing the pragmatic systems and practical skills that had always been thought of as the Western way. My involvement in the Swami Rama Project would be a chance to participate in another aspect of this same global process.

One day, years earlier, when I was camping with two Korean college students near the top of one of South Korea's highest mountains, I had a chance to get to know and learn from a high Buddhist priest, and had I pursued that possibility, I might perhaps have been sitting in a temple on some hillside instead of in Dr. Green's office in the Research Department. Near our campsite on the mountain, there was a very secluded temple where young monks were being trained; my college friends had to visit that temple to cook our breakfast. It had rained hard just before dawn, and though the sun came out by breakfast time, it was impossible to start a fire. Leaving me behind in the tent, the two friends walked the mile or so to the temple to see if they might borrow a fire to cook our rice. This temple did not welcome visitors, my friends explained as we were eating our breakfast, and they might not have been allowed to enter had they not mentioned the wet and hungry American for whom they wished to cook.

Looking up from my bowl I saw a strange robed figure in a distant tree. When the figure fell to the ground, I saw that it was a young monk, perhaps fifteen, who had been hanging by his knees from a limb, his robes falling over his head. He did this on another tree and then another, each time getting closer to where we sat. His object was apparently to get close enough for a good look at me. No doubt he had heard when my friends mentioned me at the temple. Perhaps having been raised in this secluded place he had never seen an American. My curiosity was a match for his, and I called him so we could both be satisfied. I had a series of questions for my first monk from such a temple, and I let him have them all. I asked him about right action and karma, about the wheel of births and deaths, about liberation and the meaning of enlightenment. He was surprised and uncomfortable. "I am very young," he would say, or, "You can see that I am a new aspirant." He left after that, but he was back in about an hour with a message for me. Not even glancing at me, he spoke to my companions, then hurried off to a safe distance and turned around for a long, hard stare. My Korean was weak, then, but my friends confirmed what he had said: "A very old teacher who is now visiting our temple has invited the American to the Buddhist convention to be held in Anyang on the first day of next month. There he will be recognized by someone who will show him the way to a Buddhist Master. And the Master will show him the way to the answers he is seeking."

But the real answers to the real questions belonged to another search—something that was going on in a more personal way and on a more internal dimension. What I had wanted from the young monk was something from the young monk, because the outer part of my search was a search for people, not for answers. I knew that there were monks, priests, lamas, and yogis all over the world who were possessed of a higher wisdom far beyond me. Eventually and inevitably, I would learn what they knew. What I was looking for at this time was people like me, classmates, teammates, people who were sharing my search for people. I wanted to know how many of us were conscious of where we were in the process of our evolution or had some concept of what our next steps were to be, whether we could communicate, and whether we could agree to proceed together.

I had been especially eager to achieve that communication with my peers in the Far East—not people who knew much more than I but people with whom I would be working on the same level. This was partly because I expected that new Asians and new Americans could now work more closely together, and mostly because I had been waiting a long time to talk to people with Oriental backgrounds. My grandparents had established the Life Science Publishing Company, and they and my parents studied from a personal teacher and practiced yogic disciplines. My parents' library was filled with the words and thoughts of China, Tibet, and India, and my childhood and family experience was steeped in Oriental philosophy. But never in my schooldays did I mention those things. I didn't talk about this area of my life and thoughts with my friends because then Westerners were either not interested in such things or not able to share their interests openly. My mind stored up conversations that could not be used anywhere in my social life. I longed to communicate with people about the things that seemed most interesting and meaningful to me. So when I saw the chance, I decided to spend a number of years in Korea, and I studied hard to become functional in the language because I had thought that in Korea it would perhaps be different. On the streets of Seoul I could see robed monks from distant temples, and it seemed reasonable to assume that anyone who could communicate at all with Westerners would be happy to discuss Asian thought with a Westerner. My hope was to live with people who thought and talked as traditional Asians—to surround myself not with the wise ones, but with my fellow seekers and servers, wherever they were.

Ironically, that hope was soon pushed to the back of my mind, and I became so totally involved in the Westernization of Korea—as an instructor of English, stenography, typing, and office practices, sponsor of student groups, and consultant-adviser for several universities, trading companies, and hotels —that there was no time for anything else. I did have a chance to talk with monks in various Buddhist temples after that first brief encounter with that young monk, but for more than eight years most of my days were spent in Seoul living with people who were just like Westerners or striving to become just like Westerners. They were all very eager to hear more about the United States. The Eastern ideas that interested me and that I would have preferred to talk about were not at all weird to any of them, they were simply tiresome. Such impractical concerns were certainly old-fashioned, they thought, and were probably the reason for all of Korea's contemporary problems. Americans were obviously rich and happy as a result of not having been distracted by the pursuit of wisdom.

It became apparent to me that the Westernization of the East was inevitable. It was simply irreversible fate or the natural flow of history or part of some divine plan. In any case, since it was inevitable, I felt it useful to be playing a part in helping it go smoothly—and quickly. After a few years of this work in Korea, I believed that the Westernization process was an intermediate step toward an eventual synthesis of East and West. And I came to believe that the Asian people I was able to observe so closely were really

Westerners. They were Westerners with Western pasts who for the purpose of this synthesis had been born to live their current lives in the East—as Westerners in Asian bodies.

When I returned to the United States in 1968, after living nearly ten years in Asia, I became aware of the Easternization of the West. I believed this change was more vividly apparent to me than to most Americans. For one thing, changes are always more vivid after an absence during which the gradual steps of the process are unseen, and for another, I had been observing a contrasting situation: the Westernization process in Korea. I had been involved in the trend in the opposite direction. Also, the changes that I could see here now were just what I had been longing for. I now could see that I had not been alone in my longing. Thousands of my peers, unknown to me, had been longing for the same communications and waiting for the circumstance that had at last begun to arrive. I came to believe that many of the Westerners I was now able to identify and communicate with were really Orientals. They were Easterners with Eastern pasts who for the purpose of the eventual synthesis had been born to live their current lives in their bodies of the West.

Not long after I had decided to settle for a time in Topeka, Baba Ram Dass came to join us in the Green's home for a few days, making his room in the library where Swami Rama had stayed in the spring before I had arrived. In conversations with Ram Dass I heard his observations of the Westernization process in the East. Ram Dass believed as I did that the preservation of the Eastern traditions depended in part upon their successful transplantation in the West. The time was therefore right for the new people of the West to begin to turn from the systems and ideologies that have built the military-industrial establishment and to seek new and different ways. Into this opening were coming, and would continue to come, yogis, swamis, lamas, and monks bringing the seeds of their ancient traditions. Ram Dass seemed to me a more valuable initiator and interpreter than most of the Eastern teachers who had yet appeared: perhaps no one else could so skillfully articulate Eastern concepts—could communicate so effectively with the whole spectrum of old Westerners and new Westerners.

And not long after Ram Dass left Topeka, Swami Rama of the Himalayas was to arrive to remain for some months to perform a series of psychophysiological experiments. Between his saluation at the top of the page ("Most Blessed Dr. Green") and the close of his letter ("Thy Own Self, Swami Rama") the swami had written a list of the psychophysiological demonstrations and meditation exercises he proposed to perform while "wired up" to the electroencephalograph, cardiotachometer, respiration gauge, and other electronic devices for measuring psychophysiological processes. As his secretarial assistant at the lab, I would have the opportunity to observe his techniques. In the "Position Description of Assistant to Swami Rama," Dr. Green had written: "In order to schedule research activities, appointments, and lectures for Swami Rama with maximum efficiency, it has been decided to coordinate all arrangements through an assistant." My duties, as described in that paper, included handling Swami's telephone calls and appointments, taking dictation, transcribing recordings, typing letters and manuscripts, and editing the swami's written materials.

"But your main work will be to write all this up," Dr. Green explained. "You'll be recording everything that goes on—everything outside of the psychophysiological data that's recorded in the lab—the schedule, the daily activities, all the words and explanations. We plan to have Swami give some talks and some training sessions, some explanations of beginning techniques, breathing, concentration, meditation exercises, and so on. By being so close to the swami and recording all these things, you should be able to sum up the key points or the applicable parts of his psychophysiological training system that he manages to elucidate."

Swami Rama and I were to board and room in the Greens' home; included on my position description were activities such as handling his financial transactions and special diets and general "houseboy" responsibilities that would require me to be available to the swami on a twenty-four-hour basis. It was a fascinating prospect. Inevitably I was to become acquainted not only with the teachings and talents of this Himalayan yogi, but also with the man himself.

Elmer replaced the letter in its folder and returned it to his files. He came back to his chair with one of the half-dozen or so small, gray metal boxes that were on his filing cabinet. The simple, lightweight devices that he often called "little gray boxes" were temperature trainers—biofeedback instruments—that had been built to Elmer's specifications in the Biomedical Electronics Laboratory of the Research Department. They were sophisticated, sensitive thermometers with tiny thermisters that could be taped on the skin and meters that could be calibrated to reveal even a fraction of a degree of temperature change.

With one of these simple trainers a person could sit at home or in the office and practice increasing the skin temperature of the palms or the fingertips. Watching the meter would soon convince one that relaxing deeply and imagining that one's hands are heavy and warm was enough to make the needle go up. Many migraine sufferers who were subjects in the Menninger Clinic Migraine Research Project had successfully used these temperature trainers first to ward off or prevent headaches but finally to achieve a "way of life" in which headaches didn't occur. (What actually happens to account for the results could be explained in complex physiological terminology—perhaps a rebalancing of the operational levels of the sympathetic and parasympathetic functions of the autonomic nervous system. But the wonder of biofeedback is that it works as well for subjects who understand nothing more of the complex psychophysiological processes than simply how they feel. The mother who uses a mirror as a feedback device to help her cranky boy stop fussing knows that his subjective mood and his nasty-looking face are somehow related and that by changing the one he'll change the other.) The little gray box which Elmer Green had just placed on his desk was only one of a number of training devices that patients, research subjects, or other volunteers could check out and take home to help them practice various aspects of self-regulation.

Elmer held the thermister connected to the gray box between his thumb and forefinger, and the needle on the meter moved steadily to the right. "It took a while for Swami Rama to understand what biofeedback is," he said, watching the meter, "but when he got the picture, he was impressed. When he understood that these electronic machines do nothing to the body to produce physical phenomena, but simply reflect physiological responses to changes in mental, emotional, or physical states, he became highly interested. He even talked about taking some of these instruments to the Himalayas and into the caves of the yogis. You know, these things are battery-operated and lightweight, and they can be carried anywhere. Imagine all the yoga aspirants in their caves and ashrams wired up to these trainers." As he spoke, he released the thermister and lightly pinched it between his fingers again, making the needle swing from side to side. I had a sudden ludicrous vision of a huge cargo plane dropping crates of biofeedback instruments that floated down on parachutes, swinging slowly from side to side as they descended into the Himalayas and along the banks of the River Ganges. All the crates were labeled "EEG"—that could have meant either electroencephalograph or Elmer E. Green or both.

"I've always thought that real yogis were far beyond these physiological gymnastics," I protested, blinking my eyes. "At least far beyond anxiety syndromes and tension headaches."

"The adepts are, no doubt, but think of the aspirants. They all have to start out as beginners, and they must have to begin with self-regulation of psychophysiological processes or with voluntary control of internal states. As the swami said, the yogis can learn what to do, but they have no way to monitor their progress. They have no way of knowing whether they're improving or failing until they begin to get proficient. He thinks a lot of the initial yogic training can be greatly speeded up by biofeedback. Of course, speed is probably a Western invention; but then perhaps it may be a Western contribution. Anyway, I think one of the things Swami Rama wants to do, and one of his personal motivations for coming back in the fall, is to learn about feedback techniques."

"Swami Rama wasn't getting feedback when he stopped his heart in the lab, was he?"

"No, there was no feedback. He sat in the experimental room where all the subjects are run, and he was wired up to the polygraphs in the control room, but that was a demonstration rather than a practice or a training session, and there were no visual or audio feedback signals. By the way, Swami didn't actually stop his heart, you know. In fact, what really happened was that his heart rate jumped from seventy to about three hundred beats per minute. This is called atrial flutter. In effect, he stopped his heart from pumping blood for about seventeen seconds. Dr. Marvin Dunne, a cardiologist at the University of Kansas Medical Center, identified the type of record and said that it is associated with a drop in blood pressure and fainting, and sometimes death. Did I tell you all about that heart-control demonstration?"

"Well, not really in detail."

"You know, the swami said he was willing to stop his heart that way for three or four minutes. I told him I'd be sufficiently impressed if he did it for ten seconds. As a matter of fact, I was surprised that he was willing to try it at all because he had told us when he first came that in order to safely stop his heart he had to fast for three days. Now I think that he may have two techniques. In the demonstration that he was referring to when he talked about fasting he may actually stop his heartbeat and produce a flat EKG record. But when he offered to do this heart-control demonstration I was surprised, because for one thing, I thought we had completed all the experiments we were going to do at that time, and for another, we were at the dinner table with him and Dan Ferguson, the doctor who first told us about him.

The swami was going to give a talk in the conference room the following morning, and then he and Dr. Ferguson were to get on the plane for Minneapolis. Alyce and I had taken them out to a restaurant and we were just finishing a big dinner. We were telling him how we appreciated his contribution to our research, and all of a sudden he exclaimed, 'I'm sorry I didn't stop my heart for you. I know you wanted to see that.' I said, 'That's all right, you can do it next time.' And he said, 'I'll do it tomorrow!' Alyce reminded him that we were eating, not fasting, and said that I was not willing to help him endanger his life. Do you know what he said? He said, 'My heart is my toy and I can play with it if I want to!' He finally convinced us.

"So the next day we did the heart-control experiment. Swami had insisted, and after he assured us he would only do it for a few seconds and would be perfectly all right, we agreed to go ahead. We had to start a little earlier in the morning than usual so that we could get him wired up to do the experiment, and get finished before he had to give his talk. I sat with Swami in the experimental room and Alyce and Dale were in the control room with Dr. Ferguson and Dr. Sargent, a Menninger doctor. Swami had asked Alyce to call over the intercom when his heart stopped. The verbal command, 'That's all,' was supposed to be Swami's signal to do whatever he had to do to return his heart to normal. They hadn't expected to see what they saw on the EKG polygraph. We had thought perhaps there would be a flat line for about ten seconds. So there was a delay in giving the signal, 'That's all,' because they were in there watching the polygraph and wondering what the rate of three hundred beats per minute meant in someone like Swami Rama.

"Of course I had no idea what was going on. The swami was just calmly sitting there. At the signal, 'That's all,' he established a solar plexus lock by pulling in his stomach and tightening his diaphragm. I asked him how he went about stopping his heart. Then Alyce called me over the intercom, saying, 'Would you come in for a minute and look at this record?' When I went back to the swami I said, 'Your heart didn't stop the way we thought it was going to. Instead, it started beating at about five times its normal rate!' And he said, 'Well, you know, when you stop your heart this way it's still fluttering in there.' It was interesting that he used that word because when Dr. Marvin Dunne, professor of cardiology at the University of Kansas, saw the electrocardiogram he called it atrial flutter. After Dr. Dunne had talked about the record awhile, he asked, 'By the way, where is this man? What happened to him?' I said, 'Nothing. We took off his wires, and he went up and gave a lecture!' Before he left Topeka, the swami told me that the heart-control demonstration was nothing compared to the temperature-control demonstration he had done the day before. He said it took a lot more practice for him to learn how to produce a significant temperature differential between two points on the same palm than to play around with the heart that way or even to learn to stop it."

"But such extraordinary regulation of the heart seems much more spectacular, and in a way, more important than controlling the skin temperature in the hand."

"That's how it seems. Still, when I consider that Swami produced a ten-degree differential between two points on the same palm by causing about a five-degree increase on the hypothenar eminence and a five-degree decrease on the thenar eminence, that's spectacular. And here again, the swami did not outwardly appear to be doing anything other than quietly sitting there with his hands laid palms-up on the board in front of him. Those two points on the palm are about two inches apart; and the control centers in the central nervous system are probably within millimeters of each other. That's a pretty delicate control of the central nervous system!"

I would be seeing Swami Rama himself in two or three weeks. Now that event seemed something to look forward to.

Swami

one

Swami Rama reached Topeka the same day autumn came—
on September 9, 1970. It was as though he brought the
autumn with him, as though he abruptly changed the atmosphere—inside and out. At two o'clock in the afternoon it was
just another hot summer's day. Elmer had gone to the airport
to meet the plane, and at two o'clock, when the car pulled
into the driveway, Alyce and I were in the upstairs room that
served as their library-den-meditation room lighting incense
and making final arrangements for the swami. When I heard
the car on the gravel I looked out the upstairs window and
saw the outline of his form in the passenger seat behind the
windshield. He was big—even bigger than I expected. I
watched him step out of the car, lift out a suitcase as big as
a trunk, and reach for another. I ran downstairs.

The moment I opened the front door, he called at me in a
booming voice: "Hello, Douglas! I know you!" I walked up
to him and reached out for a suitcase. Thinking I meant to
shake hands, he merely tucked one huge suitcase under his
left arm and grabbed my right hand in his. His smile was
incredible. He was wearing a white turtleneck sweater and a
Nehru jacket. He was swarthy and sharp-featured, and his
large eyes were dark and deep-set. His jet-black hair was
long and curly and glistened with oil. "Yes, I know you!"

It was a great first impression. I may have been a little
surprised by his aggressive vitality, but it was a fun and
friendly meeting. How much more awkward it would have
been for me if Swami Rama had been pompous or aloof!

The moment the swami and I had gotten his luggage to

the top of the stairs he turned to me, grabbed my arm, and said, "Well, Douglas, you will work with me. And I will take you to India!" At that same moment autumn arrived suddenly and with great fanfare, just as the swami had arrived. The sky grew dark and the wind came up and leaves rushed past the windows. I left him to open his suitcases and change his clothes while I walked out to the yard again. The heavy clouds were buzzing with lightning, and the strong wind whisked twigs and leaves in big swirls across the lawn. Once I thought that Kansas would be a dull and almost embarrassing place to live; but I had discovered and come to like the wide beauty of the state. I liked the endless green fields, the rolling hills, the countless variety of singing birds, the sunbursts, and the spectacular cloud shows and lightning storms. Now it began to rain, and I looked up into the heavy, falling drops. Billowy clouds floated by so close to the ground I could almost reach up and touch them. But much higher in the sky the darker, more threatening clouds were moving in the opposite direction! Some of the lower clouds seemed to be dragged along in reverse against their will, and I wondered what would happen if they should collide. Then came the shrieking, wailing scream of the siren. It was a tornado warning!

I ran into the house. The Greens had heard the siren and had turned on the radio.

"Please take shelter until the siren stops," the voice was saying. There was a small crawl-cellar under the house that served as the tornado shelter for this home. It could be reached either from the backyard or through a trap door in the hall closet. Elmer opened the closet door and began to shove aside the umbrellas, ski boots, overshoes, and vacuum cleaner attachments that were in the way as the radio announcer repeated the warning again and again: "This is a tornado warning. A tornado has been sighted about twenty miles southwest of Topeka. It has touched ground and is moving in an easterly direction. You are advised to take shelter immediately. Proceed to the tornado shelter in your home or in your area. If you are driving, leave your car and go to the nearest home or shelter. Please remain in the shelter until the siren stops."

Alyce was calling upstairs, trying to be heard above the wind, the rain, the siren, and the radio. "Swami? Swami, I'm sorry, please come downstairs. Please come down right away. Can you hear me, Swami?"

"Yes, yes, thank you" came the cheery response. "I am just now coming in a few moments' time!"

"You'll have to get him, Doug, he doesn't understand."

"Swami, this is a tornado warning," I shouted as I started up to his room. "Please come with us into the shelter."

He met me on the stairway when I was halfway up. He was wearing long, flowing white robes and a wide shawl over his shoulders. "What is it, what's the matter?"

"It's a tornado, Swami, a big wind coming this way. We'll all have to crawl under the house."

"No, no, no, no, no! This is not good. Swami comes, and the first thing you do, you are afraid of the wind. What is this nonsense?"

"But tornados are destructive, Swami," Alyce said, shaking her head and managing to sound both urgent and reasonable. "We don't know that the tornado will reach here; but if it does, and if we're—"

"This is impossible!" the swami interrupted. "We have not yet begun our work, and the wind comes to blow away the swami, the doctor, and everybody else? This is impossible!" He walked majestically into the living room, his shawl cascading over his outstretched arms, and seated himself on the love seat in the corner.

Alyce and I went to the hall closet, where Elmer had cleared the trap door and was peering through the opening to see whether the dirt below was wet. I had hoped that Swami would follow, but since he did not, I went back to the living room. He was still talking. "Troubles may come and go, troubles may take us by surprise, but why is it that we should have to fear? What are these announcements of disaster? What are these whistles and these speakers to drive intelligent people under their houses?" I stood in the doorway and looked at him. I was not sure how to persuade him or whether I should try. "Go do as you like," he said, "jump through the floor." He gracefully lifted his legs, and without using his hands, he folded himself into a lotus posture. Then he folded his arms across his chest. "I shall remain here in full view of the reality."

I only continued to stand there and watch him. I thought the safest possible place might be there beside the swami. But then the siren stopped. There was a silence on the radio and then the announcer changed his message. The tornado was still moving, but it had passed Topeka on the east, and now it was safely beyond us. Elmer and Alyce came and sat on the sofa. Because of the discussion and the delay no one had reached the cellar. Swami smiled. "Why is it that we should have to fear?" he asked again.

We sat quietly for a while listening to the continuing wind and watching the leaves and twigs rush past the window. After a few moments I turned toward the swami. When my eyes met his I felt that he had been staring at me. I believed he was hoping I was impressed by him. "How about a cup of tea?" he said softly. Alyce stood up and turned toward the kitchen. "No, no, Mama, let Douglas do it. Why should you jump?"

"Well, let me show him how to do it," she said.

The telephone rang. It was one of the secretaries from the Research Department. "Has the swami arrived? Then he was here for the warning? Oh, beautiful! He wasn't afraid, was he? Oh, I knew it! I knew he wouldn't be afraid."

It never got light again that day. By the time the clouds had cleared, the sun was down. But the wind and rain stopped and the night became peaceful. The stars came out and the air was crisp and clean. It was definitely the beginning of a new season.

The four of us sat at the dinner table late that night. Swami ate with gusto and finished far ahead of the rest of us; but he drank many cups of tea and told stories, and the stories continued long after we had completed our meal. Swami was a beautiful storyteller. He told incredible stories and told them with great skill while we sat fascinated behind our dirty plates and coffee cups.

"I remember one of the swamis who was trained by my master in the Himalayas. After seventeen years, Mama, he could not achieve a state of *samadhi*. We have got a systematic path. After three hours and thirty-six minutes one achieves perfect stillness of posture. If one is trained to sit in a particular posture without any movement, after three hours and thirty-six minutes one achieves that stillness. And that is one of the signs of *samadhi*. He achieved that state, but he could not achieve *samadhi*.

"The same thing happened with me. After thirteen years I said, 'Oh, Lord, I have spoiled my whole life—the best years of my life. What will happen to me? So I was annoyed on my master. I said, 'I do not want to follow you. I do not want—I will throw these books in the Ganges, and I will tell people, whomever I meet before leaving this body, that this is nothing, this is humbug. Nobody should follow and waste the time!' He said, 'What has happened to you this morning? Are you mad? What has happened to you?' I said, 'I want to achieve *samadhi*.' He said, 'Do you know how *samadhi* is achieved?' I said, 'I have tried my best whatever you have said. I have followed it to the letter. But I haven't achieved anything.' He said, 'What are you going to do?' I said, 'I want to commit suicide.'

"'You know the consequences,' he said. 'You have to come back again—and I am not going to teach you next time because I am liberated. So who is going to teach you? And you have to start from the very beginning—A, B, C, D.'

"So there is one problem with me always. I think if I come again I will have to learn again the same things. So he asked, 'Do you really want to commit suicide?' I said, 'Yes! I do not want to have this body. Let me come back again with fresh body and start. I will have a good master, a good teacher

who will not bluff me—you have wasted my time!' And such
an old man, noted saint of Himalayas. He looked at me and
said, 'I never considered you as my student and disciple. I
always considered you and brought you up like my child. I
have given you mother's love also.' I said, 'That is why! You
have spoiled me, you see? You did not—I want you to give
me *samadhi* and nothing else. Nothing I need. Take away
everything from me. I embrace death after that, but I want
to achieve that highest state when I feel that I have become
the Universal One. I am still an individual in the bondage of
this mind and body. I want to expand it.' He said, 'No, no,
do whatever you like.'

"So I dashed toward Ganges. He said, 'Wait! I will give
you *samadhi* right now.' So I waited. He said, 'Sit down. Do
you think you are fit enough to have that state?' I said, 'Yes!'
When he found that my desire is strong—that the flame of
desire is burning—he helped me there. And I did not know
what happened to me for nine hours. After I came out of that
state it was already nine hours, and I was in such a great joy
that even after that I said, 'I don't want to come out.' Because it was such a great joy and happiness that I could not
explain. Even now I could not explain today.

"But from that very day, I have noticed one thing, that I
am free from all types of fears, free from these mere diseases
and their causes. If they are there, let them remain at their
places—how am I concerned? I am different from body. I do
not identify myself with body. Body is my garment and I am
not body. So this—the discrimination between real and unreal is there, and that is firm in myself. So if we do not
achieve that highest goal of life, what is the purpose of life
on this planet? Just to live as the creatures, as animals live?
Just to live for the sensual pleasures—the pleasures which
are mingled with grief, the pleasures which are mingled with
sorrows? No, there should be another state, higher state, and
that state is the superconscious state!"

"Shall I bring you more hot water for tea?" Alyce asked.

The three of us had emptied the coffeepot, and Swami,

though he had been busy talking, had just finished the last of a whole pot of tea.

"No, no. It's all right, Mama. I have just now taken this full vessel. I will not take more until morning." But after only a moment's pause he added, "Let me have merely a half-cup."

I cleared away some of the dishes while a fresh cup of tea was prepared, and we all sat at the table again.

"My master's age—I don't say. We don't tell my master's years. But he is so aged, his body is so aged. Because he feels no need to preserve this, you see, this body. Oh, he doesn't want to wait, Mama, he stays only for me. I have told my master, 'Without you living, I also cannot live.'

" 'This is nonsense,' he says. 'We have come to this point for nothing? You have completed your preparation and I am at last able to leave thinking I have finished my part and you will go on doing your work—and now you want to give up everything? What is the matter with you?' Oh, you don't know, he is my mother, my father, my guru, he is everything to me. I have been like his own child. He raised me not only spiritually, you see, the spiritual training, but whatever I know of practical things, my daily living, it is because of him. And I have given him such trouble. I was a difficult youth. Such headaches I have given my master!

"When I went away to college in England and came back to my master, I came back still as a child. I used to try to impress him with my modern Western clothes. But he did not notice these things. He hardly would look at me. Day after day I was wearing beautiful suits for him and he would not look. I wanted my master to praise me, it's a natural thing. So each time I went to him with something different— with a variety of shirts, ties, jackets, and pants—thinking, Definitely he will be impressed with this one. Or then perhaps maybe he'll find this one to his liking. But he would not look at me, and I would have died before I would have asked him to look at me. At last I had gone twice through all my varieties of clothings, and I gave up. Let me wait some days,

I thought, and I will repeat them all again in a different order. So I went to my master in a simple kurta and pajamas, and he looked at me and said, 'You look nice today.'

"That day he watched me constantly and spoke to me lovingly. 'Why have you so long endured me?' I asked him. 'All these years I have been a headache for you. You have been my family, and I have been like a protesting child. There are others—others who would come with burning desire and steady moods. Why have you put up with me?' Such poor, frail old man, he just looked at me. 'You don't know,' he said. 'It's my karma!' "

Swami emptied his cup and gazed thoughtfully into space. " 'Don't ever leave me,' I begged my master. 'Promise me you will live until I can live without you.' And he promised. My master is such a one.

"But one day he gave me a shock. Oh, it was a horrible thing. We were below the mountains that day, below the peaks of the Himalayas, in a sunny valley where the Ganges came flowing down. We sat on the banks of the Holy River and my master spoke in Sanskrit, explaining some points of Upanishads. As he spoke he looked over and noticed a dead man in the river, and he pointed it out to me, saying, 'Let us remove the body from the water.'

" 'Why?' I asked. 'The man is dead.' My people prefer to die on the banks of the Ganges, you see, and have their bodies thrown into the Holy River. One who spends a good deal of time at the Ganges may sometimes see those who have come to leave their bodies. 'Let us be certain,' my master said, 'Come, let us check.' It was the corpse of a young man, and when he had gotten it up on the bank, my master felt the body and put his head close. 'He is such a good-looking fellow and now he has just died.'

"As my master completed those words he fell over on his back, and at once I rushed toward him. He was dead, Mama. Oh, it was such a shock! We had just taken out this dead man from the river and suddenly my master also left his body! I began shaking my master. 'Master, Master! Don't

die! Don't leave me!' The young man sat up and said, 'Why
are you shaking that old man? Why do you not come to me?
I am here, and you can do nothing for that dead body.' It was
his voice, the voice of my master! I could not think anything.
My mind was stunned. For a time I could not even move,
and when I could move again, I went on shaking my master.
The young man stood up. 'Why do you not come to me and
forget the discarded body? The young man has left his body
and I have taken it. What is the harm in it? I have done it
for you.' These words of my master came from that young
man's mouth, and he was walking to me and holding out his
arms. I cried in fear, 'Master, where are you? Please get up.
Why do you do this thing to me?'

"I could not look at the young man's face, and I just kept
holding onto my master. 'What is the matter with you?' he
asked, and he sat down beside me. 'I am doing this thing because I am doing for you. You do not let me go, you are
keeping me here. Why do you not let me take this charming
garment? Look at me, am I not more pleasing to you in this
form? I want to please you.'

"Oh, I could not look at him, Mama, and I could not speak.
I was taken with fear and confusion. I only wanted that my
master would sit up. 'Now, you know that I am in this body,'
he said. 'Why do you go on in such a foolish manner? Why
do you not speak to me? Why do you not help me throw this
aged corpse in the river?' I looked at the strange face and
the words rushed from my mouth. 'No, no! It is my master I
love and only my master. Do not torture me in this manner.
I want you as you always have been. I want you in your own
body. I could never accept a stranger as my master.'

"So the young man fell backward onto the ground, and
my own master sat up. He said, 'The body is nothing, you
know.' I was so happy to hear his voice coming from his own
body that I rushed and embraced him. 'The one whom you
call master is not this old frame,' he went on. 'Why should
you cling to this ugly flesh when I myself am willing to give
it up?' 'Because I am not so enlightened,' I answered. 'I can

feel more than the physical being, but I can see only the body; and if you leave it, then you have left me.' He walked over and examined the dead man again. 'Then let me take this younger body,' he said. 'No one is using it and I must do it for your sake. You depend on my physical existence, and I have to prolong it.'

" 'No, no, please!' I cried, holding his feet. 'I don't want to prolong it!' 'Ah!' he said. 'That is what I was waiting to hear.' 'No, no, it is not what I meant. I want only this body that has taught me and brought me up. I don't want to prolong it that much. Only until you have taught me how to let go of you.' He looked at me with those eyes—such old eyes, Mama, and we both had tears. And he said, 'No, I would not have done that thing. It was just a point I was making. You see, these bodies are real for us, and yet they are illusion. But in this earthly realm we have such attachments to these illusions, and one day I shall also have to let go of you. We will just both do our best.' "

Swami pushed his chair away from the table and watched us for a moment as we sat beside the Ganges. "I have talked so long," he said as he stood up. "Let me go now and begin my work. My master still waits for me now. The same body in the same place." He lifted his hands and put his palms together. "Good night, good night!"

two

Living in the Green's home with Swami Rama was to mean a considerable change in my lifestyle. I realized this the day the swami arrived, and I knew it around five-thirty the following morning when he knocked on my bedroom door and shouted, "Hey, Douglas! How about a cup of tea!" The tea-making became an important part of the daily routine, and wherever the swami was, I was to be nearby, ready to come forth with the hot tea and milk in a moment's notice. Swami often called it "tilk," and he preferred it in a tall glass with equal parts of strong tea and hot milk and a few healthy spoonfuls of honey. The before-sunrise teatime was an effective way for me to get my days off to a good and early start. Swami believed it the habit of all good yogis and aspirants to spring from their beds immediately upon awakening. He also believed that all sensible people are up and about when the sun comes up in order to benefit from some special ethereal quality of the sun's first rays. So I was happy to be thus awakened every morning. I could easily disregard my alarm clock, but not the booming voice of the swami and not his need for his morning tilk. Once he told me that if I could teach him the tea-making procedure, including the technique of operating the knobs on the kitchen stove, he could avoid disturbing me in the early mornings. I taught him the procedure, for the sake of his ever-expanding enlightenment, but I wanted to go on preparing his tea and to be awakened when he stirred in the mornings.

At first it amazed me to find this yogi adept, this master of "involuntary" processes, so inept at such everyday procedures as preparing tea; but I learned that Swami had been accustomed to being waited on hand and foot in India. It was not that he had insisted on it—this was the manner in which devout followers treated their teachers. Swami Rama was a particularly important swami, as he had once been a Sankaracharya in southern India. Sankaracharyas are influential spiritual and religious leaders in the Hindu hierarchy in India.

Swami Rama is perhaps the only man ever to have "escaped" from this position, having felt, as he described it to me, like a bird in a gilded cage. No one but a true scholar could ever be selected for the high and holy post of Sankaracharya; but Swami's had been a life of vigorous study, and he had spent many long days voluntarily chained to a chair so that he could not get away from his books. Sometimes he appeared to me to be an expert in all things knowable—from metaphysics to history to horticulture. Yet having his daily needs and wants anticipated and provided for without his even having to identify and verbalize them left him inexperienced in the practical procedures of daily living. Swami was an interesting combination of self-mastery and incompetence. I knew the complications and confusions of technological America would be even more overwhelming for this Himalayan yogi than for the usual foreigner, and I wanted to spare him the additional culture shock of having to make his own tea.

Living in the Greens' home also meant a considerable change in the lifestyle of Swami Rama. And it was also a challenge. On the third morning after his arrival, Elmer and Alyce went to their offices, leaving Swami and me at home. In the afternoon Swami was to perform an exercise in deep meditation while wired up for physiological measurements, and he wanted to spend the morning at home, alone and quiet, in preparation for the event.

At noon I called him from his silence and announced that I would have lunch ready within fifteen minutes. The Greens would expect us to be ready by one o'clock. As I prepared his usual meal of fresh fruits and vegetables and hot tilk, Swami showered upstairs. When everything was ready and set out on the dining-room table, the shower was still running loudly. There was no use calling him, so I sat down at the table with the bowls and plates and teacups and waited. But the shower did not stop. It continued even after I thought I heard the sound of a door opening and closing upstairs. When it was nearly one o'clock, I knew that we would be late, but I considered that a long shower might be part of Swami's preparation for what he was to do in the lab and I did not want to disturb him. Then I heard loud footsteps overhead. Swami was walking around in the library, which had now become his room. I wondered why the water was still running. I knew that even Swami Rama could not be in the shower and in his room at the same time. At any rate, I would let him go about things in his own strange way. From all the sounds coming from upstairs, I knew he was at least hurrying as fast as he could.

"Douglas!" he called suddenly from the top of the stairs. "Douglas, oh, Good Lord help me! What have I done?"

I ran upstairs and found the floor flooded with water. The shower was splashing full blast against the opposite wall and spraying on all the other walls—and on the mirror, the shelves, the towels, and the toilet paper. The first thing to do was shut the water off, but turning the knobs in either direction seemed to have no effect.

"Oh, Good Lord help us!" Swami raved on. "Why has this happened?"

Finally I figured out that in trying to turn the water off, Swami had rotated the knobs so far in the wrong direction that he had nearly unscrewed them. I revolved them both almost a dozen times before the water stopped and there was silence.

"Oh, God bless you, you have saved my life!"

I looked at him. There he stood in his finest robes and sandals. I realized exactly what had happened. When Swami had finished his shower and tried to turn the water off, he had unscrewed the knobs. Then no doubt he had stood under the rushing torrent for a harrowing half-hour or so, desperately trying to stop the water, knowing that if he opened the shower curtain the water would splash all over the bathroom. When at last he had resolved to step out of the shower and call for help, he had rushed about in a noisy frenzy while the water flooded the bathroom, and had quickly dressed himself so that at least his appearance would be as dignified as possible.

He watched as I wrung out the towels and the rugs, wailing, "Oh, my Lord, what have I done? I have destroyed the doctor's home!"

"It's all right," I reassured him. "It's only water. And I can fix everything so that no one will even notice." That was not completely true, but I did not want the haunting memory of this episode to disrupt his laboratory demonstration of deep meditation.

In the first days, Swami Rama and I spent the mornings at home, and several times he called me upstairs to sit in his room with him and listen to his tape recordings of classical Indian music and devotional singing. "You understand this music," he would say to me. "You understand because you have lived in the East." But most of the time he was wordless. Sometimes we sat in silence for hours. He would sit absolutely motionless in his lotus posture with his eyes half closed and his back and neck so straight he looked taller than usual. At those times he seemed old and venerable. And on those days we had lunch at home, and except for the day of the shower episode, we always spent a long time talking at the table. He was always obviously pleased with all that I prepared for him, and that made me feel good.

"We ought to start a restaurant," he said to me one day. "We must do this someday. You can learn some Indian preparations, and between you and me we will make endless varieties of delightful dishes. Definitely we must do it. It will be by far the finest restaurant that anyone here has ever seen."

As I listened to those words I told myself that he was only partly serious, but I believed that if I were to respond with sufficient enthusiasm it might actually happen.

The Greens' home was directly across the street from a large landscaped park that was bordered with weeping willow trees. It had a zoo, a rose garden and greenhouse, a swimming pool, tennis courts, and lots of green lawn, and a little open train with a bell and a high-pitched whistle gave people rides around the perimeter for thirty-five cents. Every lunchtime while we sat at the table the train went around and around with its ludicrous whistle, and every day Swami noticed it and remarked about it. Two or three times he ran to the window so that he could see the people as they rode past behind the weeping willow trees.

One day I told him that the Greens had ridden the train with their grandchildren, but that I had never experienced it. I had been meaning to, I explained, but had never gotten around to it. "I realize I'm going to have to see to it that I get to ride on that train," I said jokingly, "since I know that every aspirant must either satisfy or repel all desires in order to achieve nonattachment."

He listened to me with obvious amusement, but then for a moment his face grew serious and he became thoughtful. Suddenly he smiled again, and his eyes lit up. "We will do it!" he said. "Definitely we'll do it! You make all the necessary arrangements!"

"Yogis and exotic people often have several distinct natures, several aspects of their beings," Elmer had once said to me. "The swami is a man of three aspects, as I see him: a wise old man, a middle-aged man, and a young boy," and within these first days I had been able to see his three beings. At times of quiet contemplation and in our evening meditations he was a dignified and sagelike old man. Most of the time he was his bold and jaunty middle self, and at rare and unexpected moments he was simply a child. Though his highest yogic nature was probably in the aspect of the old man, I believed it was his middle self that did the demonstrations in our laboratory and performed extraordinary yogic feats. And I believed that the child in him would one day have us riding the train.

three

Elmer gave Swami Rama the title of consultant to the Voluntary Controls project, and he had his own office with his name on the door. Swami's was not a very large office, and he had it so full of cacti, ferns, and other potted plants that there was just room enough for his desk, his chair, and two or three smaller chairs in case he should have visitors. It was undoubtedly the most templelike of all the offices in the research building—or in all the clinic or administration buildings for that matter—and it was undoubtedly the foundation's only dependable source of holy smells such as jasmine, musk, frankincense, and myrrh. Walking through the fog of incense smoke into that room filled with plants, paintings, and innumerable exotic artifacts was like stepping into a shrine at an ashram or monastery. It is not easy to jolt a professional experimenter or a clinical psychiatrist, but more than a few doctors and scientists who passed through our halls were surprised and often embarrassed by Swami Rama and the various manifestations of his presence.

The swami was less disquieting to less prestigious people. The man in charge of the Menninger Foundation greenhouse liked him immediately, and that was one of the reasons he had so many plants in his office. "Well, it's nice to see that somebody's finally come here who understands plants," the man told him. And later when Swami was not there to hear it, he said to me, "Now, there's a man you can talk to and listen to, and that's unusual, believe me, and I've been here a good long time. He's as smart as any of 'em, you can tell that in a minute, but not that head-in-the-clouds kinda smart like a lot of other people I could mention." That was an interesting observation. No doubt most of the others he did not mention would have thought it was the other way around.

My office was a few steps down the hall from Swami's. It was no larger than his, but it seemed to have more work space because I only had a few small plants. If someone phoned for Swami Rama, the telephone rang in my office. With a special button I could buzz his office and tell him who was on the line. But in most cases I was instructed not to, because part of my job was to see that the swami was not disturbed. "So many people will be ringing me up. You don't know, you have no idea. Always it happens wherever I go. 'Swami, Swami, Swami.' I don't want this distraction. You tell them, 'Swami is in the laboratory now, Swami is talking with doctors now, Swami is in meditation now.' We have to do our work. I don't want to be bothered with all these people." So Swami's telephone was tucked away between some potted plants on a table behind his back, and he was not to have to think about it. Once things were properly arranged, Swami spent nearly all of his mornings peacefully enshrined in his office reading, writing, thinking, meditating, or just relaxing. The swami's afternoons were busy with his experiments in the laboratory, going over the psychophysiological measurements that were recorded on polygraphs, discussing results; but except for when he was involved in staff meetings, he had time to himself in the mornings. He needed those peaceful hours to be ready for what he was to do in the lab. So it was important that he not be bothered with unexpected calls and visits. He even made himself a hotel-style "Do Not Disturb" sign, hung it on his doorknob, closed the door, and would not answer if someone knocked. At those times I could buzz his office from mine if I needed to communicate with him, and he would pick up his phone.

In a little more than two weeks after the swami arrived, he was well settled and reasonably adjusted at home and at the office, and the Swami Rama research project had been established. It was decided that the swami would spend about two hours every afternoon "wired up" in the lab, and that a series of five afternoon sessions would be planned in detail on the first day of each week. All the people who were involved in the Swami Rama project received a copy of the week's schedule every Monday morning. Swami got a copy also, but it was my job to remind him every afternoon when it was one o'clock and time to go upstairs for the preliminary preparations. It was also my job to see that he arrived safely upstairs (without getting sidetracked in a conversation in the hall), seated himself calmly at the "wiring-up table," and had a hot cup of tilk and honey to attend to during the tedious process. Oculographic (eye movement), skin resistance (GSR), electrocardiographic (EKG), electroencephalographic (EEG), finger temperature, finger blood flow (photoplethysmographic), forearm electrographic (EMG), and respiration "pickups" were attached to the swami's body. Two brain-wave electrodes (EEG) were fastened with salt paste to the back of his head, over the visual area of the cerebral cortex, and he wore two ear-ring electrodes. This wiring up was done in a quiet corner of the third floor before the swami was taken down on the elevator to the laboratory in the basement. Downstairs in the lab he sat in a comfortable chair in the experimental room—a soundproofed room with adjustable lighting—and his wires were plugged into a twenty-five-foot cable that carried his physiological signals to the instruments in the polygraph room. It made the swami restless and edgy to sit motionless at the table upstairs while two or three staff members fussed with his hair and his skin to get the electrodes on. I thought of telling him "just be detached"; but believing that would only make matters worse, I brought him tea and did my best to make him comfortable so that he would not lose the composure and state of mind he had used the morning to acquire.

A minor catastrophe happened in one of the first laboratory sessions. It was an experiment in intense concentration in which the swami was to concentrate upon the external focusing, rather than withdrawal, of the senses. In this session he sat alone in the experimental room, and the lights were turned off completely. He was absolutely motionless for nearly an hour; even the subtlest twitch would have registered on the polygraphs in the control room. But suddenly everything jumped. At the height of his concentration Swami heard the high-heeled footsteps of a secretary on the tile floor above. The experimental room was sufficiently soundproofed—unless someone or some machine in the control room made a noise loud enough to be heard through two walls and a hallway. If footsteps on the floor above had ever before been heard in the control room it was too slight a sound to be noticed, or at least mentioned, but in Swami's ultrasensitive state the sound produced a painful jolt. It was obvious when it happened: when someone spoke to the swami on the intercom, he insisted upon stopping the session and being released immediately from all the wires and attachments.

"Oh, Doctor," he said, "I got a terrible shock! Let me be free of all this . . . this . . . all these wires. Let us conclude for today. Please, I can't do more now."

It took some discussion to determine exactly what had disturbed him, and then a little thinking and investigating to discover what had made the noise that had startled him so.

Later, upstairs, he went on complaining to Alyce Green as he helped with the removing of the electrodes and the cleaning of the salt paste from his skin. "You don't know how I felt. You can't know, Mama. This can be dangerous. I don't want to go out of my mind in this unexpected manner sitting in that basement down there. Today I have not completed my assignment, but now how can I do that type of concentration again? I shall be always nervous and looking at the ceiling, waiting for the shock to come. Oh, this can be dangerous, Mama, let us do what we can for it at once."

Elmer contacted Housekeeping, and someone came immediately to the research building to measure the area of floor over the experimental room which had never been carpeted. The next time Swami was led, wires and all, down the elevator and through the hallway to the stuffed chair in the experimental room, there was a thick carpet on the floor over his head; and unless someone should drop a typewriter in that hall, there would be no danger of another such shock for our swami.

There was a good deal more that mattered to the swami's achievements in these experiments than his comfort and tranquillity. "Spontaneous enthusiasm" were the words Elmer Green used to describe the state of mind under which Swami seemed to do his yoga best in the laboratory. We began to realize the importance of helping him maintain an interest in what he was doing, and beyond that, of allowing him a sense of control and creativity.

For this to happen, it was necessary that he learn the relationship between what it was he was doing internally and what it was he was producing in terms of the results we had to work with. A review of the polygraph records produced each day in the laboratory was incorporated into the afternoon schedule. The earlier experiments all had to do with various forms of concentration, such as concentration on an external point with gazing, concentration on a certain chakra, or concentration on the breath while performing special breathing techniques; for these experiments the brain-wave patterns on the electroencephalograph records were the most significant. Our system of showing him the records he produced after each afternoon's performance and explaining their meaning soon enabled him to understand what the brain-wave patterns were and how the four brain-wave bands are defined. He was then able to associate the patterns he produced on the polygraph charts with what he was doing internally that produced those patterns; and once having made that association, he was able to sit in his chair in the experimental room and produce whatever brain-wave pattern he wished—from delta to beta—and for whatever duration, as the strip chart moved through the machines.

The strip-chart paper that rolled slowly and steadily along

under the polygraph pens was another source of disturbance for the swami, although we did not discover this for the first couple of weeks. From the very beginning the scheduling was arranged to allow the swami at least three hours per session for sitting in the experimental room performing his various exercises in concentration and meditation. But in the beginning sessions, time after time the swami was ready to call it a day long before the three hours had passed—just when it seemed he was getting started. Since it had already been decided that it was best to let the swami conduct himself according to his own inspirations and sense of timing, Elmer was reluctant to complain. If Swami were to spend longer and do more in each session it should happen as though it were his own idea. Everyone hoped that he would eventually accumulate enough enthusiasm to want to do a few really full and worthwhile sessions.

In one of the Monday morning staff-and-Swami meetings, someone mentioned the fact that Swami was spending very little time on the machines each session, considering that at least three hours had been made available for that purpose. That allowed Elmer to take up the issue himself. "You know, there's always plenty of time, Swami," he said. "Once you get all wired up and set up in the lab, we would be happy for you to continue just as long as you want to or need to or as long as you feel that you can. You can do whatever you want to do, but what I'm saying is you can take as long as you want to do it. Perhaps you don't know exactly what you're doing. That's what we're trying to find out, to begin with. So maybe it's best for you to produce a lot of paper records, and then after each session we can go over it and talk about it."

The next day Swami called Elmer and Alyce and said, "I have news for you. All the records we got for the last two weeks must be thrown away."

"Why?" Elmer asked.

"Because I did not get into the states of meditation we had planned on."

"How did that happen?"

"If you had not told me that the paper cost sixteen dollars a box, that would have been better. This is the problem. All this paper. I am wasting all this paper. And this is special paper. Every afternoon I sit in that dark room and I am so disturbed thinking about all that paper going on the floor in heaps."

"Swami, you don't have to think about the paper," Alyce assured him. "Have you really been that worried about using paper and not even mentioned it?"

"Oh, Mama, I feel so bad! You don't know. I feel so bad."

Before beginning this series of experiments, the swami had been guided through the polygraph control room and briefed on the equipment and the procedure of running subjects. On that day there was a subject being run, and Swami could see the machines at work as the paper ran under the wiggling pens. The electroencephalograph paper was fed to the machine in stacks, and as it ran through it refolded itself in a neat pile. The EKG machine and the polygraph for recording other physiological signals were fed with rolls of graph paper that came out of the machine in heaps on the floor. If there were not enough hands in the control room to roll up the paper as it came out, it was a simple matter to avoid stepping on it until the machines were turned off at the end of the session. Swami must have been more than impressed— he must have been horrified. All the printers and stationers in his hometown could not avail themselves of as much paper each day as lay on the floor of the control room in our laboratory.

"Look, we have piles of paper," Elmer said, "boxes of it. That's the smallest of our problems—I couldn't care less about that. In fact, I would prefer it if you would use more paper each day than you are using now. Maybe we should make it our goal to use a certain amount of paper, maybe four or five times what we're using now. You could do whatever you wanted to, or could, and we would have a lot of graphs to go over each day."

So Swami overcame his anxiety about wasting paper, and

there was a great deal of graph paper to lay out across the long tables in the conference room upstairs following every afternoon session.

Soon Swami could announce he would produce so many minutes of theta, so many minutes of delta, go back up to beta, produce alpha for so many minutes—and then do exactly what he said he would do. Finally he ceased to be impressed with that achievement. One day he enthusiastically suggested that he would like to help develop the means to demonstrate the existence of additional waves or patterns that our electroencephalographs seemed unable to measure and record. He thought that by working with Elmer and with the people in the Biomedical Electronics Laboratory he could help them develop more sensitive instruments and thereby prove the existence of more significant states that they seemed not yet to have discovered.

"You don't understand," Elmer explained. "This is all there is. You can go from a flat record—that is, from zero cycles per second—all the way up to twenty-four, twenty-six, twenty-eight, as many cycles per second as you can produce, and it will be accurately indicated on the polygraph. And the whole spectrum—the entire range of electrophysiological activity of the brain—is divided somewhat arbitrarily into these four bands. That's simply a matter of definition. So zero to four hertz is delta, four to eight is theta—and this you know because we've defined these before—eight to thirteen hertz is called alpha because that happens to be what the guy got first from his subject when he was naming these patterns, and any frequency from thirteen on up is defined as beta. So there isn't anything else."

Swami was now able to produce patterns within any of the four frequency bands. But apparently he had come to the realization that he was able to do more than showed. "All this is nothing," he said, "only simple exercises. Something is missing here, there must be some more patterns—something more than this beta, alpha, theta, delta."

"Aha! there *is* something else," Elmer responded. He and

I both just got the swami's point. "You have to remember these machines are measuring the physical activity in your physical body. What these patterns are showing is not necessarily states of mind, but only states of brain."

"Not necessarily states of mind, and certainly not states beyond mind," I added, remembering Swami's saying that meditation is a state beyond mind.

For a few moments Swami sat silently in thought. I imagined him feeling he had reached the limits of what he could demonstrate in the areas of concentration and meditation. He suddenly realized that all the magnificent variations he could achieve in his internal states of consciousness could not be paralleled with equally magnificent changes in the patterns on the polygraph.

"Then what is the use of all these machines?" he asked.

"Ah, but for what they're doing, they're extremely useful. They're useful for demonstrating the psychophysiological principle, the mind-body relationship. What we're saying is that changes in physiological states affect mental-emotional states, and conversely, changes in mental-emotional states produce physiological changes. The extent to which this is true can be studied with physical measurements made by physical machines because we can see how changes in the body are related to changes in subjective mental and emotional states. This is a tremendous step, and what you are doing is useful in making this step. You'd be surprised how many people, even doctors and scientists, think we're only bodies—nothing more than bundles of largely involuntary chemical-electrical responses. And they've not only hypothesized this, they've already concluded it. We are going to have to first break those conclusions; we're going to have to smash all the premature theories in a scientific way so that science can move on. Eventually we may find higher principles: we may find how higher states of consciousness relate to the mind-body relationship. And maybe someday science can make nonphysical measurements with nonphysical instruments."

"All right," Swami answered, "let me have a cup of tea."

Just as the swami reached the point where he could sit for hours in the experimental room, letting the paper flood the control room, he also learned to sit more patiently for the wiring-up process that preceded every session.

One day when I brought him his hot tea and stood behind him, watching them rub the abrasive salt paste into his scalp, I could see that he was in a good mood. I felt that when he wanted to he could actually enjoy the attention and touching that was involved in attaching all the electrodes and thermisters. When he got up from his chair he had a smile on his face.

"You look interesting," I said. He did look interesting. He had come to the lab this day with his loose-fitting, snowy-white, yogi-looking pants that are called pajamas in India, and he was wearing sandals. He had on a thin, white silk shirt, and over that he wore the light blue jacket that was especially designed for the subjects in our project. All the wires that came from his fingers, wrists, arms, face, and head were plugged into jacks sewn in the sleeves and collar of the jacket. Around his forehead and shiny black hair he wore the white headband that held the EEG electrodes in place. Black electrical tape and black wires covered his face and hands. "I don't know whether you're from a Himalayan cave or from outer space." The swami beamed. It should be a good day in the lab, I thought.

"No, no. Leave it, leave it," the swami said as I was about to push the button for the elevator. "Why should we continually trouble the thing for me when others are going on the stairs?"

"But you're all wired up, Swami. It's inconvenient to walk."

"Inconvenience is nothing to fear. Anyway, do you think these electrodes are influencing my walking? My feet are unaffected. Coming up we may use the lift as we like, but going down we should walk from time to time."

So we took the stairs. When we reached the second floor he turned suddenly and started through the hallway. I followed along behind him. He looked through the open doors of offices and stopped to smile at people passing in the hall. He held his arms gracefully as he did when he wore his cape. Of course everyone noticed him. When he smiled at them they smiled back, partly because he had smiled first and partly because he looked so amusing.

"God bless you!" he said again and again. "God bless you, God bless you!"

God bless you, I wondered to myself, why God bless you? I had heard him say that to those of us with whom he was working, and he had often said it at home, especially before going to bed, but never before had he said it to all the research workers on all the other projects. When he had finished on the second floor we made the rounds on the first floor with me trailing behind as we wandered through the hallways.

"God bless you! Good afternoon, God bless you! How are you? God bless you!"

I began to sense that Swami had been longing to heal the painful gap between himself and all these intelligent and aloof people. Now was his chance—now that he was appropriately vested in all the evidence of his scientific efforts and at the same time looking as yogilike as ever. "God bless you" was the thing to say. These were the words to bring together the two distant worlds—the sacred and the scientific. This is what Swami wanted more than anything else. So he said, "God bless you," and he meant it.

four

With Swami Rama at home and at work there were busy times, fun times, surprising times, and even embarrassing times. But the most memorable and meaningful times of all were the peaceful moments at home in the late evenings after supper when we joined Swami in meditation. Then he was a beautiful person. This was no delirious emotional response on my part; it was the way he really was. When he sat lotus-posture on his meditation seat, with his head, neck, and trunk straight—as he always reminded us to do—he became very tall and very still, and I could feel the oldest and wisest part of his being.

I liked the clear and meaningful invocation with which he usually began the meditation, speaking first in Sanskrit and then translating in English:

> *Lead me from Darkness to Light,*
> *Lead me from the Unreal to the Real,*
> *Lead me from Mortality to Immortality.*

Swami instructed me in the proper execution of the lotus posture. Having lived in Korea for over eight years, I had become accustomed to sitting cross-legged for a good portion of my waking hours, and by legs were pliable. I was able to sit comfortably for long periods of time with my legs interlocked in what I had thought was a good lotus posture, but Swami told me that if I really wished to attempt the lotus posture I should learn to do it all the way. By way of demonstration, he pointed out to me what he claimed was the proper full lotus asana.

"You see where my feet are? The heels should press in against the abdomen like this. In this manner you maintain the locks—the solar plexus and anal locks—and you achieve the best balance and stability, which is the purpose of this posture and the reason why it is superior to all the others. It is not that this posture alone will do—no one can insist such a thing. Any posture will suit for meditation so long as the head, neck, and trunk are always straight. But either you should not do the lotus asana or you should do it properly. And see my toes? The backs of the toes rest flatly against the outside of the legs. So you may try it or not, but if you master this, you will find it superior for meditation. Once you master it, it takes the least effort. You will see how easily you keep the proper alignment of the spine. In any other posture the back will bow, and you must attend to it again and again. But here you will see the backbone remains unbending without the constant effort of the muscles."

I was able, with some effort, to sit as he did, so that my heels pressed firmly against my abdomen. It was certainly less comfortable than the half-hearted way I had been sitting, and I informed the swami of this.

"No, no, no, no! You don't know! For one moment only you are trying, and already you are making judgment? You will sit and sit and go on sitting. For a few hours you will sit again the next day and again the next, and then it will become six hours, and at last you will sit for nine without motion. If you can sit for nine hours without moving or feeling this body, then you will get somewhere. In nine hours' time you can get somewhere. And then you will know for what you have been longing. But it is work to reach even four or six hours. Wave after wave of pain will come. Pain and relief, pain and relief. First you feel uneasy, as you feel now, but then the body adjusts and you relax and settle into it."

"That's right," I said. "I'm beginning to feel a lot more comfortable already."

"Ah, but then the next wave comes. You feel you have stopped your circulation. You feel this sensation, this, this . . ."

"I know what you mean."

"But it passes. In time it passes. The body numbs, and all the sensations are forgotten. This body consciousness is gone and the body is transcended. And you may go on for two and three hours in this manner. So you sit and you think, 'Oh, now I have really done something, I have transcended my body. I feel I am suspended above my head.' But you have done nothing, because you have not quieted the mind. You must still the mind. You must gather up all the scattered thoughts and hold them still so the mind is not jumping, jumping, jumping. But then the next wave comes. You feel pain in your legs—a new and greater pain. You feel a chill in your veins and nerves, and it moves up and makes you nauseated. Again you are drawn to these body feelings. Then the sluggishness comes and you say, 'Oh, I have done enough. Let me not continue now. I shall do better tomorrow.' It will be the same tomorrow. Eventually you must endure. Sooner or later you must go beyond that point, because that is not yet the beginning. That is not yet meditation. That is not yet even concentra— Now, you see what you are doing? Your knee is coming up. This is not correct. You need a higher cushion. Raise the buttocks more, and the knee is going down. Your left knee is resting on the floor, but your right knee must do the same."

"How is this?" I asked, reaching for another cushion and putting it under me. "Is this okay?"

He gave me a long, stern look. "Of course," he answered solemnly. "But of course it is nothing. Only so briefly you have done it properly. And we are talking. But try it and stay with it until you get somewhere. Someday you will get past all these waves, and you will reach the level of the mind. Someday you will go beyond mind, and then you will begin to know what is meditation. Not before. Do the discipline. Nothing is achieved without discipline. Not even that which we already know. Do not be like those who say, 'Oh, I am sitting in beautiful posture. Look how I am doing it properly. Incense is smoking. Candle is glowing. Visions are coming. Is this not *samadhi?*' No, this is not *samadhi*. *Samadhi* is not in this room, this body, this mind. *Samadhi* is not such a thing. Work and work and work until you come to see the joy in it, and then one day you will know *samadhi*. Because you have known it before."

I tried following the swami's instructions just as he had given them. I sat for hours in the proper lotus posture, stilling first the body and then the mind. I tried it every night in our meditations, and sometimes at my *puja* table in my own room. Our evening meditations lasted not more than one or two hours, and it seemed that even in that short time I experienced all that the swami had talked about—the coming and going of all the waves of pain and relief, of transcending and falling back again.

Once on a clear and quiet Sunday afternoon I sat before my *puja* table in my room. The Greens were at the lab, and Swami Rama was outside. I sat for nearly four hours, and somewhere in that space of time I must have transcended everything—the waves of sensations, the chattering voice of the mind, the images, everything. Either I had fallen asleep or I had reached some state beyond recall, for when Swami suddenly knocked loudly on the front door, I came back from seemingly nowhere. It took me a long time to realize where I was and what I was doing. When finally I bent my head enough to look at my body, I could not make it move. After what seemed like several minutes and another loud knock at the door, I was able to unlock my legs with my hands. There was not a bit of feeling in them and not a chance of getting on my feet. I crawled slowly out of my room and across the living-room floor to reach the door. I opened it and looked up at the swami's puzzled face.

"My God, what are you doing?"

"Practicing," I said. I could tell by the swami's face that he had not accepted that as an excuse for my not standing to meet him at the door. "I can't stand up right now," I explained. "My knees just won't unbend. All I can do is crawl."

"No, no, no! Leave this crawling practice. For what do you develop this habit? It's a useless thing."

"I'm not practicing crawling, Swami. I'm practicing sitting, and I've been sitting without moving for about four hours. I have no feeling in my legs and I can't unbend them."

Swami laughed at me, and I felt at first that I would have much preferred almost any other reaction; but as he laughed I could see the humor in it myself. When he thought he had laughed enough he looked at me sternly again. "Stand up; otherwise you will be in pain. Stand up and let it pass. Stand up! Stand up! Stand up!"

Instantly I was on my feet, and Swami was laughing again.

One day we were late in getting to our meditation because Swami had kept us sitting long after supper with humorous and fascinating stories from India. At nearly ten o'clock he jumped up from the table. "Let me work alone tonight," he said, "I have made a promise and cannot wait. You go ahead with your meditation in the usual manner without me. Is it all right?"

"Of course it's all right, Swami."

Alyce, Elmer, and I cleared the dishes as quickly and quietly as possible, so as not to disturb the swami, and then went into the living room downstairs and turned off all the lights. We began our evening sitting without ritual. The house was pitch-dark and stone-still. Only moments ago we were talking and laughing at the supper table, and now we were sitting motionless in the dark. I tried to picture the swami sitting in meditation not far away. Without his presence and his invocation and his incense, too much was missing, and this night felt too different. Meditation is not a matter of mood, I reminded myself. It was not as though any of us had never sat this way before we met the swami. Anyway, after an hour or so of effort, the setting of the stage would be of no matter. It was necessary to discontinue all these thoughts, and I believe that after thirty or forty minutes I had achieved that.

It seemed that I had managed to achieve total quieting of body and mind when I was suddenly startled by a loud crash. I felt a painful jolt in my body. I opened my eyes and turned toward the sound. The crash came from the swami's direction, but of course I could not see him through the walls—I could not even see Alyce and Elmer in the dark. By the sounds that followed I knew that Swami had felt his way through the darkness to the telephone and was dialing. The crash I had heard, I now realized, had been the swami leaping to his feet from his meditative posture. What sort of meditation was he doing, I wondered, that he would get the sudden urge to make a late-night phone call?

The dialing continued for an unreasonable length of time, even for a long-distance phone call. There was a pause and another long dialing. He must have been dialing a dozen numbers in a row. Then I heard him speak. "Oh, yes, please help me. I cannot see clearly. Please. Yes, I'm trying to call Minneapolis, but this is not working properly. Can you make connection to Minneapolis? This is so urgent! Yes, I will tell you the number." He said the number slowly and repeated it several times. Another pause, and then he shouted into the phone in a booming voice: "Ah-ha! I have caught you. You are reading a newspaper! You have asked me to join you in meditation, and I am doing at the promised time—what's the matter? You have asked me to be with you for only this nonsense? For only this, this sitting under your bright lamp and reading newspaper? What is this? This is not good!"

He slammed down the receiver and came to the doorway of the living room. He was chuckling with pleasure, and I could see by his silhouette that he was peering into the living room where we remained sitting in the dark. "You see? They all try to escape. They ask me to work, and then they do not do it. But I caught him. He was not doing his work, and I caught him straightaway!" Swami laughed out loud. "I caught him! Oh, the poor man was so surprised!"

five

In mid-September the members of the training group met with Swami Rama in the third-floor conference room at the Menninger Foundation research building. There were nine of us for that first meeting, including the Greens and me. Elmer had asked that a group be formed for two reasons. It would help the swami combat culture shock and it would be instructive to us. We pushed the tables aside and pulled our chairs around the swami in a semicircle. It was an uncomfortable setting: the harsh fluorescent lights hummed over our heads, and when we sat with head, neck, and trunk straight, as the swami suggested, we looked stiff and awkward in our conference chairs; but the cold, hard floor would have been even less comfortable. From now on, it was decided, we would gather twice each week in the Greens' home, where we could sit around on cushions on the living-room carpet while Swami began his instructions on stable postures. We listened to Swami's introductory words on the mind control and meditation exercise training that was to come in the following sessions; that would be enough for this day.

"The science of yoga is known only to a few. Many people study the books on yoga, some have heard a few yoga sutras or have read the commentaries on the sutras, others have tried some of the practical exercises, but those who really understand the philosophy and the technique of yoga are few indeed. Most people in the West today think that yoga is a sort of physical culture based on the study of postures. No doubt this superficial application has somewhat helped man in society today, but the deeper meaning of yoga is something very different. I think maybe less than one percent of all people understand the true meaning of yoga. The others—either they think nothing at all about yoga or they think that yoga is standing on the head. All right. Let them stand on their heads—I also do. But let them not say this is yoga. My dear friends, to stand on your own two feet is yoga and nothing more!

"Yoga is the control of the modifications of the mind. Yoga is a system of understanding one's own nature, becoming the master of that nature and using that mastery for higher purpose. But here, discipline is required. No self-mastery can be accomplished without discipline. The first yoga sutra of Patanjali says, 'Now the discipline of yoga is being explained.' Without discipline the student will not understand even the meaning of yoga. When we watch the, you see, the superficial behavior of the people; when we consider our behavior in our communities, with our families, and in other social circles; and when we further consider our way of thinking, our inner thoughts, and our deeper awareness, we see clearly the great division between thinking and behavior. So study without discipline creates a gap between thought and action, between knowledge and behavior. The disciplined student—the dedicated aspirant who disciplines himself—is going to learn to utilize his internal resources for external expression. Doug, let me have a cup of tea."

The drinking fountain on the second floor had two taps, and the one with the red handle spouted instant hot water, so it took only a minute or two to produce a cup of tea with a tea bag in a styrofoam cup. In the few minutes that I was out of the room I reflected on the swami's presentation. This was the first I had observed him as a teacher or expounder. I had heard his voice and his words frequently—in meetings in Elmer Green's office, in our evening meditations, or on the numerous occasions when humorous and fascinating anecdotes poured from his mouth. But here he was again different—a presence somewhere between his middle being and his elder self—and he spoke more fluently and fluidly than I had believed possible. In this setting where I had seen him for the first time as a lecturer—almost like a spiritual teacher instructing and inspiring his disciples—he made it seem as though this was all he had ever done, as though this was his only real identity.

When I returned to the lecture room with his cup of tea he was still speaking in the same steady flowing manner, enunciating key words and phrases with energetic emphasis: "Man is in search of peace, bliss, wisdom, and happiness. We are all trying to achieve that everlasting happiness which is gained through knowledge which is gained through peace which is gained through method. For happiness we need peace of mind. For peace of mind we need mind control. For mind control we need method. We need a definite process with which to completely cut off the mind from the contact of the senses—from the sensations and objects of the outside world.

"So there must be the first steps along the path, and the first steps are achieved through the training of the mind. The mind is in the habit of traveling in old grooves. So now, you see, you need training—training to begin to move in new grooves upon the path of meditation. The mind should be free from all turmoils. Buddhist scriptures, Hindu scriptures, Tibetan, Tao, and Confucian scriptures all speak of ways to make mind free. In the beginning there are different methods, but they all meet in the same place. All paths lead to meditation, for there is only one goal and that goal is meditation. Meditation is the only path to freedom—freedom from anxiety; freedom from pain, anger, distress, and depression; freedom from all sorrows, all fears, and all bondages. And meditation is the only path to knowledge.

"Philosophy should support your life. A philosophy of life will lead you to your highest attainment. It will help you understand the relationship of body, mind, and soul. It will help you understand your relationship with nature; and it will help you to solve your own difficulties and problems and to help others as well. Real knowledge starts with understanding your nonself and your real self. It will be easy for you to understand your relationship with the universe if you first understand something about your own existence. You should differentiate between the nonself and the self. Nonself is body, senses, mind, ego, intellect; that which is behind and beyond all this is the true self. All things are moved from their inner conditions. Everything comes into manifestation from within. Understand this center within, and there will be no difficulty in understanding life—its goal, its currents and crosscurrents. A man having all treasures and all material happiness in the world is nothing before a man who has knowledge of the spirit or divine—knowledge of himself, of the true self.

"Now, you should have and keep a spiritual diary. You can develop yourself by writing in bold words what you have done each day. Your spiritual self will tell you what work is to be done that you have not done and what work is not to be done that you have done. In this way you will be disciplined. You will understand your major thoughts, and you will understand where you have committed mistakes.

"It is not helpful to brood upon the past. Self-condemnation is harmful. Mistakes and ignorance should be acknowledged and forgotten. You will put your mind to better use in trying to understand things properly than in dwelling upon your ignorance. One should be serious in the path of divinity, but that seriousness should not bring strain or depression. Cheerfulness is the greatest physician. One who is always cheerful will have more strength, do more work, be more relaxed, and enjoy life in a better way.

"On this path, the path of meditation, nothing is a sin. There is no sin, there are only obstacles. When you begin to understand things properly, the obstacles will be of help to you. But before self-realization anything and everything can become an entanglement. Try to remove these obstacles with purity of mind, one-pointedness of purpose, self-confidence, and discipline so that you may go on to higher things. But you should try to avoid the fruits of your actions. Use your discrimination and do what your conscience tells you is good and beneficial. Then be satisfied that you have done your best and just continue, and do not stop to search for results. The results will be there. The results will come. There is nothing that says that you must watch for them and verify them. If you watch for results then you will be distracted from your work. Those who watch for results are tempted to gather the fruits for themselves. Or else if there are no desirable fruits, then they are disappointed. So either way it becomes a burden. One will either be happy or disappointed. If he is disappointed, he cannot go on working. And if he is not disappointed, he will be tempted to take the results for himself or he will be fighting that temptation. So judge first. Discriminate first. Then act, and do not pay attention to the results of your actions—this will only become a great burden. If you do your actions for all—for men, animals, birds, insects, and plants—then the fruits of your actions belong not to you but to all of life, and you are free and joyous. Now, we should have some tissues here."

"Tissues?" I wondered.

"Let us do some practical work here now. We will begin with the first breathing exercise—bellows breathing. So you will be clearing your nose, and there should be some tissues here. Everyone should have some tissues."

Someone went across the hall to get a box of facial tissues from our project's supply cabinet. Silently Swami glanced toward the door, and then he began again: "So we begin at the beginning. And all these steps are steps on the path of meditation. They are steps, but they are not meditation. Do not think that they are meditation. They are a part of the process, but they are not the state—that state of meditation —for meditation *is* a state, a state beyond mind. We hear so many talks about meditation. People say, 'Oh, I saw this and that, I felt this and that, I experienced this and that.' But these varieties of experiences are not meditation. Meditation is beyond this. Meditation is the state of being established in one's own essential nature—this is the third yoga sutra of

Patanjali. The fourth sutra says: 'In other states the seer identifies himself with the modifications of the mind.' The aspirant who identifies with these experiences identifies himself with his mind. Such a student spends his life gathering impressions and sensations, and he remains trapped in that, you see, that which is subject to change, death, and decay.

"Now, for example, suppose I am sitting in my stable posture in some quiet corner of my house and I say, 'Now let me begin my meditation,' and then my mind begins to wander through all these recent thoughts of my daily life. So I attend to the focusing of my consciousness. But my consciousness is captured by these whirlpools of my mind, these activities of mind called *vrittis*, and these *vrittis* fool me and make themselves feel like this consciousness is my identity. So now an image comes—a tree suddenly comes before me. And this image becomes an experience, clear experience, just as if I were standing before the tree. This tree that I am looking at—I perceive that it is a sandal tree. I well know the fragrance of the sandalwood, so I respond in the appropriate manner. My mind is occupied with the sandal tree, and I am experiencing the image and sensing the fragrance. Snakes often wrap themselves about these trees, and suddenly I am aware that there is a snake in this one. I am so sensitive about the sight of snakes that I begin to shiver. My intellect is functioning, and I know that the sandal fragrance pacifies snakes. A snake in a sandal tree forgets his biting habit, so there is nothing to fear. For a moment I am relieved; but still I know that this is a deadly snake, and as I look at it, it looks fearful. Such a snake can kill a man, I tell myself, and again I shiver. The natural, primitive feeling of repulsion overtakes my intellect. I am overcome with fear. A strange, sickly feeling travels through my body. Again my intellect moves me. I am aware there was no tree at all before me, because I am just sitting with eyes closed in a quiet corner of my house. There was no snake, no fragrance. It was only a thought. My body relaxes and this horrible feeling fades away. In a brief moment I have traveled through a chain of experiences—imaginary, sensual, rational, emotional—and my nervous system in that brief moment experienced a chain of changes. But where was I? Was I at my center, that very core of my being whence I aloofly watch my actions and my thoughts? Was I sitting in a quiet corner of my house? Was I standing before a sandal tree? And where am I now? Am I sitting in my stable posture in some quiet corner of my house as I supposed in the beginning? Or am I really before that sandal tree that I have described. 'No, Swami,' you say, 'you are really sitting in the chair in the conference room giving your talk.' But is that the essence of my being that is doing these things—speaking to you, having this experience? No, my true nature is doing none of these things that my body is doing and my thought process is explaining. If these questions come before me and I try to analyze my experience, I remain entirely at one with my thought process. When we identify ourselves with our thoughts and our experiences, we have forgotten our true nature. To remember our true nature, to be in our true nature—this is meditation."

When the tissues arrived and were distributed, two or three to each of us, Swami Rama demonstrated what he called bellows breathing, an intense hyperventilation that sounded loud and powerful. Without moving his body he exhaled and inhaled loudly through both nostrils, beginning slowly at first and then faster so that he sounded like a train pulling out of the station, accelerating gradually and steadily, and finally speeding down the tracks into the distance.

"Your work starts with your lungs. Why with the lungs? Why not with your arms? By controlling the motion of the lungs, mind's movements come under control. By controlling the motion of the lungs, by increasing the capacity of the lungs, by making the lungs strong, you make the respiratory system very regular. Now, by making the respiratory system regular, you bring the vagus nerve under control. By bringing the vagus nerve under control, you gain control of the sympathetic and parasympathetic systems. There is a basic mind-body unity which exists in man. This mind-body unity exists at all the levels—conscious levels and unconscious levels. Breath is the first link between the body and the mind. And breath is the first link between the conscious and the unconscious. Why? Because the breathing is an unconscious activity that can be brought into the level of the conscious. So if you control your breath, you see—control this normally unconscious activity—by your attention, your attention develops and you are on your way toward gaining control of the unconscious processes or movements of your mind."

Swami instructed us in our first exercise, which was a beginner's form of bellows breathing. He had us exhale loudly and sharply to the count of one, emptying the lungs completely, and then inhale an equal volume to the count of three. We did that several times and then reversed the process, exhaling to the count of three and inhaling an equal volume to the count of one. He told us to do this while keeping our spines straight and without jerking the chest or the head; even this was difficult for some. Until we could do this well, he told us, we would not be able to perform properly the bellows exercise he had just demonstrated.

"So you should practice this method for one or two weeks, and then we will go on from there. And next time we will talk about your stable posture, because you should do this in your stable posture. So practice as I told you, and do not use your mouth. Mouth is the emergency gate only—not for breathing exercises and not for ordinary breathing. Why? Because mouth has no filter. The creator has provided filters only in the nostrils. You should practice this exercise, and you should practice watching the breath and see that you habitually breathe through the nostrils. Main thing is, always focus your attention upon what you are doing. In yoga, whatever you do, your mind should be there—and that is enough for today. Let us leave this place. Next time we meet at Dr. Green's place. Isn't that right, Doctor?"

On the way home I told the swami that his bellows breathing demonstration had made me think of an accelerating train. "Oh, my dear boy," he said, "you are always thinking of trains. Trains, trains, trains. One day we must definitely ride it, that train in the park. When are you going to arrange it?"

"We can do it any time, Swami, any time you want."

"I will go along whenever you want, whenever you are ready—but please arrange it. This is for you I am pushing this thing."

six

One Saturday afternoon while Elmer and Alyce were at the lab working on a report, I remained at home with Swami. When I heard his footsteps in the library upstairs I knew he was not in meditation; I thought to carry up a tall glass of hot tilk for him before he should have to ask for it. I was learning to anticipate his wishes before they were spoken.

"Ah, good, good!" he said, as he opened his door. "Wonderful! Look here, I am just now going through some of these films I have carried from India. Music films—recording reels—what do you call them?"

"Oh, you mean tapes? Tape recordings."

"Ah, yes. Now if you can help me to operate this equipment, then we shall just listen to some of this music."

Elmer had a tape deck hooked up to his stereo system in the library, and I threaded one of the reels of tape onto the machine as Swami began drinking his tea. When I noticed his loud sipping, I also noticed there was no incense burning in the room, and a voice inside me repeated the words I had just recently spoken to someone else: "They used to prepare his tea and even light his incense for him." I turned on the amplifiers, and before starting the tape, I lit many sticks of incense. I held them in my hand like a flaming bouquet, and when they were burning well, instead of blowing them out like candles, I fanned them briskly with my other hand to extinguish the flames as I had seen Swami do.

"My dear, great Doug, you are just like me," he said. "You are hopelessly addicted to this incense business. But it is a wonderful addiction, is it not?"

I only smiled.

"No, no, it is not really a case of attachment. It is simply enjoying something of this world that gives us pleasure without harming us, something that helps us without holding us back. Even the renunciates do not renounce this incense. But sooner or later all these things must be given up. All these worldly things, even the instruments of devotion, must be left behind. They can take us so far and we must continue on—beyond, beyond, beyond—always leaving behind the very means by which we reach each step along the path. I used to play sitar. All these instruments I used to play that you will hear on this, you see, this tape. And then one day my master told me to leave it. 'Why should I leave it? It is a beautiful and useful thing,' I said, 'and I am improving day by day, why should I leave it just when I am getting good?' He said, 'That is the trouble with you. You will become good; next you will become better; next you will become excellent; next you will become pleased with yourself that you are so excellent, and you will be distracted from your work. Let the musicians do their work and you do yours. If you want music, listen to the musicians.' "

I turned on the tape and Swami finished his tea, put down the empty glass, settled back on the sofa, lifted his legs into a lotus position, folded his hands in his lap, and closed his eyes. I closed my eyes too, and the room filled with fragrant incense smoke and the beautiful traditional Indian devotional sounds of sitar, tambura, and tabla.

After many minutes I opened my eyes and looked at the swami. He seemed almost too still and too peaceful to be real. I wondered if he were in meditation, or perhaps in some sort of trance. Now again he was his elder self. It was not that his face looked old, but there was something venerable about his presence.

Suddenly he looked at me, and I realized that I had been staring at his closed eyes. For a moment his eyes held mine and he seemed to be looking deep into my head. Then he softened his gaze. "Can you understand this music? Do you like it? I think you like it."

"Yes."

He closed his eyes again. "Because you are from the East."

We listened silently to the rest of the tape; I kept my eyes closed and did not look at the swami again. When the tape ended, we talked until Swami said, "All right, thank you. Tomorrow we shall hear another reel—something with singing. Now, go and leave me."

I sat out in the yard, leaving Swami alone in the house. It was good to be outside when the wind was from the north and the air was crisp and clean. I stayed out as long as I could—until the sun was low in the sky and it began to grow cold. Soon winter would be coming, and it would be too cold to sit outside at all.

I wondered whether Swami was still sitting in meditation, so I walked quietly to the top of the stairs. His door was open, but he was not in his room. He was not in the bathroom either. I thought he might be trying to make himself a cup of tea, but he was not in the kitchen. He was no where to be seen—neither upstairs nor downstairs. At last I found him in the garage.

He was standing in near darkness in a corner of the garage and he had a stick in his hand. He was poking at something in the large sink. When I turned on the light, he gave me a sheepish grin, but he went right on poking with the stick. After a full minute's observation, I realized what was going on: Swami Rama was washing his underwear in the garage.

"I can do that," I said.

"No, no, I'm almost finished, let me finish. Don't tell Mama!"

But I did tell "Mama" when she and Elmer returned from the lab. It was useless not to mention it, because Swami and I had put it all out on the clothesline in the backyard, and it would hardly go unnoticed hanging out there under the sun on Sunday morning.

"Now, why would he do that?" Alyce asked. "I asked him

several times to give me his things that needed washing. He always said, 'That's all right. That's all right, Mama.' What could I do?"

"The problem is," Elmer interjected, "he can't give dirty laundry to people like us. What an embarrassing inconvenience for a swami! Not to have anyone around of the proper caste to do the laundry!"

On Sunday morning I looked out the back window to see that Swami's laundry was still hanging safely on the line and then out the front window to see that the train was running in the park. I decided that the priority for the day should be a train ride for Swami Rama.

"Oh, you have such temptation!" he exclaimed when I mentioned the train after breakfast. "Yes, today at last we must definitely ride the train!"

In the early afternoon we walked across the street and into the park. It was a good day for riding the train: the sky was blue and the sun was warm. Swami had on his best robes. The most impressive part of his attire was the elegantly embroidered top piece. He wore it over his back, draped around his shoulders like a huge stole, but with the ends folded back over his shoulders in the front. These ends kept sliding off his shoulders as he walked along, but he was adept at flinging them in place again with an unconscious but graceful toss of his arm.

"How do I look?" he asked.

"Like a swami," I answered. "Like a nice-looking swami."

"No, no, no, it doesn't matter. Looking nice is not the point. But am I not curious to the Westerners? To the families and the children who come to the park? I do not like to make anyone feel strange. They may think me as they like, but I have not to make them uncomfortable."

"You just look natural to me, Swami. If any people get upset, it will be their own fault."

"You say that because you feel familiar with all things easily. But many people—particularly in your country, I have found—are disturbed and distressed by things different."

The starting point for the train was at the eastern edge of the park, across from the entrance to the zoo. I bought our tickets, and we waited for the train to pull in. A sign on the loading platform explained that the train made stops as it circled the park and passengers could get off along the way if they wished. There were so many children waiting to ride on this Sunday afternoon that I wondered whether there would be room for the swami and me. But when the train pulled up to the platform and stopped, Swami bolted into the nearest seat, shouting, "Come on! Come on!" He and I just fit side by side on one of the seats and the little kids piled on in front and in back of us. The "engineer," who was nearly as big as the engine, let one of the kids sit up front with him to pull the string that made the whistle blow. There were a few other adults on the last of the four cars, two of them looking like young honeymooners, but most of the grownups stayed on the platform and waved to their children. Everyone did seem to notice the swami. I didn't think they looked uncomfortable, but they did appear curious. I suppose they were not wondering, "Why is this man wearing these robes?" as much as, "Why is this large, robed figure riding this little train?"

"It's small," said Swami. "Now that we sit here, we realize it is smaller in its actual form that in our mental visions." And when the train began to move slowly away from its platform he added, "This is nothing much, actually." But he smiled when the train went through a tunnel, and when it passed over a trestle that bridged a man-made river he said, "They have designed it very nicely. It nicely suits the children." The train made its first stop and no one got off. Only a moment later it slowed for the second stop, and Swami said, "Tell me quickly, are you content?"

"Content? Yes, I'm content. Why?"

"Then let us disembark from this creature," and he leaped from his seat when the train had barely stopped. "It's a useless thing to go full circle and arrive where we started. It becomes a case of going nowhere at all. Now we have come to these fields of grass, and we can walk back in a quarter hour's time." But we had walked only a few minutes when he stopped and pointed. "No, no, just see over there. That will be something more interesting yet!"

"That's the greenhouse, Swami."

"Of course that's the greenhouse, but what is inside is the point. They should be having cactus, isn't it?"

"I guess so. I've never been inside."

"You should have looked inside, what's the matter? You've had the chance."

"Well, it's like the train—I've just never gotten around to it."

"You see? How much unfinished business we have to settle today!"

We spent a good half-hour in the greenhouse. There was no one else inside, and Swami walked boldly about looking at the plants, giving opinions about all of them. There were cacti, many kinds of cacti, but Swami was disappointed in them. "I am an expert of cactus plants, you know. I have them at my ashram in India, all around the walls—wait till you see my ashram, you will be amazed on my cactus. These here are nothing before mine! Where is their master? Poor creatures are starving! Look at them, how neglected. They are starving for affection!" And he talked of cactus plants all the way home and through the front door. "Mama!" he shouted the moment we were in the living room. "Where is Mama?" She came out of the kitchen. "Mama, I am having an idea! Let me put cactus here, all in the front. Let us remove these thickets of bushes and put cactus. Twenty varieties of cactus I'll put. They'll become by far the best in your country!"

That evening after supper the four of us sat quietly in the living room, the swami in his favorite spot on the love seat in the corner with his legs interlocked in a lotus arrangement and a tall glass of tilk in his hands. For a long time no one spoke.

"Now, Douglas should buy some furniture, and the matter should not be postponed. I will help you, Doug; I will be there, and we will select something to your liking according to my advice."

His words shocked me. What an off-the-wall thing for the swami to say in the middle of the silence—and in such confident, authoritative tones! No one could respond to this arbitrary counsel, so the silence resumed.

"No, no, this is—this should be done."

"I'm not thinking of buying any furniture," I said.

"So! Therefore I have just now put the subject!"

"But what would I do with furniture?"

"This is the point. I will arrange it so that you will have your place. Then you will have your marriage. This is high time for you to arrange your permanent home and your family. So I am going to arrange these things. We will begin with selecting furniture, and next step you will be having your wife."

"Are you going to arrange my wife?"

"I can easily arrange a suitable wife for you. You will see."

"I thought what you were going to arrange was for me to go to India."

"Either you will settle down or you will go. So I want to prepare things properly. First, we will arrange your home, and after, I will take you to India."

For some moments I reflected. This was a pretty heavy proposition on the part of the swami—a proposal to be the arranger of my life.

"Doug may have different ideas in mind," Alyce suggested. "He may decide not to go to India. Or if he does go, he may want to make his own plans. Or suppose he decides to go back to Korea, where he's spent so many years?"

"No, this is not good. This is why, you see? This is why I'm discussing the thing directly."

"You may discuss"—Alyce laughed—"but he may not listen."

"He should listen! Because I am knowing. I know what is best."

"But suppose he doesn't agree?"

"Then I will exert pressures—subtle pressures from behind. We have ways of doing such things."

That strange conversation went on for some time, and I became increasingly uncomfortable. The whole thing would have been amusing except that the swami was entirely serious. At any rate, I said very little. I did not want the situation to turn into some sort of debate, in which case the swami would only have strengthened his position.

For some days after that his words continued to ring in my ears. I wanted to dismiss them from my memory, but for some reason that was not possible. I wondered whether he really knew better than I about my future—whether he was able to see a turning in my path of which I was not yet aware. There might have been some purpose in his concern for me, some purpose that I should attend to. Yet my feeling was that I wanted him to forget about it. I wished neither to be the unquestioning follower of his advice nor the unknowing recipient of his subtle pressures.

In the unexpected episode, as in almost all of Swami's behavior, he was being his middle self. That middle self that was the performer of yogic feats was the part of him that tended to become the insistent arranger. But that was the part of him that was so powerfully persuasive. My problem was how to relate to him in a manner that would be educational and beneficial without succumbing to the powerful grip of his personality. Both the old man and the child in him were too seldom seen. His elder self seemed to be the source of his knowledge rather than his actions and did not seem to need to be persuasive. He was his elder self only in our evening meditations or sometimes during our training group sessions, and I believed he was his elder self when he was alone or when I sat with him and he was so calm and so silent that he projected an atmosphere of peace and safety. These three aspects were not simply imagined by me: they were apparent to everyone who knew him well, and they were as different in their characters as any three people are different from one another.

The child in Swami Rama was as spontaneous and natural as the rest of him, and it was really a child—not clumsy or silly, but purely and openly a child. When he was a child he laughed and moved like a child, and because he was so graceful it looked pleasing rather than awkward. That was the most enjoyable part of him, and the easiest to relate to. There was no need to be perceptive, attentive, or responsive to the playful part of him, and it became all right to say or do most anything as long as it was cheerful. Alyce and Elmer had four grandchildren living in Topeka, and they could bring out the child in him. One of the first times it happened he was sitting at the dining-room table engaged in thoughtful discourse when out of the corner of an eye he caught sight of one of the boys trying headstands on the living-room carpet.

Swami's face, his form, his total bearing changed abruptly. "Hey, man!" he shouted, jumping up from his chair. "Okay, let's go! I can do it, look what I can do!" In two seconds he was on his head, on his hands, on his head again, slipping his legs into a lotus lock, upside down and in one fluid motion as though he were made of soft plastic. Somehow when he played with the kids, he could make them forget what he was, and they would react toward him as though he were one of them. When he laughed he would turn around in a circle or jump up and down, bending his knees and springing into the air, and he would do it with no more noise or commotion than if he were a small boy.

The four grandchildren attended the same school, and on the night of the school carnival the four kids and the two mothers took the swami and me to the big event along with the grandparents. The swami became an excited child and scrambled around in the back of the station wagon with the rest of them.

The child in him didn't worry about what he consumed— cakes, pies, candy, soft drinks, nearly anything but meat or fish—and his enthusiasm for fun and tasty things to eat was used to advantage by the kids. Because of their inhibitions or better judgment, grownups usually restrain kids and put an end to most things before the kids are ready to quit. So the four children were happy to leave the grownups behind on carnival night and run here and there with the swami. When they had made the rounds of the booths they headed for the rides on the playgrounds at the edge of the campus. On their way to one of the rides they passed the car-smashing concession, and I joined them as they stopped to watch. The swami looked shocked. Schoolchildren were paying ten cents a crack for big rubber mallets to smash up a junk car. They were hitting the windows, the hood, the doors, everything, while an adult supervisor stood by to count the hits and to see that no one got hurt. The middle part of Swami would have been indignant and would have expounded his disapproval, but the child in him could only watch in painful bewilderment. He reached for his little friends for comfort, and he could only say, "Why? Why? What's the matter?"

I thought of Swami as a child in his country, and I could feel how foreign this sort of play would have been to his childhood experience. And as I watched him now I could feel him struggle to remain on the level of a companion to the children. Though he had come here elegantly attired in his flowing robes, they had proudly introduced him to their Kansas counterparts as a friend, and he did not want to be brought out of that identity by seeing this violent, destructive play.

"But we're not gonna do it," said one of the girls assuringly. "We don't like it!"

Swami took her hand. "We have not to watch any more, okay?"

So the four kids ran for the nearest ride, and Swami and I ran behind them. They all pushed up to the ticket window at once as the big, circling wheel slowed to a stop; they came away with five tickets and handed one to the swami. The attendant met him at the top of the ramp, and he saw the swami's ticket. "Are these here kids with you? Are there four of them or five?"

"No, he's supposed to come with us," they explained.

The man looked at Swami strangely. "Well, he can stand right up here and watch."

Swami seemed embarrassed, and for a brief moment he nearly fell out of character. But then he found appropriate words. "I'm saving this for her," he said. "I'm going to buy more tickets and they'll all ride again. I have sufficient enough money."

"I'm tryin' to call it a day," said the man. "That last ride was s'posed to be it. Takes a long time to break this rig down. Tell you what. These kids are the only ones on—for that one extra ticket I'll give 'em all double time."

Swami looked at all the empty seats that would soon be spinning merrily around the turning pole, and I watched him squeeze the ticket in his palm. "Okay," he said.

But just as the man was pushing the lever to put the idling engine into gear, the swami dashed through the gate and jumped into an empty seat and snapped the safety belt into place over his lap, making the children shriek with joy. Only a youngster could move so fast. By the time he was in his seat the machine was moving; but instead of stopping it again, the man only shouted at me. "He's not s'posed to be on there!"

Just then the Greens and their daughters walked up, and when the man saw they were with us, he pointed out the swami to them and shook his head. The lady came out of the ticket booth to get a better look. The swami sat sheepishly in his seat and made himself as small as he could as he went around and around. "They forced me!" he shouted

every time he came past. "The children forced me! What to
do, they forced me!"

The attendant left his lever and came close enough to
ask in a confidential and respectful tone, "Excuse me for
being inquisitive, but what is that man?"

"He's a swami," I said. "He's from India."

"Yeah? I thought he looked like somethin' on that order."
And they all got a double ride.

Swami was at times delightful and at times perplexing, but
he was always interesting. His pressuring of me never
stopped—and it was never subtle. His advice became more
constant and more insistent. He made a variety of arrangements for me, none of which I accepted, and he seemed to
want me to commit myself to his future. Several times he
asked the Greens for help in persuading me. "If he would
just let me have three years of his life," he would say. "No,
let me have him from now and then three years in India.
Such remarkable and unbelievable things I could do with
him!"

Seeing Swami on the train ride or at the carnival or playing with the children, it was difficult to believe that he could
ever be so forward and so powerfully persuasive as to be
almost frightening. His pressures were always sudden and
unexpected, and they always came as a surprise to me—and
that made it impossible to ignore them. I knew that there
were times when he was highly intuitive and there were
times when he became less of his personality and more of his
higher nature. But I could not tell whence came his advice
for me. I could only feel that when he gave it, he was being
very serious.

For a long time I thought about this. The problem was
not how to answer his demands, it was what to make of him.
If his advice to me came out of some higher knowledge,
some intuitive view of things to which I did not have access,

I ought to either listen and follow—in spite of my personal feelings—or miss a good chance. I knew that some of my best opportunities might seem unattractive to my ego. On the other hand, the swami had an ego of his own—and a very powerful one. It would be more than foolish, it would be dangerous for me to put aside my own personality only to follow another personality—only to submit myself to the manipulations of some more charismatic personality's ego.

When at last I settled the issue to my own satisfaction I settled it forever, not only with regard to Swami Rama but also with regard to any other individual in my future under whom I might be a student and from whom I might learn. What I had been doing in thinking about all this was making the best possible use of my own reason and judgment; and I realized one day that this process would never stop. Once it occurred to me, it made obvious sense: my chance to go on being a student and to continue associating with extraordinary teachers would depend upon my capacity to rely upon my own discrimination. However saintly, mysterious, powerful, or gurulike a teacher might be, he still has a higher self and a lower self like every other human; and it would be the job of my own guru—the guru within me—to discriminate between the selves. If ever I should relinquish any part of my own will and self-determination, it would have to be the conscious, purposeful intent of my highest judgment.

Once I had made this determination, I was safe. I was safe enough to go on listening, safe enough to put myself in Swami Rama's hands to a point. After all, Swami Rama knew many things that I needed to learn. He knew what I needed to do to learn those things, and I wanted to practice what Swami Rama preached. There was no limit to what I could learn from this swami or from any other swami or monk or preacher or teacher. All I needed was to be self-reliant enough to be safe enough to be humble enough to learn.

seven

With each new day in Topeka, Kansas, Swami Rama invoked increasing curiosity among the staff of the Menninger Foundation. There were a few researchers who reacted to him with mixed emotions. He stimulated their interest because they knew he could do some unusual and remarkable things, yet at times he seemed a threat to some of their preestablished conclusions about the laws of the universe and the nature of the electrochemical organism called man and to their conclusions about the supremacy and finality of contemporary Western science.

What was really threatening about Swami Rama was not so much what he did as what he said, and the swami himself contributed to the perplexity by observing the usual Indian habit of exaggerating and speaking in superlatives. He would too often say things like if one would only learn to do this or that or learn to understand this or that, then "I assure you you will be no more affected by any of these diseases and no more troubles of any kind will come before you!" In a sense, he may have been right, considering that these fantastic claims were always conditional upon achieving a fantastic level of adeptness or understanding, but many of the researchers had already drawn lines of demarcation between the possible and the impossible, and they took his overwhelming remarks as a challenge to their good sense.

Swami made another kind of challenge in Elmer Green's office one day. It was not for Elmer's sake he made it; he had begun to speak more cautiously to Elmer, because Elmer had sometimes reminded him that his statements were too far out to be impressive. There was a psychiatrist in Elmer's office that day, for whose benefit Swami boldly introduced into the conversation some very strong claims about the powers of attention and concentration. When he was questioned, Swami countered with stronger statements, and the discussion was catapulted into the realm of psychokinesis and teleportation. What followed was the typical "Can you do it? . . . Yes, I can . . . Well, prove it" sort of challenge, and the swami offered to demonstrate psychokinesis down the hall in that psychiatrist's office.

"He tied a pencil on a string," Elmer told me, "and hung it from a corner of the desk. Then he crouched down and began saying his mantra very forcefully and the pencil began to rotate. But I objected because he was blowing on it as he said his mantra. Naturally the pencil is going to move if someone blows on it. So I asked the swami if he could do it from a distance, and he said he could."

Elmer told me that the swami had claimed he could move such an object from a distance and while wearing "a mask to prevent air currents." The event was scheduled for ten days hence.

In the days that followed, the swami began to prepare himself for the "PK" experiment. There were times during those days when it seemed to me that he was feeling anxious about what he had promised to do. I would not have been surprised to learn that he regretted having accepted that challenge, I would only have been surprised to hear him admit it. I felt that Elmer and Alyce shared the same regret, not because they were deeply concerned one way or the other about how it might turn out, but because the parapsychological experiment was not part of the category of phenomena they were currently investigating. The stupendous effort necessary for the swami to live up to his challenge would inevitably become a distraction to him and would likely be a confusion of issues to others.

I could not help being concerned about how it would turn out. I kept wondering why Swami had blown on that pencil in the researcher's office, and I wished very badly that he had not done that. Maybe if he had persisted long enough and hard enough, the pencil would have moved without his blowing on it. If not, it would have been better to have tried to explain the failure than to have tried to fool anyone. But maybe he wasn't trying to cheat. Maybe his intense concentration made him chant forcefully. Maybe the pencil would have moved even if it had been too far from his face to be affected by his breath. Now we would never know what really happened. That was why I wanted Swami to have another chance, a chance to clear things up—especially since I could see that this was what he wanted. I was close enough to him day after day to feel his concerns, close enough to him to know that he really believed in himself and in what he said.

Swami practiced every day at work and every evening at home. Nobody knew just how he practiced because nobody was allowed to watch him. He continued with his session in the laboratory in the afternoons, but in the mornings he often sat alone in his office with his door closed and his "Do Not Disturb" sign hanging on the doorknob. But I could feel him becoming restless. Many times as I sat typing in my office I saw him walk past my door. Sometimes he stepped in just far enough to ask, "Any telephone calls for me?" There had always been calls—always several people who had left their names and numbers, hoping Swami would call back—so I dutifully gave him these names and numbers when he asked, even though I thought I was not supposed to, as Swami was not to be disturbed by such things.

Some of the calls I got for the swami were so bizarre I regretted turning them over to him. People would say things like "I am a very spiritual and highly advanced person—I've been traveling out of my body for years and years," or, "I'm sure that an acquaintance with Swami Rama, on the earthly level as well as in the spiritual realm, would be mutually beneficial to both of us." Some callers would keep me on the phone while they went to embarrassing lengths describing their various "experiences," but I developed some fairly tact-ful methods for limiting these conversations. Strangely enough (and fortunately, I thought), many of the callers declined to leave their names and numbers. "May I tell the swami you called?" I would ask.

"Oh, yes. Please do."

"All right, may I have your name?"

"Oh, he knows my name, just tell him I called."

"I'm sorry, but I don't know who you are."

"It doesn't matter, Swamiji knows. Swamiji knows every-thing!"

Then there were times when Swami came on the line during some of those strange conversations. Just when I would be closing a conversation with someone who had an urgent message for the swami from "on high" or with some-one who had been meeting the swami on the "astral plane" or in "dreamland" every night and wondered whether he was having the same "experience," or just when I would be ex-plaining that the swami was not available to answer the phone at that moment, his voice would come on the line: "Helloo? Helloo? God bless you? Who is it?"

Beside my telephone I had a list of names of people in Minneapolis and Chicago from whom Swami wished to ac-cept calls anytime he was in his office. All others, he in-structed me, he preferred not to know about because he did not want to be distracted. But apparently he changed his mind. One day the telephone rang when I was in his office. We could not hear it ring, but one of the plastic buttons on his instrument lit up and it caught his eye immediately. I would not have noticed it. I realized at once that he had trained himself to see that tiny light though it was almost behind his head.

"The phone!" he shouted. "Take the phone. No, you are here—let me do it." It was a call for me, so he handed me the receiver. "I don't listen to your calls," he said when I hung up the phone, "only to mine." Anyway, most of the calls are for me, by far. Who was that ringing us now? Was it regarding me?"

Swami did not have to depend for long upon watching for the light on his telephone. Something other than the instrumentation provided by the telephone company began alerting him to incoming calls. It may have happened as a result of his becoming sensitive to the telephone light or from his trying to hear my phone ring down the hall, or perhaps it was a natural product of his yogic pursuits—a sort of latent *siddhi* he decided to put to use. In any case, on several occasions that I knew about he got his "signal" even before the telephone rang.

The first time I discovered this he was in my office. "Let me take this," he said abruptly, hurrying toward the door. "It's all right, it will be useful for her. You sound that buzzer and I will use my telephone." Before he had finished his words or disappeared through my doorway, the telephone rang. It was for Swami, and there was no need to sound his buzzer. "Yes, yes, I'm here," he said as soon as he reached his phone.

A few days later he rushed into my office with a frown on his face. "Minnesota is calling and they don't connect. What's the matter? I am here, why do they not connect me? Call the switchboard. They are not doing properly at all."

"But the phone didn't ring," I protested. "There hasn't been any call."

"No, no, it's an outside call. It should be connected by the switchboard. The fault is with them. Ask them why they don't connect."

"Yes, there was a call from Minnesota," the operator told me. "Your extension has been busy. The party held for a while, then said he'd call back this afternoon."

"Well, they don't understand," Swami complained. "We have both been here all along."

"Were you using your phone?" I asked.

"No, I was only waiting."

That afternoon I picked up my receiver to call out and Swami's voice said, "Helloo? Are you there?"

I said, "Yes!"

"No, no, no! Not you! He is trying to reach me again. You see? Something is out of order."

At last I was sure of the problem and I went into his office to explain: "Swami, when a call comes in you should not pick up the receiver too early. The connection cannot be made when you are holding this receiver. We have to wait for the ring or for this light to come on; otherwise there will only be a busy signal on the other end. They will think—"

"No, wait!" he interrupted. "Call is coming! You see? The call comes and the light does not." He reached for the receiver, but before he lifted it the light began blinking. "Ah, no. You are correct! Now it works properly." He handed the receiver to me, and it was Minnesota calling.

I discussed these events with Elmer and Alyce, and they brought the matter up with the swami in the morning staff meeting. "The number of outside calls for you is increasing, as you know, Swami," Elmer said. "And it seems that you are becoming increasingly aware of them. According to what you said initially, this is just what you did not want. At any rate, this is Doug's job—to handle all these calls. If you could let Doug take care of that by himself and continue to be 'unavailable' as you originally intended—"

"Then why I am having this phone?" Swami protested. "What's the fun of having a phone if you can't answer it?"

Swami would go on preoccupying himself and me with this telephone business, I knew, and nothing would change. As long as he had a phone in his office he would watch for that light and come on the line with "God bless you" just when I was explaining to someone that he did not wish to be disturbed. And I knew that he would wander out into the lobby four or five times a day to see if there was any mail in his box. If he were to intercept a letter or a call that I was supposed to know about, it would create a problem for me. The swami's extraordinary trait of always being certain did not make him an easy person to deal with, at least on the level that I was supposed to deal with him. He might be all right, I thought, in some ashram or monastery, but this was an office and a laboratory, and I had to be able to work with him and with all the people who were dealing with him.

These thoughts went through my mind as I sat at my desk after the morning staff meeting, and they went on and on and grew heavier in my head and more frustrating until Swami came through my door, saying, "Why are you thinking these thoughts? You are independent, I am independent, we are free, and nothing can disturb us! We have nothing to complain and no one can complain of us: 'Oh, Doug is not doing this or that properly—and that funny swami is doing this and that.' What have we to care? We are free and independent, and we are above! Let the others enjoy their own lives, let me enjoy mine, and you enjoy yours!" Without waiting for a response from me, he turned and went out the door.

The main reason I was in my present position, I reminded myself, was that I was supposed to have exceptional experience and abilities in getting along with people extraneous to our culture and our ways. Therefore my main responsibility was to the swami—to be as close as I could be to what he wanted me to be and yet let him be himself. At least all my reactions to the swami were on a practical daily-affair level and not belief- or opinion-oriented. In that respect I was uncommon. Almost every person whom Swami was forced to encounter day after day was either skeptical and antagonistic toward him or else overemotionally worshipful. It was little wonder he spoke of remaining above.

One of my friends in the department was a research assistant for another project. From the day that Swami attempted that "psychic" experiment in a colleague's office, the head of that project wanted to have a private interview with the swami. Since my friend made appointments for his boss and I handled all of Swami's appointments, the two of us discussed the arrangements. The doctor wanted to spend at least a couple of hours with the swami, but I thought it should wait at least until after the upcoming PK experiment in the lab. But his boss called me directly to ask why the swami could not give him a little time some morning soon. I told him the swami's allotted time for appointments was all filled for the next week and that I had been instructed to leave him time for his practice.

"What do you think he wants to discuss with Swami?" I asked my friend at lunch.

"He doesn't want to discuss anything," my friend answered. "I know what he wants, he wants to give him a Rorschach."

"Why?" I asked. "Is that for the research you guys are doing? Does he want Swami to be a volunteer subject?"

"I'll tell you what I think, since you asked. He wants to discredit the swami. He wants to prove he's crazy."

"Do you know what I think? No, I'd better not say it. But I'll tell you one thing. If I were a swami, I sure wouldn't come over here. Some people think he's crazy, some people think he's a fraud, some people think he's their master, some people think he's some sort of god. Swami Rama isn't any of those things. He's a raja yogi from India. Americans don't even know what a yogi is."

In spite of his restlessness and all the outside distractions (which, I began to realize, he was using to counteract the disapprobation that he felt around him), the swami continued to practice every day for his demonstration of moving an object. Usually he practiced at home; sometimes I thought he practiced all night long.

On the day before the swami was to perform his experiment, he did not come out of his room. Elmer, Alyce, and I went to work and left him home alone. We canceled his one morning appointment and the regular afternoon lab session, and I wondered whether we should cancel our group meeting. It was Thursday and our training group was scheduled for that night. I did not want to bother the swami by phoning to ask, so I dropped the subject. But I did offer the suggestion when Alyce and I arrived home that afternoon and Swami came out of his room and confessed to me, for the first time ever, that he was nearly overcome with fatigue.

"Would you prefer to have the training session tomorrow night instead of tonight? I could easily telephone everyone. If people couldn't come tomorrow, maybe we could meet three times next week."

While Alyce and I had returned home Elmer had remained at the lab to make preparations for tomorrow's demonstration. He wanted to construct a device to rotate on a spindle, not hung on a string, and to design some sort of plastic mask for Swami to wear to assure that it would be impossible for him to blow on the object. Thinking of all the preparations being made and of Swami's surprising fatigue, I could feel the gravity of the swami's situation.

"No, no, these meetings are for training, and training should be regular. Why should we postpone it when it is good for all of us?"

At seven o'clock that evening Elmer called to propose postponing Swami's PK demonstration for an additional five days because he needed the extra time to get the various paraphernalia ready. He wanted to postpone the event from Friday to the following Wednesday, and Swami agreed without hesitation.

That night we had the fourth meeting of our training group. By now we had all selected and practiced a stable posture and we sat either lotus or cross-legged or in the adept's posture with our backbones perfectly straight as we listened to the swami. Again, as he had done each time, he demonstrated for us his form of bellows breathing: "Now we start with the bellows. Why do we do bellows? Often we find our nostrils closed or our throats choked or we may find our sinuses not working properly. This will increase the air in your lungs and the oxygen in your blood, and it has all the benefits I have told you. Keep a hanky or a small towel when you do it. Or you should see that a tissue box is there.

"I will show you the methods." Again he performed his

bellows demonstration. "Please do not try to do what I am doing, I am only showing you. Please do not exert your lungs much. There should be an exact time to do it once or twice a day, and bellows breathing should not be done after food—wait a few hours after taking food. These are the precautions. Everything has got precautions."

After watching Swami's examples we practiced our own form of the exercise together, and our group made such a noise in the living room that it was good there was no one else within hearing distance. The bellows was only the first of a series of exercises that we practiced each session. Following the bellows was alternate breathing. In this exercise we exhaled through one nostril (closing the other with the right hand) and inhaled to the same count through the other nostril. After several repetitions, we reversed the process. Then there were a series of relaxation exercises that were performed in the easiest posture of all. Swami called it the corpse posture. "This is the one posture," he said, "that nobody has to show you because you know it automatically from your birth. For it is simply lying on your back—which you have been doing for so much of your life since your birth. And this most comfortable and most luxurious of postures only humans, among all God's creatures, are blessed enough to do properly." Swami always guided us through the series of relaxation procedures, and afterwards he let us remain lying for some minutes on the living-room floor to be aware of the steady tranquillity within us. Then slowly and softly he would begin to speak, and usually it was some anecdote or example he had selected to introduce some point of truth. On this night the subject on his mind was ego.

"Do you know what is purity of mind—how mind can be purified? There is one thing, one function of mind, that is called ego. 'This is *me*, this is *me*.' What is this *me*? If ego gets hurt then everything will dwindle. To purify ego means to purify mind—to purify mind means to purify ego.

"Suppose suddenly I want to test someone. I will just tell him that 'You are a fool!' He will forget God's name, he will forget his beloved wife, he will forget his children, he will forget his duty—but the whole day he will remember that 'he called me a fool, he called me a fool.' So if you are not remembering God, you are remembering your enemy. A man remembers his enemy more than he remembers his lover—this is called ego. That ego should be purified. So never accept that which you don't need, accept that which you need. And need that which will be helpful to you. You see?

"This is one thing, ego, that should be purified. The whole day we are guided, we are governed, by our ego. Such and such man said this, such and such man said that. And where are you? What is your stand? Where is your opinion? A man says this and you are attracted, then he says that and you are attracted. Somebody says, 'You are good,' and I am happy. Somebody says, 'You are bad,' and I am sad—this means that I am subject to everybody's opinion and I am nothing. So you should develop your own self. Let the people give you compliments, this should not affect you.

"One day I said to my master, my guru, I said, 'This is nothing, I have done all this!' He said, 'Huh? You have done it? The sages could not do it for several births, and my dear child, you have purified ego?' And I said, 'My ego is my shoe if I wear it! If I use it, I will use it!' He said, 'No, no. Don't—this is ego!'

"So you see, this ego—this is no easy thing—and there is no point until we reach liberation that we can say we have done it. We may study scriptures, we may master this body, we may do our training and our austerities, and this ego business may be still a problem more and more. I know. This is the way with me."

Swami ended the training session and returned immediately to his room. He did not even ask me for his usual cup of tilk. I saw him again about three hours later, just past midnight.

"See my eyes," he said. "I am straining myself for this nonsense." I noticed his eyes looked painfully red. "This is all done with the eyes. It is attraction: it is done with the gaze and has nothing to do with the breath, you will see. It is all right that this thing is postponed. I will use the time. These things have been done for centuries. It is a simple thing in my country. But here there is negativity, and I am challenged."

The event took place at one-thirty on Wednesday afternoon. Swami stayed home in the morning while we made the final preparations in the experiment room where the demonstration was to be performed. The ventilators and air ducts on the walls and ceiling were taped over completely so that there could be no question as to an unaccounted-for flow of air. There was a long couch against the wall, and a large blanket was folded to form a cushion for the couch on which Swami would sit in his lotus posture. A wooden coffee table was placed about four feet from the couch, and the object to be moved was placed on the table. Elmer showed me how it worked. He had mounted two aluminum darning needles, glued together at right angles to form an X, on a small metal spindle that had a bead bearing. With a gentle push one could cause the needles to rotate on a horizontal plane about three inches above the surface of the table.

"One needle is fourteen inches long and the other is ten inches," Elmer said. "This will make it easy to observe any change in their position. I have no idea how this thing's going to move—or if it's going to move—but to make it clear in any case, I've mounted the spindle on this circular protractor."

We blew on the needles from various positions. It was easy enough to make them move at face level, but from the position where Swami would be sitting it seemed difficult to blow hard enough to make them turn. "In any case, Swami will be wearing the mask," Elmer said, handing me the nose-and-mouth face mask he had made from a painter's mask, with a plastic breath deflector bolted on the front. "And if Swami does blow, he'll be blowing on his own feet."

We suspended a photoflood light from the ceiling by its

cord and positioned it so that it would spotlight the object on the table. We placed the chairs for the observers just to the left of the couch and coffee table in such a way that everyone would be able to see the object to be moved.

After lunch we led the swami, dressed in his finest robes, to his place in the experiment room. He immediately sat on his couch and arranged himself in his lotus posture, hardly bothering to notice the arrangement of chairs, tables, and paraphernalia in the room. For a moment I felt sorry for him for what we were putting him through, but then I reminded myself that the swami had brought about all of this himself. Still, I could sympathize with him. What an awkward situation he was in!

"If it's part of your procedure to exhale forcefully, go ahead and do it," Elmer instructed him. "You won't be able to affect this thing no matter how hard you blow."

"Blow! There is no question of blow, Doctor! Pushing is not the point! The method is attraction—the object is supposed to come to me."

"But this object rotates. It's a circular movement."

"The object of my gaze will move towards, not away," insisted Swami.

"Where will you gaze?"

"Upon the very point. One of those points of needle."

Elmer pushed the protractor with his finger, moving the entire object a few inches on the table. Now the intersection of the needles was a little to the right of the swami's face and one point of the long needle was in the line of his gaze and at right angles to his face as he looked straight ahead.

"Now, if you gaze at this point and it moves toward you," Elmer said, "the needles will rotate counterclockwise."

Swami looked at me. "Bring incense from my office. We shall light some incense here—I am always having this incense. And let me have a vessel, a metal container, because I should be keeping some cold water here at my right side. It must be a metal container. Then you have to sit here beside me, and I will tell you what to do."

The incense was lit and a stainless-steel container filled with cold water was placed on the end of the couch. "Now, Doug, you will remain here at my left side. I may fall to the side, so you will have to catch me. Ah, you have to have something—you can't touch me with your hands. Definitely you must not touch me, or we shall both get a great shock. How about wood? Get something wood."

In the woodshop on the other side of the basement Elmer found a four-inch-wide plywood board about two and a half feet long. "Ah, perfect!" Swami said. He showed me how to push it against his left shoulder if he should start to tip in my direction during his chanting.

"Suppose you fall to the right side?" I asked.

"No, no, no. Only this side, the negative side. It is not possible to fall to the right. Now, where are the others?"

"They'll be coming soon."

"Then leave me and let me begin my meditation. When the others are here, you will come in together, and we will do it. Otherwise people will be walking in and out with feelings and comments, and I will be distracted."

Elmer went to inform the observers that everything was ready while I stood in the hall outside the door with the board in my hand. I rested the back of my head against the wall and closed my eyes and wondered what was going on inside the swami's mind. I wondered if I, too, should be in meditation. If it was true that Swami's efforts could be influenced by his feelings, his confidence, his state of mind, what about the thoughts and feelings of those who were to observe? Might we not also influence the experiment? I knew that the swami really believed in the possibility of what he was going to attempt to do—otherwise he would not have committed himself to such long and strenuous practice—but I also knew he felt unsure of what would happen. This was part of the reason for his restlessness. I wondered whether he had moved any objects at home in his room when there had been no one there to see it. I wondered, too, if he was still fatigued as he sat in that room now, and whether his eyes were red. But most of all I wondered what would happen to him if his experiment were to fail—if after all his efforts the needles refused to turn.

But when we entered the room he appeared calm and serene. He seemed not to notice us. He sat tall and motionless in his lotus posture on the couch, mumbling his mantra to himself barely loud enough to be heard, as we seven observers took our seats. In addition to Elmer, Alyce, and Dale Walters, the three principal researchers in our project, and another member of our evening training group, there were the doctor who had witnessed the swami's earlier inauspicious psychokinetic attempt, and a medical doctor from the Menninger Clinic. I took my seat on the couch beside the swami. I got into lotus posture and turned slightly toward the swami so that I could see both him and the object on the table.

Elmer spoke very softly. "Swami?"

Swami stopped chanting, but did not open his eyes or turn his head. "Yes."

"I'm going to put this mask on you now. All right?"

"All right."

"Oh, does anyone wish to examine the mask before I put it on the swami's face?" Elmer held the mask so that everyone could see it. No one wished to examine it further. Swami did not move or open his eyes now as Elmer placed it against his face and stretched the elastic strap over the top of his head to hold it securely in place.

Elmer sat down, and the room was dead silent. I looked at Swami's shoulder and at the board in my hands. Swami was sitting so tall, so erect that he seemed larger than he had ever seemed before. "Please don't let him tip over," I said to myself.

Swami opened his eyes wide and looked hard at the point of the needle. His eyes were more piercing than I had ever seen them, and with the rest of his face covered by the mask they look almost fierce. He resumed the chanting of his mantra and went on repeating it for a long time. When he paused to breathe, his inhalations and exhalations were loud and forceful as though he were extremely activated. Each time he exhaled loudly I looked at the object on the table just in case, but nothing moved. He used a strange-sounding mantra I had never heard before; he increased the tempo and the pitch of his chanting as he went on repeating it until finally he reached a piercing, high-pitched crescendo that ended in a sound like "r-eee-eee-eeem." Two things happened simultaneously: I felt a sensation of electricity in my body, especially in my chest and on the right side of my face, and the object moved. My first instantaneous impression was that the electric shock sensation was some sort of hypnotic phenomenon that made the object appear to move. The second impression that flashed through my mind was a vivid recall of the only other such shock experience in my memory, an incident at a mountain cabin in which some teenage friends fooled me into holding a wire attached to a portable generator and when they turned the crank, I could not let go. But now the shock faded instantly. Swami asked Elmer if he wanted him to do it again. Elmer said yes and the swami resumed his chanting, beginning softly and slowly again. I decided that what I had felt was merely an emotional response to his eerie "ee-eee" sound. Then it happened again. The same "r-eee-eee-eeem!" sound, the same intense tremor of electricity, and the needles turned on the spindle. No, it was not just an emotional response, it was a real physical sensation.

The needles had indeed moved, and everyone must have seen it, for though they had turned only a few degrees, they now rested in a different position. The needle point in front of the swami's face had moved toward him as the long hand on a horizontal clock face would move—counterclockwise—from about the nine to the seven. When the swami turned to face Elmer, I noticed his eyes: they looked wet and strained.

Swami maintained his calm manner as the mask was removed and the observers got up and left. "It was not of much use," he said to Elmer and me when there were only the three of us in the room. "The one who was doubting before is doubting even now."

"Well, don't worry about it, Swami. Whatever anybody wishes to insist isn't going to upset me."

"Swami," I said as we were going up the elevator, "I felt a wave of electric current pass through my body when you made that 'eee' sound."

He smiled. "Yes, of course, because you were sitting at my side."

"You mean you know that I felt it?"

"So I told you not to touch me, did I not?"

"At first I thought it was just imagination."

"It is real. This is current. This can be measured."

The moment Swami and I were alone in his office, his displeasure became apparent. "That was a useless thing. What is the point to do such a useless thing? That was nothing compared to the possibility!"

I said nothing. I had no idea what the swami had expected. I had no idea what the possibilities were.

"These things require the proper circumstances, when they can be done so nicely. For that, I wanted so badly to dispel all suspicions. What is the use to try to counter these suspicions and then not use the chance properly? I had no say in these preparations. I told Doctor to arrange it absolutely so there could be no doubts. I should have been wrapped with my face in a towel—then there could be no doubts."

"I don't think a towel would have been any better than the mask."

"And then I should have been put behind a glass, or a huge plastic plate, Doctor had talked about a plastic plate."

"I don't think there were doubts; I don't see how there could have been—"

"There were—I could feel it. And then this becomes a problem with these things. These things are done with visualization."

I went up to the second floor for a cup of hot water and a

tea bag, and I thought about the demonstration and Swami's feelings. I did not know enough to explain what Swami had done, but I did feel that he had succeeded. Twice the needles had moved on the spindle, and it seemed evident to me that it had not been caused by the force of air from Swami's lungs. If the needles had moved as a result of his breathing, they would have moved at a different point in time, they would have moved in the opposite direction, and the lamp suspended on its cord would have been affected also, causing the spot of light to move from the object. In addition, there was the electric current phenomenon that I felt both times when the needles turned. In any case, something had to cause the needles to move, and that something had to be explicable in natural, not supernatural, terms. It had to be real energy to act as it did upon a physical object. I could not think of any facts or theories I had learned in my high school or college science that would preclude the possibility that energy sufficient to move an object could be generated in a human body and directed through the eyes or even through thoughts. Those who chose to deny the possibility would have to rely upon their personal feelings and traditional beliefs.

"I don't think anything could have been done to make that demonstration any more convincing," I told the swami, handing him his cup of tea. "People cling to their doubts and beliefs as a matter of choice. No demonstration can ever influence anyone's beliefs, Swami. I don't know about India or other countries, but in America, people build walls around their minds in their youth—in schools and churches. They can go on learning inside their walls, but they're rarely motivated or capable of venturing out. In America there's a popular defense mechanism people use to avoid facing new possibilities—they use words like charlatan, quack, fraud, and a lot of other words. I don't think there's any solution to this problem but to let it resolve itself. If we were to prepare the control systems more elaborately, they would simply think you have a more elaborate cheating system worked out.

What it boils down to is that everyone here has already formed an opinion about you—not about your teachings or your capabilities, but about you as a person. Yet it really has nothing to do with you, it has to do with how you fit into their opinions and their prejudices."

"Next time you have to stop me," said Swami after a moment of silence. "This is my bad habit, these challenges, and I have not to make challenges. There is no use to convince anybody. This is not my work and there is no question of convince. Why should we struggle against the doubts when there are those who are ready to learn the methods? Next time, please help me, please prevent me, and do not let me create these situations."

I returned to my desk wondering how I would ever prevent the swami from doing anything. He was right: there was "no question of convince." I myself had not been convinced of anything and had no need to be. I had no need to choose between believing or disbelieving. If there were methods to be learned, I wanted to learn them—not so that I could move objects or demonstrate phenomena, but so that I could expand the scope of my learning. In order not to prohibit the opportunity to learn, I knew it was necessary to assume that anything is possible and that nothing is impossible. That would be the safest possible attitude—safe as long as I did not come to any premature conclusions about anything, one way or the other.

As I sat at my desk, I decided that attempting to prove something or to convince someone was a useless objective. Swami had said it himself: "There is no use to convince anybody . . . there is no question of convince." Any researcher—however brilliant, honest, or reputable, it seemed to me—could be accused of cheating by anyone who could not accept his claims or the results of his experiments. I thought of the people who refused to believe in the possibility of space travel, in spite of the several moon landings. Rather than accept what they could not understand, they were forced to speak of a gigantic fabrication, a clever cooperative effort on the part of government and media to fool the gullible public. But those whom they called gullible had a better understanding than they of how such things are done. I accepted the moon landings as really having happened even though I realized they might be possible to fake. I knew that space travel and moon landings could be reasonably explained by others who had studied in that area more deeply than I. And I accepted Swami Rama's moving-object demonstration for the same reason—because the possibility was a familiar one to me, because I had spent years studying the explanation before I ever heard of Swami Rama.

At any rate, experiments in space travel, healing, telepathy, and psychokinesis are useful, I concluded. Useful for discovering and communicating information. If an observer allowed himself to get caught in the question of whether the demonstrator could possibly have accomplished his end by cheating, it was his own problem. The answer to that question is always yes. Every scientific experiment in the history of the planet can be duplicated in appearance by substituting the relevant causative principles with some form of cheating. The issue in every experiment is not *whether*, but *how* a thing is done. The goal is to keep on with the endless effort to learn new things—new things outside the temporary limits of our understanding. The goal is to keep on pushing outward at those misconceived limits, to keep on being staggered, as man has always been staggered, by undreamed-of possibilities. This is what science is for.

eight

Despite all that had been said to the contrary, Swami Rama both wanted and needed contact with the public. It was more than the desire for popularity—it was more complex than this. Swami craved to teach, to guide, and to explain, and our private evening training sessions were not enough to satisfy that need. Swami had written several small books in Sanskrit, Hindi, and English. He was the founder of the Himalayan International Institute of Yoga Science and Philosophy. He had lectured and demonstrated in India, Japan, the United States, and Europe.

His current self-determined priority of offering himself to the study of psychophysiological self-regulation and various nonphysiological phenomena demanded of him what he called his "austerities," which required, in part, that he remain undistracted by emotional interactions with other people. But it turned out to be impossible for him to abandon his former identity. It was not difficult for the swami to sense that many "scientists" with whom he came in contact had feelings toward him which were not unemotional, objective, or well-meaning, and he longed for more moral support than he was getting. In a cave in the Himalayas he might have been able to practice the nonattachment of which he so often spoke, but here in the West, where all things must be made manifest and must give rise to measurable results, the swami exhibited an almost unquenchable thirst for positive emotional feedback. He had come to the United States hoping to convince medical people of his extraordinary yogic knowledge and abilities, inspiring a meeting of Eastern and Western science in the psychophysiological domain, but the impartial laboratory atmosphere with its replication of tests and demonstrations did not provide response enough to satisfy his needs.

On a Friday evening in late October, Swami Rama began his first series of public lectures in Topeka. They were held in the auditorium of the Tower Building—the administrative headquarters of the Menninger Foundation—located on the foundation's west campus near the Research Department. Except for our own project members, no other researchers attended, though the crowd always included several other Menninger people—especially the younger ones. There were always some professionals and paraprofessionals from the large veteran's hospital, some students and teachers from Topeka's Washburn University, and even some high school students. A large number of the audience were members of the local Ananda Marga Ashram and a new Topeka-based organization that called itself the Ashram Association.

Swami made an impressive appearance in public. He walked majestically back and forth across the stage in his sandals, gracefully cast his long shawl over his shoulders, and used his hands and voice in an aesthetic manner. Every Friday evening he spoke for two hours or more, but he had no difficulty holding the attention of everyone, young or old. He talked about mind, Eastern and Western views of mind, and the yogic disciplines of controlling the mind and its functions. He spoke about the meaning and the process of meditation, and in what he called the practical part of these lessons, he taught some postures, breathing exercises, and even Sanskrit chants. "I know many people think that these yogis and swamis from India have just come to force their ways and methods of meditation on other peoples and their ways of life," he announced in the beginning of the lecture. "If you will throw out of your minds this idea that this is a swami from the East and that you are from the West—that will be better. The real truth is the same truth for all, and the truth has nothing to do with religion, and the methods are for each individual to choose and develop for himself. I know that my jacket will not suit you; and I also know that your jacket will not suit me. So I assure you I have not come to teach you religion or to propagate the ideas of any religion. Yoga has nothing to do with religion. Religion is just outer form, just like these jackets. So I will not speak on religion. I don't think if Christ, Buddha, or Krishna came down today they would be accepted as they were before. They would not be much seen or heard. We depend on physical time so much we hardly get time to understand the values of life. We are taken up with these outer things— material things. We don't get any education in the university or church or even modern homes today which leads us inward. So a part of life remains unrevealed to us, and we get only the husk of life. The younger generation today is seeking, seeking something beyond this modern life because they know modern life is not satisfactory. Modern life does not satisfy man in himself. You know in the East we are suffering because of sloth—inertia. In both East and West we are suffering. We need something more. We are suffering from this one-sided progress. If there is anything like mind, then there is the nature of mind, and the modifications of mind, and the functions of mind, and the control of the functions of mind, and we should be learning about these things. If there is a possibility that these things can be studied and learned, then we should definitely be teaching them. We cannot study meditation until we have learned to control the functions of mind. But where is that university where that education is taught?

"If we ask any teachers or any university professors to tell us the meaning of 'meditation,' they will have to go to consult their dictionaries. And do you know what is the definition of meditation there? The definition of meditation is contemplation, and the definition of contemplation is meditation, so there is no explanation at all. The teachers, if they say anything at all, they can only say, 'Boys and girls, meditation means contemplation and contemplation means medi-

tation, and that's all. Don't ask any more about it.' I assure
you, the meaning of the word meditation has not been explained anywhere in the English language. So many have said
they do meditation. It is possible for a modern Westerner to
sit quietly for some time and relax, breathe, chant. He will get
peace and he will feel better. People tell me: 'I have sat for
so many hours. I have had so many experiences.' This is not
meditation, this is called concentration. Either it is concentration or it is uncontrolled impressions from the unconscious. It is not meditation.

"It is possible without sitting to do meditation the whole
day. Without sitting in one place, without having any particular posture, without leaving your office and all the
worldly duties, it is possible to do meditation. Meditation is
a definite descipline, and it has got a definite philosophy
behind it. It depends upon the strength and support of a
solid philosophy. Meditation means first self-analysis, then
self-cultivation, then self-development, then self-unfoldment,
and then self-enlightenment. Meditation is self-knowledge.
It is of the real self—beyond image, impression, experience,
beyond name or form—not subject to change."

The Ashram Association also held its regular meetings on
Friday nights, and those members who attended Swami's
lecture went directly from the Tower Building auditorium to
their own meeting place. After his first lecture the swami was
invited to their meeting. "I will go," he had said. "Some
evening after the lecture I will go and join you. Every Friday night for several weeks they reminded him of his invitation until one night he agreed to go. "I had promised," he
said to me. "We shall go today. Let us both go together. But
let us go home first for a moment's rest, and then we'll go."
The association members left so that they could get their
meeting started, and Swami and I went home with the
Greens so that he could change into his more casual robes
and have his cup of tilk.

Swami arranged himself to his satisfaction and was sitting
alone on the living-room sofa with his cup of tilk when the

car from the ashram came up the driveway. Swami got up from his seat and opened the door himself. I was in the kitchen because the swami had just informed me that he planned to have more hot tea and milk when he finished that glass. "Come, come, come!" I heard the swami say. "Just take your seats, there is time enough not to rush. Let them begin and we shall arrive." As I stood in the kitchen attentively watching the milk as it heated slowly over a low fire, I noticed there were no sounds coming from the living room. The two young men who had just arrived were probably not much beyond their teens, and they may have been at a loss as to how to converse with a swami. Or maybe the swami was sitting statuelike in his lotus posture with his head, neck, and trunk straight and his eyes closed, making the visitors feel awkward. But then I heard him take a loud sip from his glass and clear his throat; one of the visitors cleared his throat in turn.

At last one of them spoke. "We know a psychic in Topeka, Swami." But Swami said nothing. The other one gave her name, in case he might recognize it, but still there was no response.

"Do you know her, Swami? Have you ever heard of her?"

"No."

"She's really far out. She can pick up your thoughts. She can even pick up on extraterrestrial voices—like the dead and like beings from Venus and everything."

Swami took another long, loud sip from his glass and cleared his throat again. "This is a disease," he said solemnly. "The woman should be treated."

There was silence again, and the two remained speechless until Swami finished his second glass of tilk and we were in the car on the way to the meeting. Then the one who was not driving turned around and leaned over the back of the front seat. "Swami, do you know anything about drugs?"

"Drugs? Yes. In other countries I am writing prescriptions; but here, you see, I am not allowed."

"No, I mean mind-expanding drugs, drugs for tripping.

What do you think about using drugs for tripping, like to get altered states of consciousness?"

"There is not much value. Not much. And there is great risk to health and happiness. They can give a little bit of psychic experience, but there is no spiritual benefit at all. The quest for self-realization has nothing to do with any medication. Only the nonself can experience these topsy-turvy conditions—this altered consciousness. And even psychic experience—drugs hamper in the end because it is not coming in a controlled way. These drug experiences are nothing before the experiences of a yogi. Yogis are not so attracted by these small intoxications, and they are not impressed by this, you see, passivity. They want to work hard and get something more. Why should we be satisfied with such easy and helpless things? You people are attracted by these inferior means and these small phenomena because until now you have had nothing at all."

The young man may have just been making conversation, or he may have been trying to find out what kind of a guy this swami was, or perhaps he actually wanted the swami's opinion. In any case, he looked to me as though he had heard a little more than he wanted. He only said, "Hmmm," and turned back around in his seat.

All the ashram members and many others were waiting when we arrived, and it was immediately apparent that this was the swami's meeting.

"Here he is, he's here!" exclaimed someone close to the door. And another voice in a far corner called, "Come this way, please, Swami." The chairs and sofas were filled with people, and more than double that number were sitting on the floor. They had all arranged themselves facing the one empty chair in the corner, and some of the people in the middle of the floor squeezed together to allow him a path to his seat.

Swami sat quietly for a moment, watching the anticipating faces and looking as though he intended not to offer another lecture this night. Momentarily (but only momentarily) having nothing else to say, he fell back upon his frequent and familiar "How about a cup of tea?" and three or four people rushed to the kitchen. There were a few questions for him, and there was some light conversation about India. Then something that he said brought to mind one of his favorite topics, and he was soon on his way with another lecture. He even asked for a blackboard, and there happened to be one, which was brought to him along with a piece of chalk. He said that all things are one, that nothing can be separate from or outside of The One which is in reality all that exists. Naturally he could not resist expounding on this idea.

"One thing I will tell you—all right, now, let me show you. Do you know, one is the only number that exists?" When he asked for the blackboard I could guess what he was going to say, having heard it before. "All right, now I am going to explain. This philosophy should be understood, and mathematics can beautifully describe it. Now, you all know and call this 'one.'" He wrote a number one on the blackboard. "Any number has no meaning without one. Now let us put this zero. This zero has no meaning at all unless you put one ahead of it—then it becomes ten. Now you have to go and say two, three, four. Or fifteen. Or one hundred." As he spoke he wrote the numbers with chalk. Carrying a cup of tea, the hostess waded carefully through all the people on the floor and set the cup on the table beside the swami.

"Now, if you deduct one from one hundred," he went on, "it will lose its existence. It will become ninety-nine, it will not remain one hundred. Again reduce one from ninety-nine, it becomes ninety-eight. So all these numbers have their existence upon one. You may deduct two from one hundred and it becomes ninety-eight, right? Then it means that twice you have deducted one from one hundred. For two is only one and one again, two times one. One hundred is nothing but manifestations of one—one hundred manifestations of one! So in all numbers, all values, there is nothing that exists behind that but one. Either it is zero or it is one or part of one or many repetitions of one. Some people have said God created the world. God has never created the world—that is a false notion. If we try to establish this fact, we will be condemned by logic. How managed God to create the world? What was that thing simultaneously existing along with God out of which he created everything else? No! God himself exists! There is only God and nothing more!"

On those words he paused and lifted the teacup to his lips. Immediately he made a horrible face and thousands of tiny droplets literally sprayed from his mouth. He barely got the cup back on its saucer without spilling the entire contents, and as it was, he let a little fall into his lotus lap. There were dozens of gasps. "What's the matter?" he cried. "What have you given me?"

"Swami, I'm sorry!" came the voice from the kitchen doorway. "I don't know. That's tea. That's supposed to be good tea."

He carefully lifted it to his face again and smelled it. "No, no. This is some medicinal preparation."

"It's herb tea, Swami, just a natural herb tea."

"Herbal tea is herbal tea and tea is tea. If I think it is tea and you have brought another thing, you should make this clear beforehand."

"I'm sorry, Swami. I'm really sorry." But there was a hint of laughter in her voice.

So Swami laughed too. "It's all right," he said. "It's all right. Either I will have a real cup of tea or I may try to adjust myself to this preparation." For a moment he studied the numbers and arrows he had written on the blackboard. "So God alone exists in all these manifestations, and there cannot be any argument at all." He quoted a long phrase in Sanskrit. "It's a beautiful mantra. It says, 'The One manifested himself into many, and the number one goes on manifesting itself into several numbers.' The same one—this one I have first put—becomes two, three, four, five, six, and so on and on. But it is the existence of one that gives them their value. And it is the value of one that gives them their existence. So all your pleasures will have some value if you understand that One behind you. All these numbers add up to one, one total, one value. And all these values and all these existences add up to one, that One out of which all is manifest. You have to establish that One in your life—that universal One who is in all.

"In any phase of life, one should learn to be happy. And nothing should disturb man. When do we become happy? When we remember the Self within. When we recognize that we are a part of that Universal One. This 'I'—what I call 'I' is not complete. This separateness of mine, this 'I'-ness of mine makes me narrow. Do you not find your neighbor speaking that Mrs. Such-and-such is like this and that? And Mrs. Such-and-such will not speak whole night because the neighbor has said that. This is weakness. If somebody says you are wonderful, 'Oh, I am glad you said that.' No! Nothing should disturb you and nothing should give you joy!

"You say, what do you mean? A great man does not understand the language of the world? He understands. Suppose you call to a great man, 'You are a fool.' He understands, but he will not become a fool. If there is any disturbance, this is your mind, your misunderstanding, your way of thinking. If we forget all the languages of the world, we are free. There is only one Self and there is only one language—that is called spiritual language. When we learn that, we can forget these expressions of the world that say, 'He is good, he is bad, this is nice, this is pleasant, this is unpleasant.' This can be done by realization. You know all the religions of the world, all the virtues, all the means are support. Real religion is self-realization, nothing else, and that is not the monopoly of any religion. No religion is liberated. That's why religions are separate and divided. It means they are in bondage. Only human beings, those who realize the real Self, they are liberated. And religions remain in bondage. I tell you it's true." And he drank his herbal tea.

We were back home well after midnight. Swami went directly to his room to be "alone for some time, at last, to do some work." Whether for our benefit or for his, a good part of Topeka's interested public had now seen Swami Rama. Quite likely there were other men like this Swami Rama among all the yogis and swamis of India and elsewhere. I thought it was good for all of us to know what we could expect of people like him, particularly since more and more of them would be appearing in time in the United States. It was good to know what a man of the yogic discipline had to say about meditation, drugs, and religion, and to know at the same time the nonyogic parts of such people. No person's personality ever becomes a yogi. With a tremendous amount of intense effort one can reach the yogi level; this is the meaning of self-realization. But the personality goes on behaving like a personality. Just what of the yogi nature is reflected in the personality depends upon the nature of the personality and the plans for it that have been arranged by karma.

I could not know whether the swami was a realized being because, as in the words of a popular schooldays' saying, "It takes one to know one"; but I could believe that behind him there was a real yogi. For whatever reason, or by whatever cause, he had a powerful ego. He was a yogi with a big personality who behaved as a yogi on the yogi level and who behaved as a separate personality on the personality level. It seemed to me that if one saw enough of Swami Rama, one could see how this worked.

Those who had been there had seen him spit out his herbal tea and say, "So many things happen in daily life, why should we pay attention? Nothing should disturb you and nothing should give you joy!" It had been a beautiful example.

I thought all this extremely important because since people in ever-increasing numbers were looking for gurus, were eager to call someone master, it would be useful for them to know that the master is the real Self, the Self within, the Self with the capital S. Swami Rama had said this himself. The discipline of yoga, the control of mind and its modifications, the state of meditation, the achievement of self-realization—all this is the discrimination between the nonself and the

Self, the *knowing* of the Self, "and nothing more!" As a result of my association with the swami, and of all his advice and pressures, I had to settle for myself the question of who and what is the master. I could see now that this was one of the initial questions to be faced by everybody, one of the initiating steps in becoming a true aspirant. The only real Master was to be found within; and to the extent that this could be accomplished, the safe encountering of this external reflection would be no problem.

nine

As a result of his public appearances, telephone calls and messages for Swami Rama increased. One day he agreed to give a private consultation in his office to someone from "outside," and from that day on it became a regular occurrence. He had already been using some hours of his mornings talking privately with interested Menninger people, and one of the doctors at the clinic who was interested in comparing yogic medicine with Western methods talked with him occasionally about a couple of his patients. In addition to this, he had frequent private meetings with some of the members of the training group. It was my job to keep his appointment book, and now that his door was more or less open to the public, his calendar became full to overflowing. With his Ashram lectures, his instruction sessions for our training group, and now a waiting list of appointments to fill up all the hours and quarter-hours that remained when he was not either in the lab or preparing for it, there was almost no time to stare at the phone or watch for the arrival of the mail. It seemed to me that the busier he got, the more he enjoyed himself.

The only time left for him to use his "Do Not Disturb" sign was at lunch. "You three go to lunch and let me remain here alone," he said to me one day. "I have no need for midday food. If only I have a cup of tea, this is quite sufficient enough for me. Then I shall rest and do my work while it is quiet here. This is a good chance for me. You can bring me some pieces of fruit upon your return if you like."

So from that day on we informed the swami when we were about to leave so that he could close his door and hang his sign on the doorknob, and the Greens and I would go to lunch without him. Each day when we returned I would find him still in his office with his sign on the door, and I would knock so that I could give him what I had brought for him to eat and so that he could prepare himself for the afternoon session in the lab.

One day, however, he was standing in the hallway just outside Elmer's door waiting for us to return, and he looked excited. "Oh, Doctor, I have something to speak. Let me come in." The four of us went into Elmer's office. "Close the door," Swami insisted, "please close the door. I have something to tell you."

"Do you want only Elmer to hear this?" Alyce asked.

"No, no. You all hear. You all should know."

"I've brought you an apple and a couple of bananas here, Swami," I said.

"No, no, no! Who can think of food? Oh, Mama, I have destroyed something. I have destroyed personal property of others."

"What did you destroy?" Elmer asked.

"A very fine—what do you say?—a ruler!"

I felt a sense of relief. I would not have been surprised, seeing his strange combination of shame and pride, if he had said it was a desk or conference table.

"How did it happen?"

"I made a demonstration, and I have not to do that!"

Elmer had seen this done before when the swami was here in the spring. Dale Walters and one of the physicians from the clinic had each held an end of a twelve-inch wooden ruler, and Swami had broken it in two with a quick movement of his arm, touching it only with his finger, saying that it was accomplished with "the electricity of the body." What had surprised his two volunteers who held the ruler was that they had felt no appropriate mechanical shock.

"You mean," Elmer questioned him, "like you did upstairs when you were here before? Or like when you've sometimes broken pencils for the children?"

"Yes, the same way I have done it. A pencil once or twice for the children, it may be all right. But I have done a wrong thing. But one thing troubles me, that people are always calling these things tricks. So I felt not satisfied to break a mere pencil."

"Well, how did it happen?" Elmer asked again.

"It was only a few moments back, out there in the lobby, while you were at lunch. That young man was talking, the one from the college. He was telling of his own strength. I did not entirely hear the words, I actually just caught the feeling. It was an innocent thing, just simple bragging. I said, 'What do you know about strength? Do you think you are strong enough to talk in this manner?' That was a challenge to him, and I have not to do that. And he had not been speaking to me. So he was surprised. I said, 'Strength is not such a thing as you think, strength is a gentle thing. Have you heard of the electricity of the body?' I said, 'Let me show you.' So the secretary was there, Mama, the secretary whom he was telling, and now, you see, I also was bragging. Having made my challenge, I could not stop. Almost I was going to demonstrate upon her wooden file box. I would have divided it in two parts, Mama, easily I could have done it. Jokingly I said it—about the box—but suppose they would have challenged it? Perhaps I could not have resisted. This is the trouble with me. We got a ruler. Now I shall have to replace it!"

"Where is it now?"

"It remains outside there," he said, pointing toward the lobby, "at the reception desk."

Elmer went to look at the ruler and Alyce went with him. Swami and I walked to Swami's office, where he ate his apple and bananas.

When Elmer examined the ruler, he found that it had been fractured and the broken pieces hung on the twisted

metal strip of the inserted edge. Alyce talked to the receptionist and later gave me her account of what had happened.
Swami had walked through to check his mailbox and had
heard the young man talking. After listening for a few
moments, he picked up the young man as though he weighed
nothing and lifted him into the air. Then he said, "Let me
show you something." She became alarmed when he suggested the possibility of breaking her file box or perhaps a
number of articles including her handbag with "the electricity of the body." At last he settled for a sturdy, metal-
edged desk ruler, and he had the young man hold it, parallel
to the floor, one end in each hand. "Now, you see," the swami
said, moving his hands slowly and gently up along the trunk
of his body, "the electricity comes up like this." With a flip
of his wrists, he turned his hands over at the level of his
cheeks, and pointing the index finger of his right hand, suddenly and swiftly sliced his arm through the air. Instantly
the ruler snapped and the young man dropped it. His mouth
fell open, the receptionist said, and his expression of amazement was so strange that for a moment she stared at him
rather than at the ruler, as though it was the young man's
face the swami had meant to change. "I don't think you
touched it," the young man said. "I didn't feel you touch it."
Then she looked at the ruler lying on the floor. The wood
was spit in two and the metal strip was twisted. "I did not
touch it," the swami said. "Not with my finger."

Swami did wish to allow time to meet privately, or to
speak on the telephone, with those of us who studied with
him in the private training group, because this he considered
to be part of his work. One afternoon while he was at home
he spoke with Pat Norris on the telephone, and after they
had talked for many minutes, he suddenly said, "Come here.
I want you to come here. Can you come now? I want to see
you right away." Pat was a professional clinical psychologist
who worked at the Kansas Reception and Diagnostic Center

in Topeka. Because she was a member of the training group, and because Swami had requested it, she left home immediately for the Greens' residence to meet the swami, wondering what he wanted with her that could not be handled on the telephone. While Pat was on her way, the swami sat in the living room hurriedly writing something on a piece of paper. With a look of satisfaction he glanced over what he had written, folded the paper, put it in his pocket, and waited for Pat to arrive.

"Ask me something!" he said abruptly the moment Pat had sat down beside him.

"Like what?" Pat wondered. "Ask you something about what?"

"Something about anything. Just ask. Put to me whatever question you want."

She was thoughtful for a moment, supposing that the swami must at least have some topic in mind and wondering what it was. Nothing in their telephone conversation had suggested that she should have something to ask about, and now only seemingly silly questions came to mind.

"Why do you hesitate? Ask! Ask!"

So she asked some brief, simple question about her future. Swami did not offer an answer. He only looked at her blankly for a moment and told her to ask something else. Perhaps that had not been a suitable question. Trying to come up with a more thoughtful question, she asked something more specific, something about whether she should plan or could expect to continue her postgraduate studies.

"All right," the swami said. "Ask me another."

Pat felt puzzled. He had told her to ask about anything, but he apparently had no intention of making any response. He had not even seemed to pay much attention to the questions. She considered carefully for a minute and thought of a more personal question.

"Ask me another."

Pat decided that the swami was no doubt trying to learn what sort of things she felt she needed to be advised about.

But she had more or less pulled those questions out of thin air. For her fourth question she tried to think of something the swami might feel more like answering, another personal question that sounded even more meaningful.

When she had worded her fourth question as sincerely as she could, the swami smiled at her, pulled from his pocket the piece of paper on which he had written, and handed it to her.

She unfolded the paper. There, in the order she had asked them, were her four questions. And there were the swami's replies.

One cold morning in early December a member of the Ashram Association came to keep her appointment with Swami. Swami was in one of the conference rooms with our training group, who now met with him each morning for a series of talks on the yoga sutras of Patanjali, and on this day he was late in concluding the session. As I returned to my office after the talk carrying the large stereo tape recorder through the hallway, I saw the lady sitting in the lobby holding her three-and-a-half-year-old son in her lap.

On that Friday night after the Tower Building lecture when Swami had spoken at the regular meeting of the Ashram Association, this lady had approached him as we were on our way out and attempted to talk with him about her little boy. The boy apparently had chronic asthma and was susceptible to pneumonia and several times recently had nearly died from nighttime attacks. He was under the care of a doctor, but she was worried because he was not improving. The lady had wanted to tell Swami about the agony and fear of being awakened in the night by her child's wheezing and gasping for breath. She had seemed to have a hard time getting through to the swami. He had allowed himself to be distracted by the many people who came up to thank him for coming, to make some comment, or to say goodbye to him. But for some reason he had not even seemed to notice the one person who had something really urgent to say. Then, just as she had given up trying to talk to him and he had taken his leave and was already out the door, he had suddenly turned around, gone back inside, and sat down by her. So she told him about her child. The swami had slowly closed and opened his eyes a few times as though he were either tired of all the people or else feeling sleepy. Finally he had spoken softly, as though to himself: "The problem is the child's *heart*." Then he had looked at her and told her that her doctor ought to do an electrocardiogram, suggesting it might be helpful to have an EKG to examine. The next day she had an EKG taken without consulting her regular doctor.

Now she had come and brought her son with her, and when I went to tell the swami that his appointment was waiting, he and Elmer were having a conversation They went into his office. Swami took from his desk a number of pictures of holy men and told the boy he wanted to give him one. He got the boy to choose the one he wanted. The boy picked from the group a modern-looking image of Christ, and Swami told his mother to take it home and hang it in his room. She reported that she was having a difficult time over that EKG. When she had spoken to her doctor the doctor had reacted to her as though there were something wrong with her for having consulted with a swami. She had to mention the swami, she explained, because the doctor wondered why she had an EKG taken without consulting him. When she told him about the swami, he told her she might find another doctor.

Eventually, examination of the EKG by a cardiologist did reveal that there was an abnormality or a malfunctioning of the child's heart.

"How did you happen to think of the EKG?" Elmer later asked the swami.

Swami recalled the night when he had sat beside the lady after his talk at the Ashram Association meeting. "I called the boy, and he came to me in his astral body. I said, 'What's the matter with you?' And he said, 'In this life I have a defective heart.'"

At this writing the boy's condition is greatly improved, and his mother attributes his well-being to the fact that the EKG incident forced her to change doctors and led her to the "ideal" doctor for her boy, the fact that the swami "blessed" the boy and continued to meditate for him, and the fact that the picture of Christ still hangs in his room.

Swami's attempts to help one of the research psychologists turned out less fortunately and led to a conflict within the Research Department. For many years the psychologist had been under medical care for a crippling disease, and because his doctor had concluded there was no hope for real improvement he had asked to talk to Swami. Swami thought something might be done with yoga. He had ideas about some breathing techniques that the psychologist could practice without interfering with his current ongoing program of treatment, and the psychologist was at least interested enough to spend several hours with the swami hearing his ideas and instructions. But that one researcher who had been trying to give the swami the Rorschach test for so long interfered. He demanded that Swami be prevented from seeing the psychologist and from making any further pretenses in the area of health and healing. What about the psychologist himself? Well, he was not sure. The swami had said some puzzling things but if there was any truth to anything he'd said, it sounded encouraging.

That was just the problem, said the swami's antagonist in a meeting in Elmer Green's office. The swami was cruelly creating false hopes, and he would not stand for it. One of the physicians from the clinic—the one who had been meeting frequently with Swami Rama and the only one who knew him well—was sitting in on this meeting, and when that notion was voiced he spoke up. "Wait a minute!" he said. "What's wrong with hope? Hope may be a very important factor. No one can argue that hopelessness is more humanitarian than hope. How do we ever know there's no hope anyway?"

Nevertheless, Elmer asked the swami not to see the psychologist again. I thought I knew what had climaxed the upset. To help the psychologist, Swami had wanted to work with what he called "prana" and "the electricity of the body." Anyone who knew the swami at all had to agree that there seemed to be some validity to his ideas about "the electricity of the body," and that the yogic concept of "prana" was the result of a recorded continuity of centuries of scientific and empirical research by yoga scholars and adepts. But Swami had written down some of these ideas in English in his own words in the form of a series of lessons, and he had given some of these pages to the psychologist, who showed them to others. I knew this had happened because before each of the few times the swami met with the psychologist he had asked me to type up what he had written in longhand, and he took the pages with him. The first two pages of Lesson 3 contained the swami's explanation of "prana," which he thought would help his friend understand the yogic therapy which Swami hoped would help him:

When the balance between the flow of the right and the left nostril is upset, the "pranic" energy is affected by it, and the result is some sort of physical ailment, sometimes trivial and sometimes serious. If we want to cure ourselves of disease and restore the balance of life, we should try to restore the balance between the flow of breath. The breath flow should therefore be carefully studied for the purpose of getting rid of diseases. Not only does breathing oxygenize the blood but it also stores up "pranic" energy. The breathing not only coordinates the positive and negative currents of the body but also attracts desirable and undesirable conditions. This is done by the operation of the magnetic law of attraction and repulsion. Now, ether, as is proven by modern scientists, contains all the things we need for building and repairing the bodies. When we breathe, we draw oxygen from the air and nourishment from the ether. Now, if we bring about proper balance between the magnetic currents, as nature intended, we can produce "pranic" energy to meet every demand of the body; but if there is an excess flow of one of the two, there will be a proportionately lesser flow of the other. This will not produce enough "pranic" energy because, like electricity, "pranic" energy is produced by the union of the positive current with a proportionate amount of the negative current. This "pranic" energy, if it is wasted, causes diseases. Thoughts of happiness, hope, faith, courage, and strength help us in conserving "pranic" energy. Thoughts of sorrow, fear, and worry deplete this energy.

"I never heard of anything like this before," said the puzzled psychologist many times. He said it to me, he said it to the swami several times, and he must have repeated it to his colleagues when he showed it to them to see how they interpreted it. Elmer and I agreed that it would have been better if those words had not been written in that way—at least better for the feelings of those Western scientists. Both of us knew the swami had not simply made up his ideas. We believed he was expressing a truth with which he was familiar, but the way he expressed it was misleading. He had made it sound as though all diseases could be cured by breathing more or less through the left or the right nostril. Typical of the statements of so many healers that have angered many conventional physicians, it was too simple, too all-conclusive, and too insistent. But it was also true that the swami had expressed himself in a rather typical Indian manner, and his words would not have been so shocking even to the scientists among his fellow countrymen.

What the swami had meant by his words was something

quite different from how they were interpreted by the man they had angered. Western science is as fanatic in its own direction. I could tolerate either extremity, and I could not help but wonder how an intelligent person could allow Swami's mannerisms to get in the way of the real issue. The real issue was that a member of the Research Department was highly inconvenienced by a physical ailment that Swami felt confident he understood something about and could at least arrest, if not cure. I believed there was hope, and it bothered me to think that a person could be presumptuous enough to kill that hope without even a trial of the technique. I was sure that what had spurred the hostility was more than a concern about false hopes, and that there were no dangers. Swami could have done no harm with his simple yogic exercises—they could not in any case have made the man worse. My own opinion was that what Swami's antagonist was really afraid of was not what he might fail to do, but rather what he might succeed in doing.

The swami, however, was more saddened than angered. He had really liked that psychologist, and he had said so many times. He talked so much about that man, both at home and at work, that I knew he felt more enthusiastically hopeful about what he might accomplish with him than about anything else he had done at the Menninger Foundation.

I tried to console him by telling him what I could about prejudices. I told him about the opposition to Aldous Huxley, who had brought himself out of almost total blindness by using unconventional and unorthodox methods, and about a healer under whom my grandfather had studied—a "quack"—who was jailed for advocating a "fraudulent" healing technique which was in fact a pressure-point system somewhat like acupuncture that had been successfully used by millions of people all over the world, especially in the Orient, for centuries. I told him about the monumental campaign against acupuncture that was financed by American aid in Asia in the late fifties and early sixties—an American effort that I had learned of in Korea to eliminate that "dangerous superstition" lest it should spread to the West. "But fortunately," I said to the swami, "American medicine could not control what was going on in China. If they had had their way, acupuncture would have been outlawed in every corner of the globe where it has been practiced since ancient times, before it could spread to the United States. But now it is too late, and in years to come, it will save countless American lives. I lived nearly ten years in Korea, and I knew over a hundred doctors well. I saw first hand the incredible power and authority of Western medicine. It's a kind of commercialism and an abuse of power. You must know about this. The same thing must be going on in India."

"It is not going on in India," he said softly. "There is no such power or influence there. In my country there is no competition or hostility between various opinions and methods—you will see one day. We respect all the disciplines. We respect all the methods, all the paths, all the sciences, and all the religions—and they are all good and useful. No person has the right to hold himself in authority over another, saying he has not to seek hope elsewhere. No doctor, however highly reputed, could dare say, 'This patient is mine and mine alone.' If he sees that he has not sufficient success he is required to encourage all the methods, the fruits of all the studies and disciplines—herbs, asana, pranayama, mantra, everything. If he withholds or prevents some possible alternative, claiming that here or there there is no hope—this is oppression. No one has the right to do this. No one has the right to prevent hope. In my country we respect all the knowledge. We know that all the small sciences—chemistry, physics, anatomy—are only a small part of the higher spiritual knowledge, only a small part of the vast scriptures from which they were taken. Yet in my country there is such sickness and suffering. This is because, you see, there is no money. Here you have so little knowledge and so much money, and this is a strange thing, very strange thing. Anyway, this is not the point. I wanted to bring help. I wanted to bring comfort; this is my work. What is the use to help one person and make anger and confusion among two or three others? My desire is to create joy and nothing more."

For a moment he was deep in thought. There had been sadness in his voice and somehow he had sounded more genuinely distressed than I had ever heard him. I believed what he had just said about comfort and joy. In spite of his exaggerations and occasional strange behavior, I knew that he had meant those words, that they were true.

Swami left before Christmas. His plans were made in November when Elmer talked with him about a world-wide yoga conference that was to be held in New Delhi. Our research and training schedule had been laid out for the rest of 1970 and for 1971, but in our discussions with the swami it became obvious that he really wished to make the trip back to India. If he were to leave in time to make the conference in New Delhi, he would have to make hasty preparations. It was decided that the work schedule could be postponed until early 1971. The swami said he would be back, but I wondered.

At this time the swami was staying at the Holiday Inn, which was conveniently situated about halfway between the West campus, where the research building was, and the Greens' home. He had insisted on taking the room at the Holiday Inn upon his recent return from a short trip to Chicago, and he remained at the inn ever since. The Greens had reminded him of his welcome in their home, but he was determined to try to live more individually and independently as he had learned Americans do. It was not in the swami tradition, he told us, to stay in one place for a long time. Besides, he thought we were seeing him frequently enough at work and at the evening training sessions at the house, and we should have the comfort of being free of him the rest of the time. It did make life a little easier for me, and I supposed for him also. The staff at the Holiday Inn, I learned, found him fascinating and entertaining, and they were happy to wait on him at every opportunity—even with his frequent late-night and early-morning teas. Furthermore, I realized such matters as his laundry were no doubt less awkwardly taken care of.

So it was in his room at the Holiday Inn, as I sat talking to him only two days before he left, that I began to wonder whether he would ever be back. The following day would be his last day at work before departure, and it would be a busy day. He planned to wind up his series of lessons on the yoga sutras, and he had a number of appointments. Most importantly, it was arranged that he would take a number of portable biofeedback training instruments that were being prepared for travel by the Biomedical Electronics Lab to the New Delhi conference, and he had been instructed on how to unpack and repack them and how to set them up for demonstrations. Swami was arranging his own personal luggage on this night, and as he puttered around with his things, he spoke as he had not long before when his well-intended efforts had brought him the discomfort of being opposed. Only now he spoke in an uncommonly subtle manner. It was as though he wanted to convey his disillusion and despair without having to outwardly admit it.

I could understand the swami's point of view, but I could understand the conservative scientists also. I could not agree with them, but having been brought up in the same situation, I could understand them. They, like Swami, were products of their culture. Neither the swami nor those who opposed him had ever seen anything like each other before and they could not understand each other's extreme viewpoints. Actually, the swami had gained the attention and interest of some of the doctors and scientists in various departments of the foundation as well at the veterans' hospital, the state mental institution, and several large universities in Kansas and Missouri. In addition to this, there were many such professionals among his followers in Minneapolis, Chicago, and other cities. These people outnumbered those who resented him and were certainly equally intelligent, equally well trained, but much less prejudiced and opinionated. Why, I wondered, should it have been necessary for him to be admired by everyone? Was this just an additional ego problem? Why could not he, and his antagonists as well, have gone on about their various separate projects without being bothered by one another's strangeness? And particularly the swami, who always spoke of "living in the world and yet remaining above"—why could he not have ignored those who were opposed to his presence and simply attended to his lab demonstrations and to working with those who were learning from him? But as I sat in his motel room watching Swami empty the drawers of his bedside table and place the contents carefully into his suitcase, I realized I knew the answer to these questions. The swami responded to everything. That was the essence of his character and all his behavior. He responded to my unvoiced thoughts. He responded to incoming calls even before the phone rang, and he could not help but respond to all the efforts being made to contact him—the very thing from which both he and Elmer had wanted me to protect him. He responded to all the moods and conditions of the Greens and their family. If someone was tired or sick, he felt it. Within the walls of the research building there was resentment against the swami's presence—perhaps against the swami himself. All these feelings reached the swami, just like my thoughts, the telephone calls, and everything else; and unavoidably he responded.

"Did you see this?" he asked, taking a small box from the drawer.

"Maybe," I answered, waiting to see what was inside.

"No, never. You did not see. How could you see this when I have purposely not shown it to anyone?" He took it from its box and put it on his finger. It was a ring with a ridiculously huge setting that looked something like a pearl but must have been glass. He extended his arm so that I could see it more closely, and he tilted his head and acted as though he were watching himself with admiration as he aesthetically rotated his hand in the air.

"You're right," I admitted. "If you had ever worn that thing I would surely have noticed."

"Thing? This is not mere thing. And it is not mere ring also. This is not for wearing, not for, you see, spectacle. What do you call this?"

"I don't know. What is it?"

"I don't know. This is a thing to be used for practice. With this I have trained easily in my country. The focus, you see?" He slipped the ring over his thumb, and holding out his arm, he fixed his eyes upon the glass ball. "Here we train how to concentrate the attention—gazing, this is called gazing."

"Crystal ball!" I said. "That could be called a crystal ball, is that what you were trying to say? That looks like a crystal ball, only a crystal ball is much bigger."

"Ah, yes. It is one and the same."

The swami and the crystal ball, I thought to myself—that was the image that accompanied my first encounter with the word "swami." I could still see it clearly: a thin-faced man with dark, deep-set eyes, a Vandyke beard, a turban, and long, thin fingers that hovered gracefully over a crystal ball. Such an image was once commonly seen on little lunch-counter machines that dispensed fortunes and answers to questions for only a penny apiece. Probably this was still the most popular stereotyped concept of a swami.

"This is the process I used some time back when I tried to prepare myself for that simple attraction test. With this I nearly destroyed my eyes. You saw my red eyes. Here is not so suitable for doing those things. Because of distractions, you see? In my country I was always in proper form. Then attraction is a simple matter. These people don't know. Repulsion is much more difficult, and I have never mastered it properly, but attraction is a simple thing." He removed the ring from his thumb, returned it to its box, and put the box in his suitcase. "I don't mind being put to the test—this is what I wanted—but I did not want to create this anger and anxiety. So many of your intellectuals are afraid to approach even the gates of many gardens of knowledge. This is not the case in many countries, you see, and I had no idea about this."

Swami had a very busy last day at the office. In the morning, in the conference room down the hall, he gave us the last of his lessons on the yoga sutras of Patanjali and then held private meetings with some members of the training group. He also had an unscheduled meeting with a visitor from Portland, Oregon, a man representing a foundation that had helped to fund the research. In the afternoon he and I cleared up his desk as best we could, and then he returned to his room at the Holiday Inn, taking with him the things from his office that he wanted to have along on his trip.

In the afternoon I sat for a while in his office arranging the papers, books, and supplies that had been left on his desk so that they would be safe until he got back. Among all the papers and pencils there remained his incense burner and several boxes of incense, and on the desk, the telephone stand, the bookcase, and the shelves under the window there were a number of religious and art objects that I wanted to leave as they were and hoped would be safe. And I had promised to take care of all the plants. "Now, I leave all these things in your hands," the swami had said.

After I had finished my own work for the day I borrowed a dymo set from biomedical electronics and began to punch out names and addresses on plastic tape for the swami's luggage. His own personal baggage and all the biofeedback equipment packed in suitcases made up a great deal of luggage to be labeled. This was the first time I had used the dymo, and it turned out to be a much more tedious task than I had guessed. It required a fairly hard squeeze on the handles to make a clear impression on the plastic tape, and it must have required a thousand squeezes to punch out all the necessary labels. Before an hour was up I noticed I was beginning to get blisters on my hand, and I still had piles left to be labeled. When the Greens and everyone else had left for home and it had grown dark outside my office window, I remained at my desk, squeezing the dymo. What had started this project was that Elmer had wanted to label the suitcases from the lab and all the electronic instruments inside them, partly to protect the equipment and partly to make it easier for the swami when he tried to take the strange-looking machines through customs in his country. Many times I punched the words "Property of the Menninger Foundation" and "Research Department, The Menninger Foundation, Topeka, Kansas, U.S.A." Then as an additional favor to the swami, I decided to make identification labels for him to attach wherever he wished on his suitcases and personal belongings. So I punched out many pieces of tape saying "H.H. Swami Rama" and several saying "H.H. Swami Rama, Research Department, The Menninger Foundation, Topeka, Kansas, U.S.A." I even made a few that read "H.H. Swami Rama, Himalayan Institute of Yoga Science and Philosophy, Kanpur, India."

Anyway, Dolly Gattozzi was practicing in the lab downstairs, and I had to wait to give her a ride home. Dolly is a science writer with the National Institute of Mental Health. Recently she had come to Topeka to study the biofeedback research project and the work with Swami Rama. She was also a guest in the Greens' home, and since she had come to Topeka, she had joined the sutra lectures and participated in the training sessions. Sometimes in the evenings, when our Psychophysiology Laboratory was not in use, she spent hours wired up to the electroencephalograph practicing some of the techniques that the swami had taught together with methods we had used in the laboratory to control the production of alpha and theta brain waves. This night she stayed downstairs for over two hours, and I had decided that as long as she was down there I would go on punching labels for Swami's luggage.

It was nearly seven o'clock when she came into my office,

carrying the polygraph paper that attested to her success for the evening. "Well, these are my results," I said. "Look at my hand." By this time I had produced three large blisters on three fingers. They were bright red, very raw, and very painful. Dolly thought I had been foolishly careless to allow that to happen, but I explained I did not realize it would be such a painful task until it was too late.

"Well, let me do it for a while," she offered. "I'll know when to stop."

"It's all over now. Let me just finish this, and we'll go. I want to drop these off for Swami on the way home."

"Why not just take them home? Swami's coming over to meet with the training group at nine, you know."

"I know, but he's leaving early in the morning. He should have these right away so he can get finished with all his luggage. That's why I didn't want to stop. At first these were only water blisters and I thought I could be careful enough not to break them. I guess I got carried away."

"I guess you did," she agreed.

I realized that I had indeed foolishly overdone it as I drove us down the hill from the west campus toward the Holiday Inn. I could not use my right hand. It was painful enough even when I didn't move it.

"Are you going to just drop these off?" Dolly asked. "Or should we get into putting them on all his luggage for him and be really late for dinner?"

"Let's just drop them off. The people here help him with everything."

But Swami was not in his room. We decided to leave the bag with all the labels at the front desk with a note for him, so we went around to the office. "Swami's in there, I think," offered the man behind the desk, pointing toward the dining room. "At least he was a little while ago."

Dolly and I looked in through the door, but the lights were dim and there were many people inside. Then came his booming voice from the farthest corner. "Come, come, come! I am here! Why do you stand peering?" Many heads turned, first toward the swami and then toward us. Dolly and I stepped back away from the doorway, and Swami came out to the lobby. "Why, why? What's the matter? Why do you hesitate?"

"We're on our way home, Swami," I said. "I just wanted to tell you I left the labels for your luggage at the desk. There's a note in the bag explaining how—"

"What he really wants to tell you is how he sacrificed for you," Dolly interrupted. "Doug, show him your hand!"

"It's okay," I said, briefly holding up my hand.

Swami gave an indifferent glance. "For what purpose are we standing here? I have some guests inside. Come join us, why do you hesitate?" We explained that we were late for dinner and that we would soon be seeing him at the house, as he had promised to come for late evening tea with his training group people. "Thank you," Swami said, shaking my hand. "Many times thank you, thank you! I have never told you I appreciate, but really I appreciate."

"You've said it, Swami. I should say it too." It was a long handshake, and it felt to me like an expression of farewell. The only other time Swami had shaken my hand was when I first met him. After that, it had always been the traditional Indian gesture. When at last he released my hand, we started for the door. "Anyway, Swami, we'll see you at the house tonight." As I reached to push on the large glass doors I realized what had happened. I stopped and looked at my hand. I felt my fingers with my left hand. I turned to look at Swami, but he had gone back inside. "Look!" I said, holding my hand out for Dolly to see. The three painful holes in my hand had disappeared as though I had dreamed them. There was no sign that the blisters had ever been there!

That night we all sipped tea with Swami Rama, and I rubbed my hand again and again to remind myself of what he had done less than three hours earlier. As a result of my rubbing, or perhaps my thinking about it, the pain of the blisters suddenly returned; but when I looked at my hand, the pain went away. There was no sign of the blisters, and if I had not remembered the spots, there would have been no way to tell where they had been. I pushed hard on those three spots, but now I could feel nothing, not even the normal feeling of pressure. Swami caught my eye. I realized he had noticed what I was doing—probably what I was thinking—so I stopped checking my fingers and drank my tea.

Before he left, Swami gave us instruction in a different type of meditation exercise. It was different from anything we had done before, and Swami told us it would be dangerous for anyone who had not been trained. "If you give this to anyone, I am not responsible for the consequences," he warned us. Nevertheless, I was to record his words and make a copy of the recording for each of the members of the training group. As I was preparing the machine for recording, I discreetly examined my hand just one more time, and again I was surprised. On the three points where first there had been blisters and then there had been nothing, there were now three hard calluses. I wanted to look closer, but Swami was watching me. "Come on, are you not ready? Let us begin!" After the exercise there was a long silence. Then Swami said quietly, "Now I take my leave."

That was the last we saw of Swami Rama in Topeka, Kansas.

India: The First View

ten

On October 25, 1973, Dr. Green and a team of researchers and documenters left for India, carrying along in their luggage what may well have been one of the world's most sophisticated portable psychophysiological laboratories, all neatly packed up in suitcases. As a result of an eleventh-hour turn of events, I was with them. I was no longer an employee of the Menninger Foundation, since I had left during my work with Rolling Thunder, an American Indian medicine man; but unofficial as I was, it felt good to be with the Voluntary Controls Program again—and good to be going to India!

We came down in New Delhi as the sun was coming up. Swami Rama must have gotten up in the first hour of the morning, because he was there, standing just inside the terminal building, with a big smile on his face. I recalled that it was not unusual for Swami Rama to begin his day shortly after midnight, and I thought he looked well, as usual. His thick, well-oiled hair, his white robes, and his smiling face glistened in the early morning and made us seem the more tired and wrinkled. We were not the only group the swami had come to meet at the airport. Over a dozen others from Minneapolis, Madison, and Chicago had arrived on this flight. These people were from his ashrams in these cities, followers of Swami Rama who had come to attend and participate in the All-India Yoga Conference in Kanpur to be sponsored by the Himalayan Institute of Yoga Science and Philosophy. Our party had plans of its own: a ninety-day itinerary that included traveling nearly the entire perimeter of India. But the yoga conference was first on our agenda, and the Greens, Elmer and Alyce and their daughter Judy, were scheduled to speak.

The customs procedure went smoothly and quickly with the swami managing everything, standing behind the long counters, supervising his American guests and his government's officials as well. We were soon on our way toward the capital city in a caravan of little Indian cars. That was a ride not to be forgotten: the first look at India in the first hours of the day. The airport road was empty at this hour except for a few cows who crossed the road in front of our cars to demonstrate their right of way. But as we neared the city the streets became crowded, first with street people bathing and cooking by the roadsides, herding their animals here and there, and then with city people riding taxis of all descriptions and driving bicycles, scooters, and autos of all sizes to their daily destinations.

This was not unlike my first ride through the streets of Seoul, Korea. In those days taxis drove beside and between bicycles and bullock carts. That was before the traffic became mechanized and automatic—before Westernization modernized the city and took the life out of the streets. But the life was here in these streets in all its vivid reality. India would be like Korea once was: traveling here would mean passing right through the midst of the processing of living, passing people brushing teeth, washing plates and pots, answering nature's calls.

Swami led his caravan of cars and his twenty some-odd guests to the Lodhi Hotel, where he continued to be very much in charge of everyone, assigning rooms to his various guests and assigning duties—like separating the luggage—to his younger disciples. Apparently, in Swami's opinion, the process of getting arranged and settled was confusing to others, and he gave his commands with insistent repetition. As I watched him I felt that a great deal of the confusion was being created by the swami himself. Invisible now were the two aspects of Swami I liked best: the old man and the

child. Here was only his middle aspect—the robust executive. Swami must have become aware of my feelings as I
was watching him because he took me aside there in the
hotel lobby, right in the middle of all his administrating, and
said to me in a quiet voice, "You are my brother and you
have come to my country. If you need anything, ask me.
Don't say anything to Doctor. Just ask me for anything, even
money if you need it." That was still the middle self of
Swami. Not that he hadn't meant it. Even if he had said it,
just as confidentially, to all the others, it was meant and
was a kindness. But the old man would not have needed to
say it, and it would not have occurred to the child.

We landed in Kanpur the next day at what could just
barely be called an air field; but at first it seemed as big and
busy a place as New Delhi's International Airport because
there was a huge crowd of men, women, and children standing in a row, looking happy-faced and festive. Those in back
craned their necks as they all stared in our direction. I
thought maybe they were wondering what all the Americans
were doing here. When the youngest members of the crowd
could contain themselves no longer, it became apparent
who these people were and what they were doing here. Suddenly all the children came rushing up to Swami Rama, running along beside him, touching his feet as he walked. Swami
stooped to pat their heads. All these people were Swami's
disciples. Most of them stood now holding their hands together in the customary Indian greeting.

Elda Hartley, the film maker in our party, looked at me and
shook her head. "I was wondering who the big celebrity
was."

There was a great deal of greeting and introducing and
shaking of hands as workers pulled cartloads of our luggage
across the field, and garland after garland of bright-smelling
yellow flowers were placed over Swami's head and piled as
high as his neck. Swami called out in Hindi to some of the
dark-faced and distinguished-looking men (who I would
later learn were his closest disciples from his Kanpur Yoga

Institute), and the men started toward one of the parked cars. When the car pulled up to where Swami was standing, he instructed those of us who had arrived with him to count our suitcases and see that none were left behind, and then he opened the door, nudged the driver, and jumped in behind the wheel. He grinned at us, stuck out his tongue, and briefly allowed that mischievous, childish expression that I had missed in him to pass over his face. Then he spun out and sped across the field toward the road in a cloud of dust.

Our arrival date in India had been arranged to coincide with the All-India Yoga Conference sponsored by Swami Rama's Himalayan Institute of Yoga Science and Philosophy. But unknowingly we had come to India at a good time for some interesting first impressions. During our stay came the religious and festive days of Devali—a romantic combination of ceremonial worship and fireworks. The Devali ritual includes worship to the deities Lakshmi and Ganesh. Lakshmi is the goddess of wealth and prosperity. Ganesh is the elephant-headed son of Lord Shiva, and he is the remover of obstacles. The city of Kanpur spent several days decorating streets, buildings, and gardens with holy images, streamers, autumn flowers, and strings of colored lights. This busy but despairing industrial city appeared misleadingly bright and cheerful to us as we went here and there through the streets on evening outings.

Those of us who had come to India together spent that week of the yoga conference in Kanpur living with an Indian family in a private home. Our eight-member group consisted of three psychologists, Elmer, Alyce, and Judy Green; film maker Elda Hartley of Hartley Productions, with two assistants, film director Harvey Bellin and still-camera expert Tom Kieffer; writer Dolly Gattozzi; and me. We were the investigation and documenting team that was identified—from our arrival at the Lodhi Hotel in New Delhi to our departure three months later—as Dr. Green and party.

One of the most impressive things about the yoga conference was the big tent. It was not as tall as a giant American circus tent, but it was much more exotic. Its colors and design made one think of Arabian knights and camels. The tent was set up on the lawn of a Kanpur park, and there was plenty of grassy area all around it for the overflow of people. Inside, at the front end of the tent, there was a four-foot-high platform large enough to accommodate a speaker's rostrum, a long table for those officiating, and about twenty-five very comfortable armchairs for speakers and honored guests. There were what seemed like countless rows of folding chairs facing this platform, but the first two rows were made up of stuffed sofas for the dignitaries in the audience. Electric lights and speakers were strung along the poles from front to back. Thousands of people came from east, west, north, and south to sit in those chairs to listen to swamis, yogis, doctors, and scholars.

"Ladies and gentlemen," said the master of ceremonies as he began a long introduction in Hindi and English to present the one who was chairman, arranger, leader, and Master. Again people placed garlands of brilliant fresh flowers over the head of Swami Rama as he walked to the front of the platform, just as they had done only moments ago when he had come to sit in the largest chair at the center of the official's table. Again Swami quickly removed them. He stood looking tall and stern at the ocean of expectant faces before him. He lifted his arms under his flowing white robes and put his palms together. There was a profound hush throughout this huge crowd. Then in the silence he had just created he said in a quiet voice, "I salute the divinity in you," and then again I could feel the dignity and beauty that I had known in Swami Rama.

On the second day of the conference the Greens talked about biofeedback and self-regulation—about their research on voluntary control of internal states. They demonstrated their biofeedback machines—the small, battery-operated instruments they often referred to as trainers—and they displayed the portable psychophysiology laboratory that we were to carry thousands of miles throughout India. The huge crowd of students, teachers, doctors, yogis, swamis, and tourists listened attentively as the Greens explained how they planned to measure skin potential, skin temperature, respiration, and heart, muscle, and brain activity of yogis and advanced meditators who had achieved extraordinary physiological controls.

Over the past many years, the Greens had demonstrated their monitoring and feedback equipment and presented their hypothesis on volition and self-regulation to many thousands of Western scientists and laymen. No doubt most of their listeners had been amazed, in varying degrees, to consider all the possibilities in the area of self-regulation— such as the possibility that one can regulate the pace of one's heart with one's will. But this audience, I realized, was different: what amazed most of these people was not the idea of volition and self-mastery but all the remarkable electronic equipment.

Every one of the thousands of men and women who were able to crowd into this huge tent or within speaker range on the lawn outside demonstrated an intense interest in all the speakers—both American and Indian—and in all they had to say. It seemed that virtually everyone who came that first morning and left at noon for lunch came back again in the afternoon and again each following day. Not once was there a falling away of attention or a restlessness in the huge crowd.

This conference, I understood, was an activity to promote the practice of yoga in India. It was, in a sense, a huge revival meeting—part of the new, world-wide process of reviving the ancient wisdom of the East in all its spiritual and practical forms. Having studied with Rolling Thunder and other American Indian medicine men before coming to India, I now knew that there is also the ancient wisdom of the West—even the ancient wisdom of what we have recently named "America"—and there is the concurrent revival of that ancient wisdom. The next steps, I thought to myself, might bring about a marriage of wisdoms.

I recalled once having heard someone say that the essential difference between the East and the West could best be described in terms of manifestations of emotion versus manifestations of intellect. I remembered that because it was one of the neatest East-West statements I could think of. Now I felt it made sense to believe that yoga is no more Eastern than Western. If the wisdom of the East or the wisdom of the West were to be put into practice in this world, if any wisdom were to be made manifest intellectually as well as emotionally, if there were to be growth of bodies and minds, of individuals, societies, and nations, it would have to happen in the East as in the West: the result of a global coming-together of which this All-India Yoga Conference was only a small part.

We nearly missed our train out of Kanpur. Swami Rama was to have provided cars to convey us from the ashram to the Kanpur station, but the transportation never arrived. Our Kanpur host, whose own car was at the company, managed to borrow a couple of cars and drivers from his neighbors. We frantically loaded the fragile laboratory and our own suitcases and tore through town for the station. We arrived at the station just in time to run down the tracks and step on the slowly accelerating train.

It is possible to reach Rishikesh on some sort of train from somewhere, but most trains stop at Hardwar a few miles downriver, and continue from there to Dehradun. The usual procedure for Indian pilgrims traveling north to these holy cities on the Ganges is to take a train or bus to Hardwar, where they can begin their worship and take their first dips in the sacred water. From there it is an easy ride of forty minutes or an hour by taxi, jitney, or bus, to Rishikesh. Our party was to disembark at Hardwar and wait there for the vehicle that was to take us to Rishikesh and then on to

Chandigarh and Calcutta, and so on the rest of our Indian journey. So we stepped down into the station platform in the first light of early morning and rode through the streets of Hardwar to the Tourist Hotel on the Ram Ghat. There we waited for four days for the vehicle which Swami Rama had promised to have sent there (but never arrived).

Here we were properly broken in for our India tour: we sat cross-legged on a hard wooden floor and ate curds and rice and hot curries with our fingers; we shopped in the marketplace for fruits and nuts and tried using a half-dozen Hindi words from Judy's guidebook; we had things stolen right out of our hands by mischievous red monkeys, who found us unsuspecting and delightfully easy to sneak up on; we caught sniffling, eye-watering colds from breathing soot, charcoal smoke, and cow-dung dust, and we learned to drink our daily five or six cups of milky, sticky-sweet tea.

But Hardwar had its enchantment and I liked it. Here we were at last on the banks of the Holy Ganges, the setting of so many romantic tales and mystic legends. All along these banks were the bathing *ghats* where people came in steady streams to offer flowers and coins to the swift current, to lift handfuls of water to their lips and pat wet hands upon their faces and heads, or to immerse themselves completely— shirts, pants, trunks, pajamas, saris, and all. Along these banks, in the temples, or at the river's edge, even in our tourist hotel, evening *pujas* always followed the setting sun. Each night in my room I opened the window that looked over the Ganges, watched for a moment the quivering image of the moon, and then went to sleep to the sound of the river's rushing.

When we decided we had waited long enough in Hardwar, we hired two taxis to take us to Swami Rama's ashram in Rishikesh where we could check on the progress of our vehicle arrangements. We left with no regrets, anxious to see Rishikesh and beyond, and hopeful that breathing would be easier for us once out of Hardwar. It was a pleasant ride from Hardwar to Rishikesh, and I was encouraged. The air was fresh and clear, the temperature ideal, and this was a scenic ride through forest country. Elda Hartley had an eye for beauty in every form, a trait which was to become her trademark on this trip. She was particularly enraptured at times like this when the sun, shining through the trees, softened the air and cast golden light beams and long, black shadows.

After nearly an hour, we passed a few small buildings and a couple of fruit and vegetable stands and stopped at the side of the road.

"Where are we?" someone asked.

"This is Rishikesh," our driver said, "the center of town."

I looked out at the holy city. The road was mostly dust. We had stopped beside a lot with a fallen fence. Inside were a couple of cars that looked very broken down, a considerable accumulation of paper litter, and one rather sooty-looking cow. On the other side of the road was a small shack with a sign that said KOFFEE KORNER.

I felt a mild disappointment, but I reasoned it out. I knew I couldn't judge Rishikesh from a taxi window. Whatever was here was deeper than appearances, I supposed, and this was not a sightseeing venture anyway.

We had hired our taxis to transport us to Rishikesh, and now we were here; but we hoped the drivers would be willing to take us right on to Swami Rama's ashram, where ever it was. Even in India one does not expect fluent English from a clerk, a policeman, or a driver, and it is a pleasant surprise whenever it occurs. "Had you told me earlier exactly where you wanted to go," our driver scolded, "we would not have come all the way into town. We passed the turnoff back there, and now we'll have to double back a ways."

The two cars made tight U-turns in the road and went back to where a large sign pointed left to Ram Nagar. We went down a long narrow road that seemed to be going out into the country. The Ganges was close by now, but out of sight behind the houses and trees. We were watching left and right, sure that we would see another sign eventually, but our driver stopped to ask directions. He spoke to an old man who was wearing the same faded orange robes that we had often seen in Hardwar. This man had big, bushy eyebrows, a long white beard, and a walking stick.

The old man spoke in Hindi and pointed down the road. Then he opened the door and got in beside me, pushing me over against the driver.

"He doesn't have to show us, only tell us," said Elmer Green from the back seat. "I'm sure we can find it."

"This swami wants to go there too," the driver said.

Another swami! (I didn't know it then, but there were hundreds of these people walking around in Rishikesh.)

Swami's ashram was no disappointment. It fit the mental pictures I had developed years ago in Topeka, Kansas, where Swami had talked of it frequently and so vividly, tempting me to return to India with him. There were dozens and dozens of cacti, just as he had said. They bordered the inside of the fence around the ashram, surrounding the building itself. I recalled our visit to the Gage Park greenhouse in Topeka when he had told me that nobody could raise cacti to compare to his. "They are all nothing before mine," he had said. I remembered the time he offered to landscape the Greens' entire yard and living room "with over twenty varieties of cactus plants."

I was staring now at Swami's plants, and one of his disciples was watching me. "Swamiji loves cacti," he said.

"I know."

The swami had been informed that we were here, and he was ready to see us. We were led through the front door into an empty anteroom, where we took off our shoes. Then we filed into an inner room and found the swami seated on a thronelike arrangement of cushions and bolsters, wearing a majestic-looking wine-colored cape, looking like a modern maharaja. Incense burned at his right and a telephone sat waiting at his left. A beautiful hand-made rug bearing the emblem of Swami's International Institute of Yoga, Science and Philosophy took up most of the floor, and I supposed that no one ever sat or stepped upon it. There was enough floor space remaining for a border of cushions and a path to get to them. We took our seats on these cushions, joining others who had been listening to a lesson—the American disciples whom we had met before.

There was some conversation about why didn't we wait in Hardwar, leaving everything up to the swami. Then he used his telephone to arrange rooms for us at the guesthouse of the mahant, now that we were here. We knew the mahant, whom we had met in New Delhi. "Mahantji," everyone called him (but they said it so fast it sounded like "manji"), and this, we learned, was his title, not his name. Mahants are religious leaders. Like trustees of the holy cities, they are high enough and important enough to be called saints. They are the hereditary custodians of temples and temple property, all the wealth the propery represents, and all wealth it brings. "That's the man who owns Rishikesh," someone had said of him in New Delhi. He had paid for all the rooms at the Lodhi Hotel, our plane tickets to Kanpur, and the train to Hardwar.

"How about a cup of tea?" suggested Swami Rama. More than a hundred times in Topeka during 1970 and 1971 I had heard those same words. But now the tone was different: it was an invitation, not a request. Here someone else would make the tea.

When it was ready we sat around a long table in the dining room while Swami's American disciples asked us about Hardwar. After tea we were led up a narrow concrete stairway into the top of this main ashram building and out on to a rooftop balcony where we could look over the land.

Even this land that was now Swami Rama's ashram had been provided by the mahant. It was even more beautiful than I had envisioned in my mental picture. Surrounding this building and the one adjoining—the lodging rooms for the disciples—was an open yard, swept clean and kept clear except for all the cacti and a variety of flowers and one round garden table complete with a huge sun umbrella. Beyond this yard the terrain dropped off to a sandy, rocky beach and then to the edge of the Ganges.

We had seen this same river in Kanpur and in Hardwar, but I liked it best here where there were no concrete walkways or steps leading into the water as there had been at the bathing *ghats*. Here it could flow in the quiet privacy of trees and mountains, turning to follow the contour of the land. That turning added to its beauty. There was a sharp bend in the river upstream from where we waded, making it look as though the river had turned this way to pass near Swami Rama's ashram.

In spite of all the beauty, it was a relief to leave the ashram, and I was glad that we would not be staying there. It was awkward and difficult to relate to Swami Rama or even to observe him while he was surrounded by all these people who considered him their master. After all the talk about self-regulation, and the internal search for the master within, it was embarrassing to see the swami indulge in this bizarre Americanization of the guru-disciple principle.

We stayed for about three weeks in Rishikesh, still waiting for some sort of vehicle to take us on our way.

During the first week we stayed at the guesthouse, talked with Mahantji, and visited the ancient temple there. Then we took rooms at a Tourist Bungalow on the other side of town from Swami's ashram.

One morning not long after we arrived, a young Hindustani watchman at Swami Rama's ashram began chanting and continued through the day. In the evening he marked off a square plot of ground just down the path from the ashram yard beside the grove of mango trees. In the center of the square he dug a shallow pit, and in the pit he built a fire. He constructed an altar of stones, and before the altar he lit a candle and many sticks of incense, then seated himself facing the altar on a mat beside the fire burning in the pit.

That evening Swami Rama and one of his assistants drove

up the hill to the Tourist Bungalow, where we were gathered in one of the rooms for tea and conversation. He told us about the watchman who was at that moment performing his ritual at the ashram. The young man would sit there through the night in a trancelike state of intense concentration while others maintained the candles, incense, and fire. By dawn, we were told, his body would have become like a temple, and he would lick some hot object with his tongue to show that he would not be harmed. We were to arrive at the ashram at midmorning to watch this happen. There could be no physiological tests: his body could not be touched—by electrodes or by fingers—and no one would be allowed within the marked-off area. But we could observe with our eyes and our cameras.

The watchman was a devotee of the Divine Mother who performed his ritual for his personal worship, but this time Swami Rama had instructed him to do this so that we might see it.

In the morning we walked quietly down that path and saw the watchman sitting there in his enshrined area just as he had been sitting for more than twelve hours. I respected him. What he had been doing for all these hours represented a magnificent effort, and had I not felt that respect, I would have felt that our being here like this with our cameras was cruel and mocking.

The swami, who only minutes ago had been instructing us not to step across the marked boundaries of the square and not to allow a sudden or uncalm act or thought, was himself being most uncalm. He vigorously directed those of his disciples who had brought cameras, loudly criticized those who had not, and shouted in a voice that resounded up the path to scold those who had not yet come down. When at last Swami was satisfied that everyone was where he or she should be, he sat down beside Mahantji, just outside the boundary line, directly facing his young servant.

The plump Indian woman who was the ashram cook arrived carrying a tray; she walked right over the boundary line and into the sacred square, where no other person had stepped. She sat down beside the young man, who looked at her with a loving look—she was part of the ritual. Taking a piece of food from her tray, she put it gently into his mouth. He stared at her with a deep, steady gaze as she continued to feed him with her fingers, and his large, black eyes filled with tears. He then turned his face away as though he could see her no longer and nearly closed his eyes.

Suddenly he looked up at Swami Rama and began to yell at him in a sharp, angry voice. He was leaning forward and shaking his finger at the swami. Everyone seemed shocked. For a moment I felt an almost electrifying fear. Why had he become so angry, and why had it happened so suddenly, in the midst of his ritual, and what could he be shouting at the swami? I was sure that nothing like this had ever happened before. But Swami calmly watched until his servant stopped shouting, then leaned over and whispered something in Mahantji's ear. The young man glared at them. Swami waited for the mahant, who looked thoughtful for a moment, nodded his head, and spoke only a word or two in Hindi.

The watchman, still looking intense, took some ashes in his hand and licked them from his palm. Out of the glowing coals he took a flat piece of metal about eighteen inches long and rubbed it vigorously on his tongue. His expression softened and he looked peaceful again. With slightly trembling hands he reached again into the pit, took a handful of hot ashes, and thrust them into his mouth. Again he licked the hot metal, allowing the ashes to fall from his mouth. In a moment he sat quietly just as he had been sitting when we arrived. When Swami stood to walk back up the path, everyone stirred. People crowded up around the boundary lines, and the watchman gestured, inviting them into his square. Elda got some close-up footage of the man's tongue while others examined the piece of metal, which had cooled enough by now to be carefully touched. Some wanted to question the man, but he either could not speak or did not want to. No one was sure what his tongue was supposed to look like in its original condition, but if it had been burned it was hardly apparent.

I walked up the path and found Swami Rama sitting on the wall beside the steps that led up to the yard. It was the first time since Topeka that I had seen him alone. I sat down on the steps. Now, in the absence of all the followers, Swami was calm and gentle and spoke to me with a friendly warmth.

Later, Elmer and Alyce told us what Swami had said to them about what we had seen that morning. The woman who had entered the ritual had represented for the watchman, in physical form, the figure of the Divine Mother upon whom he had been steadily focusing his attention for more than twenty-four hours. Those were not the words of the watchman that had been shouted at Swami in the watchman's voice. The young man was then functioning as a medium, according to Swami Rama, and the Hindi words that we had not understood had included instructions for some changes and a demand for a promise. Swami had not explained what he had been commanded to promise, only that he had declined.

"I was supposed to promise her," Swami had said, "but I didn't. She demanded a promise, so I told Mahantji to promise, and he did it. I'm not going to promise anything."

eleven

Judy Green and I paused at the side of the road to view the Ganges. We had just hiked down the hill from the Tourist Bungalow, where we met the road out of Rishikesh. It was no more than a half-hour's walk along that road to the Koffee Korner, the nearby post office, or fresh-food stands; some of us had made that journey several times.

But today we turned the other way, planning to follow the road about two or three miles upriver and cross over the Ganges on the iron rope hanging bridge called Laxman Jhula. We were pausing here to prepare for a long, uphill tread. Here was a clear view of the Ganges with nothing between the road and the river but open green fields.

We spotted an orange-robed sadhu coming down the road, and both Judy and I turned to watch him as he approached. These fellows dressed in orange no longer attracted our attention as they had a week or so ago, for we often passed dozens of them on the road during our frequent walks into Rishikesh. They lived in the ashrams, in the hills, and on the banks of the Ganges, often coming on pilgrimage from the holy cities in the south. Mahantji maintained a mess hall for these sadhus, so they came into town at scheduled hours in the mornings and evenings for free food. At those hours crowds of sadhus could be seen taking their meals in that large hall while crowds of them were walking along the road carrying their mess kits filled with rice and *japatis*. They seldom seemed to notice other people, even we odd-looking foreigners; and we in turn were beginning not to notice them.

But this man coming down the road caught our eye because he was watching us. As he came closer, we knew he intended to stop and make conversation. Although he looked to be in his forties, he had a youthful face—not the kind of face that disguises one's age, simply a youthful face. It was slightly square-shaped and uncomplicated. His head was covered—not with a turban or hood, but with one end of the extra piece of yardage that he wore over his shoulders—and his legs were bare to just above the knees.

"Excuse me, but may I ask you people where you are from?"

We could tell already that we were not the first Americans this man had spoken to. His manner and speech were natural and easy. He was the first who had not tersely growled, "Your native place?"

"Then are you attending some ashram here, or are you tourists, or . . . ?"

We were tourists here, and it was not easy or necessary to offer any more complicated details than that, except to say that we were a party of eight.

"Maybe you are interested in our religion or our yoga, or you are looking for some interesting places to visit?"

It seemed this man wanted to be our tourist guide, and at that moment neither Judy nor I needed one. In fact, we would probably never need a guide, as we had already discussed. Although we realized the benefits of having someone who could interpret and explain, we also knew the advantages of being left alone—alone to enjoy the solitude of a serene mountain path, alone to contemplate personal impressions in some quiet temple. And today we wanted exercise, not education. We just wanted a brisk walk up the hill. So we sent him off to meet Harvey Bellin, who was at that moment in Rishikesh looking for photogenic subjects in the sadhus' mess hall.

"Very fine. Then I am just now going," he said.

"Harvey will be happy to see you."

"I am Swami Sivanandapuri," he informed us. "I have been headquartered at the Sanyas Ashram in Hardwar after leaving the Sivananda Ashram here. But I've come back up to Rishikesh to meet Westerners." He tore off a corner of a newspaper he was carrying to write that information down for us. We did not reciprocate with like information about ourselves; we only repeated Harvey's name and described his mustache and blue shirt so that the swami would be sure to find him.

The swami smiled. He didn't think he could miss finding the American amongst all the sadhus. As he continued down the road toward Rishikesh, we started our uphill climb.

Relieved by our graceful escape from what could possibly have been an awkward situation, Judy sighed. "Poor Harvey." She was thinking about a little, bald-headed, bespectacled swami who had first attached himself to Harvey and then to her. The persistent swami had approached Harvey somewhere near the guesthouse when we were staying there, and Harvey had invited him in—probably at the little man's insistence. We had not been long at the Tourist Bungalow before he learned where we had gone, and there he began seeking our company. We called him the Scholar Swami because of his large glasses and constant discussion of books. After talking about them for a while, he would begin to ask for some. He would inquire which books we would be willing to give him now and which we could promise to send him at our earliest convenience. At first we didn't mind his coming so often, but it was his constant presence that got to be a problem. Soon we developed the habit of watching for him and warning the others. He usually went to Judy's room, and after the talk had proceeded from which books did she like to which books could she offer to her regrets that she couldn't offer any, he would consent to be satisfied with notebooks and pens.

After that experience Judy was afraid we had just gifted Harvey with another orange shadow. But I was not sure; we had not really known who or what this man was. He had not directly implied any interest in being our guide. Instead, he had only said he was familiar with this area, inquired what our interests were, and mentioned that he wanted to meet Westerners. I had the feeling that I would be seeing a lot of this man.

It took a long time to hike to the turnoff to Laxman Jhula. The steep, winding road seemed at times to go unnecessarily out of its way. Although it was bordered with trees, over-looked the river, and carried little traffic, it was not a good road for walking. When a bus came from one direction, another bus would come from the other direction, and the two always managed to meet at precisely the point in the road where we would have been standing if we had not scrambled off into the trees.

When we reached the turnoff, we discovered we were high above the river. At any rate, it looked like an easy, peaceful road leading down to the bridge.

The hanging bridge itself began to sway very slightly as we got toward the middle. It was not because of us, we dis-covered, but because of the train of donkeys laden with building bricks who had stepped onto the bridge. It was a gentle motion. We gazed into the depths of the peaceful river flowing below us as we let the donkeys pass.

We stepped off the Laxman Jhula bridge on to the grounds of the harsh concrete ashrams and temples, popular for tour-ists and for seekers of liberation and prosperity. The temples and ashrams here did not communicate the delicate beauty or the still serenity that I had learned in Korea and Japan to expect of such places. The temples here—like hotels, offices, warehouses, and terminals—were cold, stark, square-cornered concrete. In fact, they reminded me of government buildings on military bases. Pictures and statues of an assortment of deities painted or clothed in loud primary colors served as decoration. Inside the ground-floor halls of these buildings, people gave offerings of coins and flowers and made their supplications (which they emphasized by clanging bells to signal the gods), but we did not go inside.

On this side of the Ganges there was a path leading from Laxman Jhula to the boat crossing downriver, and our plan was to walk down this path and ride back across on the boat. It was much more pleasant walking down along the path than hiking up the steep dusty road. The Ganges was invisible from most of the path, though it was never far away. Mango trees and a variety of other exotic fruit trees whose names we could not remember grew thick on both sides of the path, and they provided cool shade and comfortable homes for dozens of chattering monkeys.

Just beside the path not far down from Laxman Jhula were a dozen or so strange-looking old men whom we guessed must have been devotees, yogis, pseudo-yogis, or fakirs because of their long, matted hair, their bodies covered with ashes, and the sacred symbols painted on their foreheads. Whatever they were, they looked professional, as they had settled as close to the path as possible with their containers ready for offerings. They all had some paraphernalia: assorted pictures of their gurus and gods, incense to burn and bidis (cone-shaped hand-made Indian cigarettes) to smoke, rice bowls and dishes, mats for sitting or sleeping. Some even had a blanket. Most of these characters had drums or flutes —something to pound or toot. One old man had a musical instrument consisting of a string on a stick and a bow; he even had a snake in a basket, who would no doubt dance for a price. Some of these old men were on mounds of dirt leveled at the top to accommodate their mats, and one man had an old army cot; most of these oldsters, however, had settled against the bases of the largest trees, the roots of which spread out above the ground like gigantic gnarled hands providing places to build altars and keep dishes and cigarettes.

We walked past these old fellows without stopping to give coins, only returning, "*Hari Om!*" to those who cried it first; but when we came to the little man at the end of the row we stopped. This was someone we knew!

Swami Rama and Mahantji had offered to find us a yogi or two who would be willing to be wired up to the portable psychophysiology laboratory. But the most impressive yogis remained secluded in faraway forests or in high mountain caves and were difficult to find. Furthermore, the roads through the Valley of Flowers and into the Himalayas had been closed to foreign travelers because of recent border problems between India and Red China. So one Sunday morning they brought us a little man from across the river. He had long, matted hair and ash-covered skin, and he did his meditation on a bed of nails. The Greens wired him up on the rocks down by the Ganges below Swami Rama's ashram, and his temperature, heart rate, brain waves, respiration, and various other physiological functions were observed as he concentrated, meditated, or simply lay back and relaxed on his bed of nails and smoked his bidis He was our first subject. If there was anything interesting about the man it was his unusual appearance; the fact that he had taken a vow of silence that was to last twelve years and the fact that at least a few of his nails were indeed very sharp were also intriguing. From a physiological point of view, however, he was quite an ordinary person, and Mahantji admitted that he was just a "commercial yogi." At any rate, it had been a useful practice run, and the little man had given the Greens a good chance to test out their equipment in an outdoor setting.

Now here he was on his bed of nails, sitting on his haunches with his feet on the spikes, busily working on one of the sharp points with a metal file. We watched him for a few moments. If he had glanced up, he would have recognized us, and we could have said, "Hey! How's it goin'?" But he never did look up. Instead, he just kept filing, testing the sharpness with the pad of his thumb, and filing some more. Once he paused to light some incense off his burning candle, then lit himself a bidi and continued filing, never glancing toward the path. So we took a couple of pictures, which apparently he didn't notice, and strolled on.

"Well, at least he made a little change," Judy said.

After watching our friend for a short while, we had decided to donate a few coins. A number of Indian pilgrims who came down the path stopped when they noticed us watching the old man, and when we had tossed our coins in the bowl they had contributed likewise—every one of them. They had no doubt felt that the favorite attraction of foreign tourists was worth their money too.

Back at the Tourist Bungalow, Harvey mentioned Swami Sivanandapuri at the dinner table before we even had a chance to ask. The swami had found Harvey and spoken with him, and Harvey had informed him where we were staying—even revealing our room numbers.

"We didn't talk very long," Harvey said. "He just asked about us and said he'd like to meet us all. He wanted to know what I was interested in. And he gave me his name and asked me how we could be reached, so I told him. Then he told me about meeting you two on the road."

"Well, Harvey, looks like you've done it again!"

"No, I think he's a nice guy."

"Then we won't have to apologize for arranging that meeting."

"Yeah, I like him. You'll see. I guess he'll be coming up here."

Harvey had guessed right. Swami Sivanandapuri was on his way as Harvey spoke.

After supper we had just washed up and were sitting on the steps outside our rooms when we noticed a robed and hooded silhouette in the distance. "Oh-oh! Is that Scholar Swami?" Judy jumped to her feet, ready to disappear somewhere, anywhere.

"No, that's Harvey's friend," chided Elda. "Go meet your friend, Harvey. Tell him you've been waiting for him."

Harvey sauntered toward the approaching figure as Elda said, "I know why Harvey's so impressed with that man—he told me about it. He'd walked right up to Harvey and said, 'Excuse me, you're Harvey and I'd like to meet you. I know about you and your party.' Harvey was almost believing he'd been sent a swami from heaven."

So Swami Sivanandapuri was our guest that night. And the following afternoon he was back again, carrying a harmonium and a few Indian songbooks. They were not the usual type of songbook: they were translations and explanations of Hindu chants and mantras—songs from the Ramayana and compositions by the revered philosopher Shankaryacharya. Swami Sivanandapuri was no virtuoso on the harmonium, but he could accompany himself well enough, and he knew all these songs as well as the stories behind them. He encouraged us to sing along. If only there had been a few weeks to spend with him, we might have learned a number of the enchanting Indian songs.

That evening I left the others and carried the harmonium and one of the songbooks to my room. I put the harmonium on the bed, sat cross-legged in front of it, and opened the book to a song I was anxious to try. Just after I had begun, Swami Sivanandapuri heard me and was at my door.

"May I come in?"

I closed the harmonium as the swami sat on the edge of my bed. In the conversation that followed I learned he had come up from the south some years ago and until recently had lived and worked at the Sivananda Ashram just up the road. His duties involved foreign correspondence and translation of letters, but what he had enjoyed most in his work there was communicating with Westerners. The attachment to the ashram he had not liked. There were always too many letters waiting to be done and too many people waiting to receive them. Soon he began to create mental images of these people and to translate and compose sentences in his mind when he was trying to meditate. For that reason, and possibly others he did not reveal, he left the ashram and went to Hardwar, where he found he was always looking for Westerners, especially Americans. Whenever they were scarce in Hardwar, he came back up to Rishikesh. He did not really want to settle anywhere. His hope was to help India and America become close friends again—this time not only on a political level, but on a cultural and spiritual level as well. As he talked, I realized this task had become this swami's *sadhana*. He thought that by meeting Westerners, by showing them friendship, making them feel wanted by the spiritual teachers, leading them to whomever and whatever they wanted here, he was doing his work in the world.

"The only thing that will save India—" he said emphatically, then added more gently, "maybe America, too—is for many young, new Indians and many new Americans and Europeans to become very good friends." He looked at me for approval and then quickly went on, "But I did not want to make you stop your songs."

He offered to leave the harmonium and books overnight so I could practice more. On second thought, he offered to let us keep them for a few days so that we all might learn some songs now that the chance was here. Soon he would have to take these things away, since he had borrowed them himself, but until then we could all enjoy them.

"And I'll try to be available to you," he offered, "whenever you want to learn more songs and mantras."

If he had been the Scholar Swami I might have felt endangered by those words, but they had been only an offer. I knew this swami would not try to teach me anything that I was not trying to learn. And if I did want to learn a song, I knew he would not insist on choosing which song it was to be. As I looked at him sitting on the edge of the bed I could feel that he was unassuming and unimposing. He was easy to like, and I liked him.

"But this would not be to spread religion," he continued, "only joy. We have only to spread joy—and all the works and the results will come."

Swami Sivanandapuri did indeed make the effort to be available. The next day when we returned from several hours of mailing letters, cashing travelers' checks, and shopping, he was standing on the steps of one of the rooms and he came to meet us.

"I've taken one of those rooms in that building up there," he announced, pointing to another section of rooms—the ones with a common bath. "I've engaged it for the duration of your stay. It was getting cold sleeping by the river. Besides, I thought I should try to be nearby so long as you are here. I won't bother you, I like to be alone. I'll just be nearby."

twelve

Early one morning five of us walked up the road to the Sivananda Ashram, with Swami Sivanandapuri as our guide.

Elmer, Alyce, and Elda had visited the Yogi Niketan Ashram the previous afternoon, and while they were there, an Indian professor had told them about Swami Nadabrahmananda, a devotee and teacher at the Sivananda Ashram, whose spiritual *sadhana* was the discipline of music. The professor had called him the world's greatest musician. This was likely another example of the kind of exaggeration Westerners often hear from Indians, even those who claim to be nonattached and holy. But the musician swami was worth hearing and seeing, if it could be arranged. He was reputed to hold his breath through a half-hour set of complicated ragas on the tabla, and he might be willing to demonstrate his talents wired up to our lab.

Elmer and Alyce had told me about the musician swami, so I mentioned him to Swami Sivanandapuri, because I wanted to hear his opinion.

"That sounds too much like a circus," Swami Sivanandapuri said. "But you should go to see him anyway. You might enjoy it and you might be impressed. But let me take you to see another musician at the Sivananda Ashram. Swami Vidyananda Saraswathi. He's a musician in the traditional sense. Let's go to see Swami Vidyananda Saraswathi first for a realistic introduction to devotional music, and then you go see whoever you like."

It was a reasonable response and a helpful suggestion, I thought. I would be happy to go.

"But we'll have to get up early. The morning devotion begins before sunrise."

So Dolly, Judy, Harvey, Tom, and I were up at 4:00 A.M. to follow Swami Sivanandapuri along the road through the darkness up the driveway that led around to the back of the ashram, then up the narrow stairs to the third floor of an old concrete building painted yellow with dark-green wooden shutters. Ironically, Elmer, Alyce, and Elda, who had first heard of the musician swami, were the only ones not here to get their "realistic introduction to devotional music."

The playing had already started as we quietly ascended the stairs, and we heard musical instruments and chanting voices. We walked across a veranda and into an empty ante-room, where through the open doorway we could see Swami Vidyananda Saraswathi sitting on a mat on the floor, playing a veena over which he leaned to see the pages of a large book opened on the floor before him. He was a saintly look-ing swami—elderly, slender, gentle—with wispy long hair and a silvery beard, and he wore the traditional cloth. There were two other musicians sitting at right angles to the swami. To his right was a woman who also played a veena, and to his left, a man who played the tambura.

About fifteen people sat facing the swami on the other side of the small room. They were not watching, they were par-ticipating, for this was a morning *puja.*

Swami Sivanandapuri stepped into the doorway, put his hands together in a greeting of respect to Swami Vidyananda Saraswathi (who did not notice), and then seated himself among the worshipers. Dolly and Judy followed Swami Siva-nandapuri inside, while Harvey and Tom remained in the anteroom to set up their Nagra IV recorder and Sennheiser 805 microphone. I stepped back out onto the veranda.

I gazed into the sky as it was just beginning to acquire that faint luminescence of early morning. The air was still cold, but the rapid walk up the hill had made me too warm, so I pulled off my coat and heavy woolen sweater. The early morning air touched my skin. It was invigorating. For a few minutes I sat on a wooden bench on the veranda, listening to the sounds of chanting floating out into the dawn.

When I went back in, I found Harvey just inside the door holding his microphone pointed toward the musicians. I made myself comfortable on the floor in the doorway and settled my eyes on the woman with the veena. She was sitting under an open window across the room from me. From where I sat I could look into her face. It was a peaceful face. Behind her round glasses were deep, dark eyes. She too followed the music from a book on the floor in front of her, turning the pages in unison with the swami. In her concentration she maintained a steady expression as her fingers plucked the strings in quick, staccato motions. By watching those fingers I could separate her notes out from the music that filled the room. Closing my eyes I could pick out any one of the three instruments and concentrate on it, or I could hear them together, in unity. The music was composed of patterns, and the player's synchrony made patterns of patterns. If this music was spiritual, it was its logic that made it so. It was like Bach: elaborations of structure perceived at first as a sequence of patterns and variations, but ultimately experienced as a single design. Or like the process of creation: a chain reaction of manifestations striving through variations and repetitions, climaxing in a complete expression of existence. I recalled Swami Rama's speech to the Ashram Association in Topeka, in which he said that *one* is the only number that exists, that all other numbers are repetitions of *one* and all numbers added together become *one* in its total form.

These thoughts went through my mind as I listened. I stared at the steady face of the lady playing the veena as the early morning light glowed through the open window above her head. A bird flew past that window, and I realized that now their morning songs could be heard also, along with the music and chanting of the morning *puja*.

This was not merely a performance. Swami Vidyananda

Saraswathi and his people were not entertaining themselves or us. They were not rehearsing and they were not playing for the sake of the music. They were worshiping. This was a spiritual *sadhana*, an exact and precise discipline, a form of meditation.

As the playing and chanting continued, more light came through the open window and the singing of the birds grew nearly as loud as the music in the room. Suddenly the music stopped—with no climax, finale or resolving chord, simply a note after which there was no more. But it continued inside my head. My mind had picked up the pattern and continued to move with that rhythm. Or perhaps there was an echo that lingered in the room.

The musicians were stone-still, and I did not take my eyes off the lady's face for what may have been several minutes. When Swami Vidyananda Saraswathi moved, my eyes followed him. He lay his veena on the floor, lifted his clasped hands to his face, and leaned forward until his forehead rested on the floor. I closed my eyes. There were only the echoes and the songs of the birds.

Swami Nadabrahmananda had his own building in a different part of this ashram compound. When Elmer, Alyce, and I climbed up the long stairway that was the front entrance to the ashram and inquired where we might find Swami Nadabrahmananda, a young man led us to the small cottagelike building with the familiar yellow paint and dark-green shutters and asked us to wait beside the locked door while he went to fetch the swami.

Swami Nadabrahmananda was a short, round man with a big bald head. "Many devotees playing tabla almost like me," he said. "Many yogis doing *kumbaka*. But nobody's doing both at same time—playing tabla, doing *kumbaka*—only me. I play thirty minutes program, thirty-five minutes, I see my god, no blinking eyes, no moving body, no taking breath, only see god." He spoke in a sharp, clipped manner in a voice reminiscent of a percussion instrument. "I keep coin on top of head. If I'm taking breath, coin fall down."

He told us he would be pleased to have us bring the portable psychophysiology laboratory, bright lights, and movie cameras into his little cottage and test his heart rate, respiration, temperature, brain waves, and so forth while he performed. "Yes, in past times many doctors testing me." He showed us photographs that had been taken during such demonstrations. One picture showed him sitting with his tabla in an airtight glass box. There had been a lit candle in the box, he explained, and when the candle went out for lack of oxygen, he had begun to play. "Yes, many doctors have interest. Sometimes other country's doctors. No musician swamis are doing these things. Only me."

The performance began at nine o'clock the following morning. The three heavy suitcases that contained the psychophysiology laboratory had been carried up a ladder to the loft where the swami slept, and there was just enough room up there for all the equipment and two of the Greens, who sat looking down at the swami from above. The long wires that were attached to various parts of the swami's body ran across the floor and up the ladder to the loft. Many other wires and cables ran here and there across the floor, connecting cameras, lights, and sound equipment. But with all this, the room seemed no less templelike than it had the day before. Now the swami's students, disciples, and admirers crowded the room, squatting or standing wherever they could find a space, watching the preparations with anticipating faces.

While cameras, lights, and microphones were being positioned and electrodes were being attached to the swami's skin with salt paste and black tape, one of the disciples took the swami's keys and unlocked the heavy carved chest that held the special set of tabla. He also unlocked a tall cabinet with glass doors and removed a small wooden box, which he placed in front of the swami. Swami Nadabrahmananda unlocked this box himself and took out a turning key, a coin about the size of a half-dollar, and the portrait of his deity, which he unrolled from its cloth wrapping. The disciple stood the heavy chest on end a few feet in front of the swami and placed the holy picture on the chest so that the swami's god was in his line of vision, just at eye level. Swami Nadabrahmananda tapped the tops of his tabla and made some slight adjustments with his turning key. The thermisters that are normally attached to the subject's fingers were taped to the swami's feet so that his hands would be free to play.

"Are you comfortable, Swami?" Alyce asked. "Nothing is too tight or pinching? We don't want you to feel restricted or distracted by all the tape and wires."

"It's all right," he answered. "I am feeling nothing during playing, and I am not moving body, only hands. If I make motion, coin is falling down." The coin was passed around for the experimenters to examine so we could see that there was no gimmick—nothing to cause it to stick to his smooth, shiny scalp.

Swami Nadabrahmananda positioned himself on his cushion, straightened his back, placed the coin atop his head, rested his hands on the tabla, and fixed his large eyes upon his god. Hartley Production's big, bright lights clicked on.

"Sound is rolling," said Harvey.

"Camera's rolling," Elda answered.

And the swami began to play.

The performance lasted thirty-five minutes, and it was spectacular. Swami Nadabrahmananda was indeed a magnificent musician. He began in a slow, steady rhythm, creating with his fingers and the heels of his hands a complex structure of tones and pitches. He produced a pattern so precise and so consistent that as it was repeated again and again, I was able to follow it exactly as though I were prefabricating the plan in my own mind. Suddenly the rhythm doubled and after only a moment it doubled again, but the pattern never faltered, and my mind was able to make the jumps. It felt exciting. Now the swami's hands moved at an amazing pace. But the rest of him was as still as a stone statue, and his eyes did not blink once. The rhythm was doubled again and yet again. It seemed impossible. My skin tingled and I felt myself smile in disbelief. Then he lifted his left hand from its tabla and quickly moved it over to join his right hand. He held his hands together by entwining his thumbs. He had made this move without breaking the steady focus of his eyes upon his god and without breaking the tempo. Now the pitch was heightened as eight fingers played upon a single tabla. The swami's hands were like a bird hovering over the tabla with fluttering wings. Only the fingers moved.

In this manner he played on and on, and after several minutes I was again able to follow the speed, and the pattern became clear in my mind. As I wondered to myself how the two hands I was watching could possibly produce the sound that I was hearing, the swami released his thumbs and gently lowered his left hand into his lap. Still the tempo was unbroken. Only one hand, now nearly invisible, maintained the incredible rhythm.

I stared hard at the moving hand, then at the unblinking eyes, then at the motionless body. I supposed the swami might be in a trance. It was true that his eyes never blinked, and if he was breathing it was impossible to tell it. When the left hand returned to its own tabla, the sound became instantly melodic as fingers, palms, and wrists produced a variety of tones. Gradually the tempo decreased, and the precision with which this was managed was as beautiful as the tones of the tabla. In the same way he had reached the unbelievable tempo, he descended from it step by step, mathematically, spending only a moment on each level: 128, 64, 32, 16, 8, 4—stop. The two hands came up, palms together, in salutation to the deity upon whom the eyes had been affixed for over half an hour. The half-century of preparation, practice, and performing was a gift to God. "*Namaskar*," said Swami Nadabrahmananda, and he closed his eyes.

It was over, but we who had been observing only sat and went on watching, and I realized that I too had been motionless for over half an hour. The swami opened his eyes and looked up toward his loft where Elmer and Judy sat with the lab, and he smiled as though he were anticipating some rewarding verbal feedback. No comments were immediately forthcoming, as Elmer and Judy were busy shutting down the equipment, labeling records, and making notes in the logbook. So he asked, "What is the result?"

"The results?" Elmer responded. "We won't know the results until we get back to the United States with all our records and process them through our computers." The information that was picked up from the swami's body while he was performing was recorded on magnetic tape and could not be analyzed until months later when it would be transcribed on polygraphs in the laboratory.

"And I did not breathe, Doctor? There was no breathing, isn't it?"

"Well, as I said, we can't be sure about anything until we get back to our laboratory, but in any case the whole thing seemed to go very well."

I knew that the respiration harness attached to the swami's body not only fed the Teak recorder but also activated an ultrasensitive read-out meter on the operator's panel—and that had sounded like one of Elmer's diplomatic, noncommittal responses.

"Well, I believe he may once have been able to perform that entire set without breathing," Elmer later said to me. "In fact, I believe a lot of yogis may achieve some extraordinary capabilities and then for some reason not maintain them. It's like an athlete who breaks a world's record and then retires to do something else. In Swami Nadabrahmananda's case, since he's probably in some altered state of consciousness, he may not be aware of whether he's breathing or not. As far as I could tell he was breathing normally, but earlier tests seem to have indicated that he was not breathing at those times."

When, months later, Swami Nadabrahmananda's records were examined on a polygraph, it was confirmed that he had been breathing normally. But it was also apparent that his heart rate had decreased, rather than increased as might have been expected. And even more interesting, his brain waves had been predominantly alpha and theta while he had been busy with his spectacular performance—a brain-wave pattern normally associated with semiconsciousness or meditation.

thirteen

Our party of eight often went separate ways during the extra days spent waiting in Rishikesh for the arrangement of the vehicle that would take us on our journey throughout India. We seldom went anywhere alone except into town, to the bank, or to the post office; sometimes two or more of us went for a stroll while the others stayed inside reading, resting, or making travel plans. The film crew—Elda, Harvey, and Tom—often took the cameras and the sound equipment and went off to find subjects to shoot. "When I see something photogenic and beautiful I want it on film," said Elda emphatically. "And when I get restless, I've just got to shoot something!"

So she beckoned to her men one midmorning. "Come on, boys, let's get the show on the road. It's getting late already."

"Where are we going?"

"I thought we'd go across the river and see what we can see."

They were back just as supper was being prepared, and what they had seen was Tat Walla Baba.

"I think he's the first real yogi we've seen so far," Harvey said to me.

"What about Swami Rama and all these swamis we've met already?" Tom wanted to know. "Maybe they've accomplished as much as he has."

"I doubt it," Harvey assured him. "Anyway, I mean the first real practicing yogi who's just being what he is without putting any kind of a trip on anyone."

"He does have his trip," Tom rejoined, "and maybe you're impressed because he's so far out."

"What do you mean, 'far out'?" I asked.

"Naked," Tom replied.

"Well, all he wears is a jockstrap," Harvey explained to me, "and he has real long hair that touches the ground."

"And that might just be some kind of a trip," insisted Tom.

Harvey continued, "He lives in a cave and all he does is meditate, year after year. He comes out for a while every day and sits under a banyan tree so people can see him if they want."

After supper we all gathered, as we often did, in Room 10—the residence of Elda, Dolly, and Judy—because that was the largest room. Arranging our metal folding chairs in a semicircle around a small coffee table set with cookies from Dehradun and tea, we sat facing a large map of India that Dolly had scotch-taped onto the wall and we talked. I think it was looking at that map that started our conversation of how far we could get and return on a one-day outing, and we eventually found ourselves discussing plans for a day-long sightseeing drive; since we had this free time, plus the use of one of the Mahant's jeeps, a day's drive seemed a welcome idea.

"I don't think I'll go," Harvey said. "I think I'll stay here and spend the day in the hills across the river."

"You're still thinking about your Tat Walla Baba, Harvey?" Elda asked.

Harvey turned to me. "Don't you want to do that, too?" Wouldn't you rather stay here than go with the whole group?"

I had once discussed with Harvey what I considered the good and bad points of traveling en masse. As useful as our team arrangement was for the carrying-out of our project here, a party of eight was a bit too much, I felt, for any in-depth sightseeing or meaningful relating with people; the business of synchronizing interests and opinions among ourselves was too preoccupying. Harvey and I had decided to take what opportunities there were to be alone or in a group of only two.

"We can talk to Sivanandapuri," he said. "I know he'll be glad to take us up to Tat Walla Baba's cave. I don't think I could find it by myself, and we'll need him for interpreting, anyway."

After Harvey's description of Tat Walla Baba, the possibility of meeting such a person was enticing.

When we had finished our tea Swami Sivanandapuri arrived with his songbooks under his arm, and Harvey and I had a chance to talk to him about taking us to Tat Walla Baba.

"Oh, Harvey!" exclaimed Swami. "You've made an excellent suggestion. What a wonderful idea."

So the three of us made plans to start out at eight-thirty or nine in the morning—allowing an hour to cross the river and hike up the hill to find the baba under his banyan tree. Our swami guide explained that although Tat Walla Baba was withdrawn from the outside world, he conducted his physical life with consistent regularity—especially where others were involved. Therefore we might expect to find the baba under his tree beside the path every morning at ten and every afternoon at four. Visitors could be sure to see him only at these allowable moments. At no other time was he seen.

We drove off in the morning with our swami guide and our driver through Rishikesh past the sadhu's mess hall to the guesthouse, and then back again through Muni Ki Reti, stopping on the way for ten liters of gas—then past the turnoff to the Tourist Bungalow and on to the boat landing. All the way dozens of orange-clad persons stared at our swami with a variety of expressions—and opinions, no doubt, as to the meaning of a fellow renunciate riding in a chauffeur-driven jeep along with two Americans.

Our driver let us off as close as possible to the place I later named the Tonga Terminal. Tongas are the one-horse open carriages that provide the only means of public transportation available in Rishikesh, Muni Ki Reti, plus places between and beyond. We asked our driver to wait for us there among the horses. Harvey glanced at his watch; it was well past ten. In any case, we could not stay with Tat Walla Baba a moment past high noon. Swami translated that, should our driver leave for any reason, he should be back no later than twelve-thirty.

I was surprised to see a crowd of people standing at the boat landing. "Maybe you have not been here in the morning. At this hour there are always hundreds of pilgrims crossing over to those ashrams," explained our guide. "In the evenings they are all crowded like this on the other side waiting to come back. But look, there are three boats working now."

Each of the three largest ashrams on the other side of the river owned and maintained a motorboat for the sole purpose of carrying pilgrims free of charge to their places of worship, but I had always been here at midday when there were fewer pilgrims crossing and there was only one boat working.

One boat was loading passengers on our side of the river, while another unloaded on the opposite bank, and a third boat—with only three or four passengers—was halfway across the river. Its bow was pointing toward us but the current was pushing it downstream. At the middle of the river the boatman turned the rudder to put the stern below the bow and drove against the current. The boats always crossed in V-shaped paths.

The pilgrims had formed a fairly orderly queue, and with three boats in operation it was a short wait for our turn to cross the river. We were among the first to board our boat. Judging from the one that had left before us, I guessed there would be thirty or even forty people packed onto this small vessel. We sat on benches made of slats that ran down both sides and the center of the boat.

Someone behind me grabbed my left shoulder, gripping me hard. Alarmed by the forcefulness, I turned to look just as a middle-aged man stepped onto the boat at my side and over the middle seat. When an elderly lady did the same, then a young boy, and another lady, I finally realized I was sitting near the loading point where the people boarded the boat. They were using me as a support. They stretched out their arms as they stepped to the floor of the boat and up onto the middle seat, and hands reached out to meet them. People were holding one another by the arms and legs, around the waist, or even by the head. They used one another's limbs and torsos as though they were their own. It was a natural, instinctive act (the way I had often seen it done in Korea), as though when people are crammed in such close proximity, moving together and toward the same end, they begin to function as the one being that we really are. It could not happen in the conventional West, I reflected, because our artificiality has replaced natural behavior: naturalism has become embarrassing.

Where did all these pilgrims come from? Displaying a variety of skin colors and costumes, they must have come from all over India. They had probably come up from Hardwar for the day to visit temples and ashrams and to dip in the river in this holiest of places along the holy Ganges. I had observed in Hardwar that most of the buildings were lodging houses or inns called dharmshalas where worshipers could stay rent-free. I had seen no such places in Rishikesh, so I assumed this was a one-day side trip for the pilgrims.

As our boat pushed off, everyone shouted in a single chorus as though it had been rehearsed for the count of three, but I knew it was spontaneous and I assumed it was a long-time custom: "Ho, Mother Ganga!" People sitting along the sides of the boat dangled their hands in the water. We were sitting too close together for any of us to turn sideways, but some managed to twist their bodies and lean back enough to get at least one hand in the water. Others scooped handfuls of the river to their lips and patted water upon their foreheads and hair while they urged their children to do the same. But the youngsters who could reach the water were satisfied to submerge a flattened hand to feel the force of the churning. Coins were tossed into the river as into temple coffers: the Ganges was herself a deity.

The boat bumped against the sandbag dock, and the rope on the bow was tied to the stake in the river bank. Harvey and I paused while disembarking to look again at the many pilgrims taking their holy dips in this sacred spot, immersing themselves to the shoulders regardless of what they were wearing. Swami Sivanandapuri hoisted his angle-length robes up to his knees, and with one quick fold and a twist they stayed in that position—looking rather diaperlike; then he walked briskly up the long, concrete stairs to the front of the now familiar Gita Bavan.

The Gita Bavan was one of a long row of ashrams and temples that these pilgrims had come to visit. We strolled past the several ashrams and the concrete pavilion at the end of the row where sadhus always sat in the shade, and then turned toward the hills. We crossed the path that led to Laxman Jhula and hiked through a dense orchard of mango trees. At the end of the orchard was an open gate, and beyond it was a path that led into the forest, through a valley, across mountain streams, and finally up the side of the mountain. Hoping Tat Walla Baba might answer some questions, Harvey carried a cassette recorder. For an offering we carried bananas and lemons.

We came to a place where the path was especially steep, but huge rocks had been used to build steps along the side of the mountain. I wondered if some of Tat Walla Baba's disciples had constructed this mountain stairway—or even Tat Walla Baba himself. Halfway up these stone steps we looked down upon the rusty roof of a shack made of sheets of old corrugated metal with a padlocked wooden door.

"This is the sleeping baba's place. We can see he is not in now. This part is only the entrance; the cave goes way back under here." Swami swung his arm past the stone steps we were standing on. "When he's here he's either sleeping or unconscious or half conscious. Then his door is open, but few people go in. I can go in because I know him, but no one can talk to him. When he wakes up to this world, he locks his door and goes somewhere."

We came to the last of the stone steps to where there was only the dirt path again, but it leveled into a more gradual path that looked like a ledge cut into the mountain. Climbing along the side of a hazardously steep slope, we could reach out and touch the mountain wall that went vertically straight up at our sides. To the left was nothing but open space, and we had only to peer at the ribbon of a stream in the valley below to know our fate if we fell.

"You see up there? Well, you can't really see it, but Tat Walla Baba's cave is in the side of the mountain up there," pointed Swami. All we could see directly above us to the right of the path was a wall of wooden poles and sheets of burlap that flapped in the mountain breeze. "You can't see Baba's cave because of that. That's a kind of room Baba's disciples built, and that goes back into the mountain too. You see, they've built this outside part with a roof on it, and the inside part has the mountain for a roof. A little higher up there, up above this roof, is Baba's cave."

In another fifteen or twenty yards the path was leveled by the plateau where Tat Walla Baba had built his shelter. Continuing along the path, we passed this curious-looking structure; I scanned the entrance, wondering how the place looked inside and how Tat Walla Baba could possibly climb from there to his private cave above.

"You see the top of that tree? That's Baba's tree. In just a moment you will see Baba." As we walked on, the tree came into view about ten yards in front of us, and sitting alone and still at the base of the tree was Tat Walla Baba.

To me he looked like a fat-bellied Buddha sitting lotus posture under his banyan tree. As we approached I noticed that although his eyes were open he did not move, even slightly.

Swami Sivanandapuri slipped off his rubber sandals, walked up to the tree, prostrated himself upon the ground, and placed his hands on Tat Walla Baba's feet. The baba blinked almost unnoticeably and glanced down at the swami with a look of indifference. Slowly turning his head, he looked at both of us. His eyes alarmed me; they were not sharp and piercing, but almost hazy. But they were shiny and strangely colored like a tiger's eyes, and so large and open it seemed I might look right into his head and he into mine. Our eyes met for only a few seconds and then he looked quickly to the ground. Swami motioned for us to come closer.

"You have to take off your shoes here," Harvey whispered. Around the tree there was a cleared area of hard ground that looked as though it had been swept clean, but there were no seats or mats to sit on. Even Tat Walla Baba sat upon the earth. We placed our offerings of lemons and bananas at the baba's feet and put our palms together in salutation. The baba motioned for us to sit on the ground in front of him.

I looked closely at him—at the matted hair piled on his head like a turban, dusty with ashes, his wide forehead, dark brown skin, huge stomach, and callused feet—but he did not look directly at us. For nearly an hour we sat facing him, and his eyes never looked any higher than our chins.

Harvey turned on his recorder and we waited, perhaps thinking Tat Walla Baba would begin talking or ask if we had any questions, but the baba only sat there like a Buddha. It was not as though he were assuming a pose: he had been sitting that way when we arrived and he was only being natural. He looked so natural that any other posture would have been a pose. So relaxed, so at ease was he that it was comforting to sit near him. Harvey turned off his recorder.

The babbling stream in the valley far below sounded louder and clearer as we sat in silence, listening. The only other sound was the singing of birds; we could hear hundreds of them performing their songs. There were birds in the mountains above us, birds in the valley below us, and birds in Tat Walla Baba's banyan tree. We sat motionless.

Our being here would not change this man's reality. It felt

as though we had always been here. In a sense, I felt that
Tat Walla Baba might not perceive us as separate beings.

I would have liked to have sat there in silence for our entire
visit with Tat Walla Baba, existing in the still presence of
his intrinsicality, but Harvey broke the silence, asking Swami
Sivanandapuri, "Is it all right if we ask some questions?"

"Yes, put your questions. Ask anything and Baba will
answer." Harvey turned on his tape recorder again.

"I'd like to know what sort of path Tat Walla Baba would
recommend for Westerners. It's not very likely that anyone
could live in the West as he is living here, or even approach
this lifestyle. What sort of spiritual path or what yogic discipline is appropriate for those of us living in, say, New
York?"

The swami began the translation, the baba kept his eyes
on the ground, and Harvey's eyes darted back and forth
between them.

Tat Walla Baba spoke, surprising me once more. He
sounded like a recording played at slow speed—in reverse. I
had never heard anything like it before. But his unaffected
and calm voice began to feel pleasing to the ear. Swami
translated, this time in English: "Baba says all these disciplines, all these various paths, they are all valid. Bliss is an
internal thing, independent of surroundings. In anything and
everything of this external world, pleasure and pain both are
there. Both are to be found, according to the attitude, according to the consciousness. But pleasure is within, Baba
says, and the body consciousness is pain. True bliss is in the
eternal. So how to reach there? You are there. So Baba says
do your duty in your place. This is your path. This doing of
one's duty is karma yoga, the path of nishkam karma yoga.
Do your duty without attaching to the fruits. This is the
way of bliss."

"What is Baba's own spiritual discipline? What is his personal *sadhana*?"

We heard the shuffling footsteps of someone coming up

the path; Swami, Harvey, and I turned to look, but Tat Walla Baba did not move. She was a middle-aged lady dressed in a light blue sari. I thought she was Indian, but when she came closer it was obvious she was a Westerner. The swami began his translation, and the lady sat down on the ground just outside the cleared circle.

This time the response was short. "Baba has followed the paths of Raja yoga and Bahkti yoga, and he has his master who is living near Nepal. Baba has meditated in his cave for thirty-five years. Before he came into his own spiritual path he was bound to *samsaras*. Then he became changed through the paths of devotion and yoga discipline. But the real world does not change, Baba says. Reality is ever the same. Only the mode of mind changes."

The translation finished, the swami beckoned to the lady and pointed to a place beside him. She stepped out of her blue toe slippers and into the sacred circle and sat down again. Swami looked at her as though he expected a comment from her, but Tat Walla Baba only gazed at the space between us.

"Oh, you go ahead," she said speaking in a European accent. "I only want to listen."

Harvey looked at me. "You haven't said anything. You must have some things you'd like to ask."

"No, I'll just listen too. I haven't been thinking about questions, and you're doing great."

So Harvey carried on with the questions. "What is the proper attitude toward the suffering of others? What is the meaning of helping others in relation to the meaning of suffering?" This time Harvey stopped his recorder for the translation process and turned it on again when the swami began to speak English.

"Baba says it is good to help others. Suffering is caused by karma, but it is good to help others. This is also karma. Suppose you are going to plant a mango tree—you are going to get fruits of mango. So you get fruits of your action. If a man takes salt, he must drink water. If you have done good deeds, you will get good fruits. But Baba says only by these good deeds, only by getting these good fruits, you will not free yourself from this cycle of birth and rebirth. The only weapon to cut off this bondage is nonattachment. Dedicate yourself. Success comes from the path of devotion. You must find bliss within yourself."

"What is the form of this devotion? How, specifically, does Baba do his *sadhana*?"

"Baba says there are two kinds of sanyasis: those who try to gain fame as teachers; and those who, like him, just try to find their own happiness. If you are happy you can give happiness to others. First Baba wants to have no attachments to anything. He just wants to live in this bliss."

Again Swami Sivanandapuri spoke to the woman. "You put some questions to Baba."

She looked at the swami, then at Tat Walla Baba, and back again at the swami. "What do you do if your guru is dead?"

"May I ask Babaji?"

"You see I'm—I think I told you before, Swami. My guru is Yogananda. Now I live in Los Angeles and my guru is dead. So I don't know if I should—I like this baba, but—" She thought for a moment. "Well, ask him what I should do since my guru is dead. I want to keep my guru, but I want to make progress too. I'm all right here in India, at the Sivananda Ashram. But I have to go back in a few days. I've tried to get something. God knows how I've searched. My lady friends with me—they don't care about a thing. They think this is all nonsense. I don't know why they ever came. Being a lady, and all alone, how can I search for my spiritual path? It's so difficult, you can't imagine. And Los Angeles! Swami, you just can't imagine Los Angeles."

So the swami related the woman's concerns to Tat Walla Baba. "Baba says before you go back you can get an initiation."

"But who would do it? This baba? Wouldn't that be wrong? Wouldn't I then be faithful to him? Are you not supposed to have only one guru—even if your guru is dead?"

"Baba already says your guru is not dead, and you have not to worry about that matter. He says your obligation is to yourself. Your Yogananda remains within you."

After a long silence the lady spoke slowly as though she were thinking aloud. "I did think about it. Maybe I should move to India. I could arrange it. It is much more spiritual here, isn't it? Swami, please ask this baba. Isn't it most spiritual in India?"

The swami's question resulted in a quick reply: "Baba says God is not the property of India."

Another long silence, and then Harvey spoke again. "Can you ask Baba what his mission is?"

"To reach *samadhi*. He has no mission or desire in this world, but he will communicate anything to help anyone who comes here."

"Would he describe for us a typical day in his life?"

"Babaji begins his day at five o'clock with meditation. At ten o'clock he comes out of his cave and sits here, and if anyone wishes to see him, he is here. If anyone wants him to talk, he will talk. At twelve o'clock he will be alone. Daily he takes food in the early afternoon. Then he has time for work or rest until four o'clock, when again he is sitting under this tree. In the afternoon he stays here one hour, until five o'clock, and after that he does his devotion, *budjen*, *puja*, meditation."

"What does Baba recommend for concentration? What are the techniques of concentration?"

Tat Walla Baba always began his response without hesitation, responding with a subtle smile that showed his teeth as he spoke. His manner seemed to indicate that in thirty-five years of sitting alone in his cave or occasionally with seekers under his banyan tree, he had listened to and thought about all the questions in the mind of man; but he talked as though he had no need to talk, no need to press a point—as though he were willing to go on listening to questions and sharing

thoughts for the rest of eternity and equally willing to drop
these questions and answers and forget them.

"Baba says that the technique of concentration is to do
your duties, get free of the results, and clear out your
thoughts. Withdraw the energy from these senses which fix
themselves on external objects. When the mind receives a
kick from the outside, it goes within. Whose servants are
good, he is happy, Baba says, therefore lock up the servants
and be happy. Be free from attachments."

Swami Sivanandapuri touched his fingertips, tilted his
head, and began to chant softly in a high-pitched voice. He
sang in Hindi; I could not understand. I could only hear,
again and again, *Siva-hum, Siva-hum.* Was this part of the
translation? I looked at Tat Walla Baba, who as usual was
not reacting, not moving, not looking at anyone or anything.

I, who had not spoken at all, entreated of Swami, "Do that
again."

Swami resumed the ritualistic pose and began chanting a
line and then translated: "I am the Lord Siva always blissful." Again he sang, then translated: "I am not in these four
states. I am not mind, I am not intellect, neither mind-stuff
nor the ego. Also I am not in the senses. I am the ever-blissful
Lord Siva." He finished the chant: "I am not with any desire.
I am not having any form. Always in perfect balance. No
bondage, no liberation (the two are not working, these two
are just modifications of the mind). I am the Lord Siva. I am
Siva, ever auspicious. I am Siva, ever blissful."

I looked at Tat Walla Baba, amazed to see he had changed.
The turban of hair that wound around his head was no more.
His ash-plaited hair hung in ropelike strands down his front
and back and lay in ringlets at his feet.

"Be free from attachments," Swami repeated. "It is not
necessary to renounce life, only to be nonattached. Baba had
described it as a drop of water on a leaf of a lotus. The drop
remains on the leaf; but freely it rolls around, nonattached.
This is the way, Baba says." Swami looked at the lady and

directed the translation to her: "Baba says peace is only within. It cannot be given by a baba or a guru. I will tell you about initiation, it is beginning a new step. But I will explain later, because just now Baba will go to meet the stream coming down way up there, and he will be alone."

Tat Walla Baba and the swami stood up together, and we scrambled to our feet. Swami placed his palms together and touched his thumbs to his forehead, and we followed. Even as he stood Baba's hair reached the ground. I stared in amazement. He appeared so large and so solid, yet he stood so gently, holding his hands loosely with his palms outward and fingers extended, holding his arms slightly away from his body as though the long hair that draped over them were a robe or shawl. Again his eyes met mine, but only for a few seconds. Tat Walla Baba rewound the strands of hair around his head with the ease that comes from experience. He adjusted the band around his middle that held the small piece of cloth that was all he wore, and bent his neck to gaze toward the top of his mountain.

"Should we go on up to see the American Baba?" Swami asked as we were putting on our shoes. "He speaks English quite well and you can talk to him directly. He's just a little ways farther up the path here."

"Is he really an American?"

"No, no. He has reddish hair and freckles on his skin so he looks rather American. 'American Baba,' we call him. It just came to be his nickname," explained Swami.

The lady walked with us until we came to a point where the path disappeared around a big rock.

"Come, it's just a few more meters beyond here," assured the swami.

"You'll be coming back this way, won't you? I'll just wait here for you," she suggested.

"No, come along. We'll just spend a few minutes with the baba up here. We'll only be a short while."

"Good, then let me just remain here. I have seen him the other time when we came here, you know, Swami."

The American Baba did not have a cave like Tat Walla
Baba's cave, but he did have a cavelike cooking area in the
side of the mountain. In that spot sat a young Westerner
with long hair and a beard, making *japatis*. This baba's
private quarters was more like a pit with an awning over it.
We sat on the ground just outside the awning while the baba
sat on a wooden platform about two feet high, so we had to
look up at him and squint our eyes in protection from the
sun.

"Where are you from?" asked the baba.

"The United States."

Without our having asked any questions he began a
speech; but after only a few short sentences, he switched to
Hindi. Soon he was talking so loud and fast I wondered if he
was angry. He was very dramatic compared to Tat Walla
Baba.

Swami Sivanandapuri looked at us, perhaps anxious about
our reaction to this baba, who was wildly waving his hands
in the air and going on and on while we sat politely, squint-
ing in the sun and not understanding anything that was said.

"I think we should be starting back," the swami interrupted. "So I will begin the translation at this point. Baba
says that all these people going here and there, all this
traveling and searching and searching, all this asking of
questions and seeking of answers means nothing. All these
languages and translations are nonsense. He does not care
about all these nations, and he does not even care about war
and peace. All these things belong to the unreal. All these
things are of the external world only. We must renounce all
these things. We must go to the reality. We cannot be liberated if we go on and on asking questions about this nonsense world. Traveling here and there is not the point. There
is no truth in India. There is no truth in the United States.
Truth is to be found within only. So in this external world
there is nothing to seek."

The swami's voice came to a weak halt long before he had
spoken as much English as the baba had Hindi. Without

notice or care, the red-headed baba started up again, shaking his fists in the air. I looked at Swami Sivanandapuri, and he smiled at me. We had excited this poor baba, I thought to myself, and all we were doing was sitting on the ground with our shoes off and our mouths shut. I wondered whether the illusion of our external presence had made him uncomfortable by reminding him of all the things he thought he did not care about. Well, hopefully he had found a little secret pleasure in the unreal stimulation that our unreal visit offered.

"Did you find him interesting?" the lady asked as we joined her at our meeting place by the big rock before starting our hike back down the path. "He is slightly interesting, don't you think? But I have seen him once, so I know what he says. I like this baba much better, don't you?" She pointed to the ground where Tat Walla Baba had sat as we approached the banyan tree. "I'm more impressed with this baba. I find him much more real."

There was no waiting for the boat back to our side of the river and no waiting for the jeep. Our new friend rode with us, as she wanted to join us at the Tourist Bungalow for lunch.

We led Swami and the lady into Room 11 and arranged the folding chairs around oranges, bananas, cheese, nuts, and cookies. The swami talked to the lady about initiation and offered to arrange a time to take her alone to Tat Walla Baba. "He just wants to give you a spiritual push," he assured her.

During lunch we talked about the city streets of Los Angeles and New York, about the saints and yogis in the mountain caves of the Himalayas and the foothills, and about Mahatma Gandhi. I mentioned Martin Luther King, and the lady looked shocked.

"But he was a communist!" she exploded.

"No, he was not a communist."

"Oh, yes, he was. That's the trouble; you people just don't understand. I have experienced Communism in my own country. Most Americans just can't possibly realize—"

"I can sympathize with your experiences, or try to, but they have nothing to do with Martin Luther King. In fact, what you experienced has nothing to do with any ideas or ideals. King was not a communist any more than Gandhi, or any more than your Yogananda—and I'm sure every idealist has been called communist by someone. Those people were far beyond being communist, or capitalist, or any other kind of '-ist.' I know that none of their speeches or writings could accurately be used to support communism or any other political power structure."

"I thought he was a good man," offered the swami, and Harvey diplomatically changed the subject.

Instead we talked about monkeys and birds and the beautiful November weather so the lady could enjoy her lunch. Despite her strange ideas, I liked her for her warmth and friendliness.

"I met her some days ago," the swami told us later that day, "before I met you, actually. Once I took her to see Tat Walla Baba and this morning she found her way herself. Baba has agreed to give initiation, so I will arrange the time. He may give her some methods and I think he may perform *puja* for her personally—so tomorrow or Thursday I will take her there without you, if you don't mind. I'll be needed for translation."

I wondered whether her pending spiritual initiation with Tat Walla Baba would help her clear up her sociopolitical confusions.

In the early morning on Friday, November 16, we got word from Manoharlal Dudeja that a vehicle and driver had been arranged for us and would be leaving Kanpur for Rishikesh that night.

"Within a few days we should at last be leaving here," I said to Swami Sivanandapuri. "You know, we've been here fifteen days today, and that's a lot longer than we'd planned, but I'm sorry to leave."

"You have a good trip planned," the swami said, "and a lot to see."

"But it will be mostly driving. I don't think we'll stay in one place long enough to get to know anyone like I've gotten to know you. I'd like to be able to spend a month or two here—to have a chance to really talk to you and Tat Walla Baba and some of the others here."

"Come back. Definitely you should come back."

"This is a long way from home."

"You should come back for the Maha Kumbh Mela in Hardwar in the spring. You would see all the sages and swamis you could ever hope to see if only you could come back for the Kumbh Mela in the spring."

We were sitting on my bunk in my room and Swami had the harmonium beside him because we thought this might be our last opportunity to record the swami's songs. Earlier that day, before we had heard the news about our vehicle, Swami had taken us to a small village just below Rishikesh, where a group of elderly sadhus devoted to Shiva lived in a sort of commune. There Elda Hartley had filmed him sitting on the ground in front of one of the huts singing Shankaracharia's poem, "I am the Lord Shiva always blissful," and giving the explanations as he had done for Harvey and me under Tat Walla Baba's banyan tree.

"If I am ever able to come back, I will write to you, Swami, and let you know, and if I go again to see Tat Walla Baba we'll go together."

Swami put a finger to his temple and pointed at me as though he had suddenly remembered something he had wanted to tell me.

"You should have heard the conversation when I took that lady back to see Baba. She wanted to talk about spiritual progress, like having a guru or having a chance to get initiation, and she asked if these chances meant that some people advanced at a faster rate than others. Her opinion was that the whole world was advancing, that evolution meant spiritual progress. She said she believed that scientific progress in

the West must be a sign of spiritual advancement, and Baba
agreed it could be so. He said it could be a step on the path
for some individuals or societies, but it could also lead to
attachments and illusions for others. So she told Baba about
the astronauts landing on the moon as though she expected
him to be astounded by such news. And do you know what
Baba said? Baba looked at the sky and he laughed out loud
and he said, 'This going to the moon is a joke! So clumsy. So
childish. Build a box, put some bodies inside and send the
box to the moon? This is funny! You want to travel to the
moon? We have been to farther places. Men sometimes move
their bodies here and there. But it is not the other way
around. We are not confined to these bodies. Only naïve
children would build these awkward containers that breathe
fire and make explosions to propel their bodies into the
cosmos!' "

India: Deeper Meanings

fourteen

It was the evening of April thirteenth and the Woodlands
Café looked the same as when I had last been here nearly
three months before, on January twenty-third—the last night
in India for our party of eight. The waiters in dark trousers
and orange jackets and the customers dining at the tables
had not changed. Now, sitting in this room, that last supper
seemed only hours ago; only this time I had come back to
India alone. This restaurant is my gateway to India, I
thought, and if I should come many times to India, I shall
always begin and end my trip with a South Indian meal in
the Woodlands.

"You came back," said a voice over my shoulder. It was
the waiter I had made friends with when I was here before.
He had written down his name for me: it was P something.
Now I could only remember the P. "Where are the others?"

"They are in America," I answered. "I came alone this
time. How do you remember me after all this time? You must
meet so many people."

"Of course completely I remember you. I remember all of
your party."

The headwaiter was standing by my table with his pad
and pencil in hand. There were many men in orange jackets
who served food but only one man who took orders, and I
was keeping him waiting.

"I'd better order," I said.

"Are you staying here?" He spotted my room key on the

table. "Oh, yes. I will go to your room. I am busy now and I am not the waiter for this table, but I will finish in one hour."

I ordered the meal that Elmer Green and I had tried on that January evening—a tray filled with soups, curds, and vegetables prepared with curries and other spices, and sweet shredded coconut to be picked up with small round *puris* (I preferred them to the larger, greasier *japatis*) or to be mixed with rice and eaten with the fingers. Elmer and I agreed this was one of the tastier meals we had experienced. Dining in solitude, I began to think of the people I would like to invite here, but most of them would never see this faraway place. I picked up my check and looked at the menu again and realized that all the prices had increased at least 25 percent in less than three months.

I left the necessary rupees to cover the meal and tip and walked back through the lobby and up the stairs to my room. I glanced around my room and laughed to myself. I must have been in a daze when I checked in; I had taken everything out of both suitcases and my shoulder bag and arranged it all neatly in the closet, in the drawers, and on the top of the dresser. I had even set out the contents of my toilet kit on the shelf under the bathroom mirror. Now I had to repack quickly because before sunrise I had to check out and get down to old Delhi in time to catch my train for Kanpur. I wanted to finish packing before my waiter friend came to my room. I would probably talk to him as long as I could stay awake. On this trip I had not slept at all for the entire twenty-six-hour plane ride from New York to New Delhi. I could hardly have felt sleepy taking the taxi ride from the airport and through the streets of New Delhi. It had been a beautiful ride with the bright green lawns and flowering trees adorning every street and blooming bushes and shrubs and colorful gardens everywhere. But now, after that big supper in the Woodlands—which had been my first meal of the day—I was beginning to feel sleepy.

P. Suresh, whose name I finally remembered, was late getting off work. I had finished repacking my belongings and I was paging through an international edition of *Newsweek* magazine when he knocked on my door.

"I'm sorry I'm late," he apologized. "So many people got sick at my last table."

"Got sick? What happened?"

"Oh, it's a common thing," the waiter explained, "a common thing with the rich. They have got to spend always so much, you know? They come with guests and they have got to make their best impression. They take too much food for the capacity of the human stomach. It makes trouble for the waiters." I had not heard of anything like that since the days of ancient Rome.

Room service brought us cokes with ice and a small plate of semisweet cookies. It came to about a dollar's worth of rupees.

"So you came alone. How long will you stay?"

"In India?"

"Just here."

"Oh, I'm leaving tomorrow morning for Kanpur. I'll be in India not more than two months this time. Mostly in Hardwar and Rishikesh, I guess."

"But definitely you must come back here before leaving India."

"Sure I will. I always do." I wondered why I said "always." This was only my second visit.

"Have you booked your transportation?"

"Yes, my Kanpur friend reached me here this afternoon and told me to take the morning train, and the front desk got first-class tickets for me." I showed him my two tickets for train fare and seat reservations—perhaps to assure myself that they were still safe in my passport case.

P. Suresh stayed longer than I had expected, but as we talked my sleepiness left me. After two hours of conversation he told me that his friends were waiting for him behind the restaurant where he always parked his scooter, and they would be wondering what was keeping him.

"You mean your friends have been waiting for you all this time?"

"They don't mind," he assured me. "They don't know what room I'm in, so they have to wait. Now I will take leave, and I will see you in the morning."

"No, I'll be checking out early, long before you come to work."

"But I'll be waiting at the front desk."

Soon after P. Suresh left the telephone on my table rang. It was Bipan Dudeja. He was checking to see whether I had managed to get my reservation to Kanpur on tomorrow morning's train. I already had my ticket in my room, I reported. I had arranged it through the hotel clerk at the front desk as he had suggested. That was all he had wanted to know. He would be at the station waiting for me when my train arrived in Kanpur.

Bipan had called me earlier in the day (while I was making the mistake of unpacking all my things) because after my airline reservation had been confirmed, I had sent him a cable telling him I would be checking into the Lodhi Hotel on this day. Bipan had insisted I leave for his place on the first express train in the morning and had advised me how to get my ticket in a hurry. I had had to pay considerably extra to have a train ticket delivered to my room on such short notice, but I was glad I had done it because now everything had been arranged and communicated, and by this time tomorrow I would be in the Dudeja's comfortable home.

The Dudeja family—Bipan, his parents, and his two younger sisters—had been our hosts in October when we were in Kanpur for the All-India Yoga Conference. Mr. Dudeja and Bipan had been here at the Lodhi Hotel in January to say goodbye to "Dr. Green and party" on our last days in India. When I had told him I planned to return to India in April for the Kumbh Mela, Mr. Dudeja had advised against it. He felt that the frantic crowds and the chaos at the Kumbh Mela would defeat my purpose. It would be an opportunity to see a massive (and almost tragic) spectacle, but not an opportunity to really communicate in depth with anyone. "In any case," Mr. Dudeja had insisted, "if you do return, return in the spring before it becomes too hot. And if you really want to go to Hardwar, you just do one thing— you arrive at this hotel and then you contact me first. I will help you and I will arrange accommodations for you in Hardwar. If you go there unprepared, it will just be a mess. There will be *lakhs* and *lakhs* of people."

If things were to work out as I hoped, I would be able to get accommodations in Hardwar just after the main pandemonium of the Kumbh Mela, but still in time to see plenty of sadhus and sanyasis. From there I planned to go on to Rishikesh. I hoped to find Swami Sivanandapuri, and through him, Tat Walla Baba and others whom I had seen before and wanted to see again.

As promised, P. Suresh was waiting at the desk downstairs, but there was only time to say goodbye and to assure him I would be seeing him again. Soon after, I was sitting on my comfortable first-class seat on the train called the Calca-Mail and I was headed for Kanpur.

For over an hour I waited for Bipan at the top of the steps outside the Kanpur station. During the first ten or fifteen minutes it bustled with travelers, the people who came to meet them, and the peddlers and porters who stand by for their brief, intermittent chances to hustle for their lives. Then the station was empty except for the ticket clerks who sat inside their windows and a couple dozen rickshaw boys, beggars, and children of the streets. This was a familiar place, I reflected as I sat, although I had been here only once some five and a half months past when "Dr. Green and party" had dashed up these same steps to catch the night train for Hardwar. I knew I was the only foreigner to get off the train this day and the only foreigner to have come through this station in many days or even weeks.

Westerners are seldom seen in Kanpur, and I knew I looked curious and rich to all these rickshaw boys and beggars who were crowding around me, pushing in uncomfortably close and staring at me. They wore ragged clothes and their bodies were covered with dust. But their eyes were dark and deep and beautiful.

I sat on my suitcase at the top of the steps so if Bipan came to meet me I could be easily found. Either he had not come or had somehow missed me. If necessary, I could hire one of these rickshaw boys and take a ten-minute ride to the Dudeja's Hotel Valerios. But that could wait.

This was a chance to be with another "kind" of people—people who represented a very large percentage of the world's population and were therefore as typical of India, as typical of humanity, as any other people. It was a chance that would not come often, because if any of my friends were with me they would not let me talk to these beggars and "rickshaw wallas," and they would not let them talk to me. Those friends would understand my desire to communicate with swamis and yogis—even with people who live as hermits in mountain caves—but they would not understand why I would want to communicate with these people. I did want to communicate with them as much as with swamis and yogis, not because I had something to learn from their words but because I had something to gain from their presence, because all people should communicate with all people, because the distances and separations between people are painful and dangerous.

Unknowingly, they were making me feel a little uneasy by pressing so tightly all around me and staring at me so intensely. But I longed for them because they were really very far from me, so far from me that it was "inappropriate" for me to be sitting here with them. And, whether they knew it or not, it was out of longing that they pressed around me. Their deprivation was a deprivation of love—there is no other deprivation.

I moved my hand toward a boy of ten or twelve, and he jumped back, stumbling into two smaller children behind him who were holding on to his shirttail. I shook my left hand with my right so they would get the idea. I had done

this last time in Tirupati and other places. "Shake hands!"
shouted an older boy, pushing forward and holding out his
arms. Then they all wanted to do it. Another boy of ten or
twelve wiggled forward from behind on twisted, crippled
legs and held out his arm, but not to shake hands. He held a
rusty tin can. "Money," he said. An older boy gave him a
kick, and he fell against the concrete and skidded down the
steps. "Don't!" I blurted. A still older boy grabbed the of-
fender's ear and twisted it, watching my face for a sign of
approval.

"Don't," I repeated.

They all looked at me quietly, and for a moment no one
moved. I was sitting on one of my suitcases and they were
standing so I could look directly into their faces. An older
boy muttered something in Hindi that sounded as though it
were intended to be provocative and pushed the boy in front
of him, trying to make him fall on me, but the boy held his
balance and on one else moved. I extended my arm to one of
the youngsters who had not yet shaken my hand and motioned for him to sit down. He sat down and took my hand,
and then most of those who were standing sat on the bare
concrete or on their haunches. The handshaking was resumed.

"My name is Doug," I said. Most of them could understand that sentence, and they began calling out their names
or pointing at others and announcing theirs. One little boy
shouted a name and another boy reached to put a hand over
his mouth and they all laughed. I guessed the little one had
called out some nickname that was an embarrassing or forbidden word, but I hadn't understood it anyway.

A dignified-looking man in a gleaming white kurta ascended the stairs with his driver behind him. They both
shouted and waved their arms and looked surprised when
the beggars and rickshaw boys only backed up a few paces
but did not scatter. They did not know we had begun to be
friends.

"You are from?" demanded the dignified man.

"I am just coming from Delhi!" I answered in a loud Indian voice, hoping to sound as though I had lived here for years yet knowing it was not the answer he expected.

"Your native place!" he demanded again.

"Oh, U.S.A."

"Why do you stay here? These boys are disturbing you."

I reassured him, "They're not disturbing me."

"Where do you want to go?"

"Hotel Valerios."

"I'm having my residence quite near there. If you'll just wait twenty minutes I'll give you a lift."

"That's all right, I can take a rickshaw."

"But I'm offering you comfortable conveyance."

"Well, I have sort of promised."

"To which did you promise? They are all after you!"

"The first one who asked."

The dignified man shouted something in Hindi over the heads of the boys, who did not look at his face. "I have instructed them not to overcharge you. They are wretched boys and they will take you for your money. You have not to pay more than one or two rupees."

"Thank you," I said.

"I'm coming back this way in twenty minutes' time and I'll take you if you're here."

"Thank you," I repeated in earnest. But I did not intend to be here.

As soon as the man and his driver were out of sight the boys surrounded me again. I wanted to continue our communication where we had left off, but now they knew I was a potential rider and cared only which rickshaw I would hire and how much I was going to pay.

"Let's go!" insisted one, grabbing my arm.

"No, this man!" shouted another, pointing to the one who asked me first.

"Money! Money!" shouted the little ones.

"That's right, *that* man," I said. He ran for his rickshaw, wheeled it to the bottom of the steps, and ran back up for my luggage. I stood up. "Okay, goodbye," I said. Then I put my palms together and brought my hands to my face and looked again at all those eyes. "*Namaskar!*"

Probably not many Indians had greeted these commoners in such fashion before. That gesture and that Sanskrit word had become a frequent expression of respect for greetings and farewells; but what it really meant—and what I meant —was "I salute the divinity within you!"

I sat with my feet on my two suitcases and my shoulder bag in my lap while the rickshaw boy peddled past the station, over the tracks, and onto the busy street called Mall Road. When we reached the hotel, he unloaded my suitcases and I held my shoulder bag. The sign read NEW VALERIOS HOTEL; it was new indeed. I remembered the front of this place as a plain, dark wall with an old wooden door in the middle and a dirt area where cars, scooters, and bicycles were parked every which way. I was surprised to see a neat row of cars and potted plants and three small steps leading to a painted concrete floor with delicate glass tables and wrought iron chairs arranged under a colorful canvas canopy like a French sidewalk café.

"Please four rupees," demanded the rickshaw boy. His pathetic expression was for effect, but it was not entirely unreal. I gave him four rupees.

Bipan Dudeja and his father, Mansharlal, were waiting inside. I stepped into an air-conditioned room with beautifully carved tables and chairs, couches with velvet bolsters, beaded curtains, and soft indirect lights. Since the Woodlands Café I had not felt such wonderfully cool air.

"Ah, come, come, come! Sit down, sit down!" Manoharlal was waving at me from a corner table.

"How did you get here?" asked Bipan.

"By rickshaw."

"I met your train—how did I miss you?"

"I don't know. I waited on the steps out in front."

"Oh, that's not the front," corrected Bipan, and from his explanation I learned it had been the rear of the station I had seen both times I had been there. I had been waiting in the wrong place, but it had not been for nothing.

"Anyway, he's here," said Manoharlal. "Have something to eat." He waved for the waiter.

The sweet corn chicken soup that I had been looking forward to and a tall, frosted glass of fresh lime and soda revitalized me. I had come safely to India, to Kanpur, and to the Dudejas who had been our first hosts in this country. Everything would go smoothly from here. Lodging would be arranged for me in Hardwar as well as an interpreter and travel assistant. Meanwhile I would stay in the air-conditioned guest room at the Dudeja residence.

Owing to the usual slowness of communications, it was ten days before we boarded the night train for Hardwar. Except for the smothering heat, they were pleasant days spent with the Dudeja family. I greeted old friends from my previous visit to Kanpur, shopped for additional supplies, and watched developments in remodeling and decorating of the hotel.

One day Mr. Dudeja made arrangements by telephone for me to meet an elderly swami who was visiting Kanpur. Bipan drove me in one of the family cars to a wealthy home where the swami was guest. First he sent his driver in to inquire. The swami was receiving guests, the driver informed us, and we should enter through the side entrance and up the stairs.

The stairs led to a small room where we found the swami seated on a hard wooden bench which served as his bed at night. A half-dozen local visitors were seated on the floor at his feet so that they had to look up at him. The swami nodded to us as he talked; we left our shoes on the top step and sat on the bare floor behind the others. We created a mild disturbance because the swami had his visitors get up and spread out the blanket to accommodate us, and then he interrupted his talk long enough to ask me my "native place" and why I had come.

"Now I will return to Hindi because I am giving guidance

to this old woman, and though you will not understand, you should wait patiently for your chance."

So he spoke in Hindi for ten or fifteen minutes, waving his long, robed arms through the air with swamilike elegance. At the proper times everyone nodded except me, and Bipan nodded only slightly.

The swami was a tall, thin man with short, white hair and a clipped beard. His face, neck, and hands were lined with age; the rest of him was covered with the traditional orange cloth. Though his movements were graceful, his face looked stern, as fits a scholar of the East. To me he looked like a retired high school principal.

His Hindi words built up to a crescendo, and then without warning or even the slightest pause in his voice, he cast his eyes on me and said, "What's on your mind?"

Nothing, I almost said, but that would not have sounded convincing. Apparently this was my turn to ask a question, but I had not prepared one. It would have been more convenient, I thought, if I had some problem and needed help or if I could have said I'd been in pain all my life. These are the people swamis usually like to talk to. Manoharlal thought this would be a swami worth seeing—a former scholar and statesman who entered the path of renunciation—and I was interested in talking to any swami I could. I wanted to hear anything of interest to the West—to carry back those words and repeat them. This, I supposed, was what was on my mind.

"Right now I don't have any personal questions, I just wanted to meet you. People in my country are becoming interested in the thoughts and ways of the East just as people all over the Orient are busy trying to Westernize. I don't know what will come of it, but I like this sharing and I hope it will increase through every possible channel of communication. I just came here—I mean, to India—to listen, to get whatever messages—"

"The message of the East is the message of eternity. Eternal bliss." He paused for a long time, hoping I would reflect upon the deep profundity of those few words. I had already reflected upon such words, but I reflected upon them again. "Those material things that you develop in the West are temporary and therefore they are not real. You people are always trying to find happiness in that which is not real, and you do not know true happiness. Now our people become misled and they also become confused about reality. They try to find happiness in these superficial things. Our people were once contented, even those who had nothing. Now they have learned to fear, to fear losses, fear starvation, fear death. So in seeking external happiness, they become unhappy. Real bliss is internal and eternal. You see what I mean by the message of eternity?"

He paused again. Maybe he thought I would raise a question or challenge his wisdom. I had nothing to say. I would like to talk with this swami some day, but not here, not now. I believed in the essence of the truth to which he was referring, but that truth apparently had far different implications for me than for him. So I waited.

"You have come so many miles trying to find happiness and at a cost of so many dollars. But I do not think you have found the happiness you are seeking. Happiness cannot be bought with dollars. Happiness cannot be found East or West or here or there or anywhere."

We went on for a long time in this manner—without my saying anything, and him everything. His sternness reminded me of the old man in the hills above the Ganges who we called the American Baba. For a moment I wished that I had prepared some questions, but then I realized that whatever the question, the answer would be the same. So I patiently listened to those words all over again, and several times I nodded my head. When at last the swami paused, Bipan quickly whispered that we must leave. The driver was waiting and he had to get back with the car.

We thanked the swami and left. Within minutes we were drinking cold, fresh lime and soda in the air-conditioned restaurant in Bipan's hotel.

"What he said was the standard thing, you know. This is what all the swamis will say, especially to a Westerner."

"I don't want to take issue with those words. I just want to hear some other words; something beyond that."

"I know. But there were people there, so he felt like making a speech. And that's the only speech he knows."

"I've heard that speech so many times that I could say it just as well."

"Do you agree with it?"

"I agree, but I feel like saying so what? That's the important question. So what? What to do now? What do we do in the meantime? What do we do between here and happiness? Withdraw? Renounce? Escape? What do we do about our health and our earth and our children?" These are what I considered important.

"I don't know about your country, but we have problems in India that have to be solved. There's no denying them or escaping them or meditating them away."

"What I think is this: this whole external world is very real. Temporarily it exists, as a real aspect of the permanent reality behind it. I don't think there's any such thing as escaping or withdrawing from the external world. It's the door to the rest of reality. Freedom from worldly problems comes as a result of solving them. If one individual thinks he can withdraw his senses and turn himself outside in and personally enjoy eternal bliss while the problems grow worse, he's only furthering the illusion of separateness—and furthering all the problems. There's a new saying in the United States that if you're not part of the solution, baby, you're part of the problem."

I met Hridaya Singh on the same day I left Kanpur for Hardwar. Mr. Dudeja and Mr. Shukla assumed they had made communication with Mr. Ram Panjwani in Hardwar, though they had received no reply, and Manoharlal Dudeja deliberated a long time about who to send with me. "He must be excellent in English and he must also be diligent and truthworthy and faithful . . ." Then he thought of Hridaya Singh, who was a sales representative in a pharmaceutical company of which he was a silent partner. We were in his private office at the time, and he called on his inside line to have Hridaya Singh sent in. I had not understood what he said on the phone nor what he said to the man who came into his office, so I did not guess what they were talking about until Manoharlal looked at me and pointed at Singh and said, "Will he do?"

"Of course." I nodded.

"You can send him back once you are settled or you can keep him with you as long as it suits you."

"How long can you stay?" I asked him.

He looked first at his boss and then at me. "As long as you like."

"When can you leave?"

"Any time," he said. "When do you want to leave?"

"Just now."

"Then take my car," Manoharlal said, "You will find my driver just outside. Go together, pick up all your things, and then go to the hotel. I'll be in the restaurant."

"Call me Singh," Hridaya said as we looked for the driver.

"Okay. Call me Doug."

I waited in the car while Singh went in to gather up his belongings. The impatient driver waited no more than two minutes before he began honking his horn.

"Don't honk. Give him time. The poor man had only a moment's notice and suddenly he's got to go off somewhere for a month or more with some foreigner." But the driver either did not understand or did not care, and he sounded his horn again and again.

Singh came out struggling with a large bedroll and one little attaché case.

"Are you really going to need that big bedroll in this heat?" It looked like a huge, square sleeping bag folded into a tight G and fastened with canvas straps. On our winter trip we learned that nearly all Indians travel with bedrolls. We had seen them tied to the tops of every car and taxi on roads for nonlocal traffic. So hotels and dharmshalas, and maybe even private homes, expect most of their guests to arrive with their own bedding. I thought these bedrolls had thick quilts and could not imagine their usefulness in temperatures well over one hundred degrees.

"But this is the only luggage I have. Some shirts and pants are packed inside."

I looked at the attaché case. If he had any clothing along at all it would have to be in the bedroll. The awkward thing turned out to be a convenience. Neither of us ever carried it anywhere because there was always an abundance of porters, and instead of a thick quilt there were blankets for both of us—not for covers but for padding on train seats and hard wooden beds.

At the hotel Singh waited outside the restaurant door and would not come in even though I was inside for two hours talking to Manoharlal and enjoying a big lunch. Once I stepped out to try to persuade him. "It's cool and comfortable in there and I'm having something to eat. You should eat or you'll be hungry."

"You should not think about me in that way. I'm supposed to think about you. Anyway, I had taken something just before I met you."

He spoke in the typical abrupt and clipped manner, but I was used to that now. The only difficulty in understanding him was the softness of his voice, which made it hard to hear him. At any rate, his English was excellent, and he smiled when he talked. His face looked like Gandhi in his twenties. I could not know how he felt about his sudden assignment, but my guess was that he was going to be easy to travel with.

By three o'clock that afternoon we had arranged to share a taxi with two successful-looking businessmen to ride to Lucknow for fifteen rupees each. Right then we established our system: I would pay all the expenses, but Singh would handle and keep track of the money and give me an occasional accounting to record in my book.

I left Singh with the luggage in the main waiting room of the train station and followed a porter through the crowd to the first-class ticket windows. I thought my foreign appearance would be helpful if tickets were scarce. But it was no help; the tickets were more than scarce. This station was not selling tickets for the train to Hardwar, and not reserving them—not even for ten days hence. That long line of people at the ticket window must have been going elsewhere because after nearly an hour of waiting that was the news I got. So I went to see the stationmaster. I had learned that sometimes the stationmasters had what they called a quota for foreign tourists. I never knew which one was the stationmaster, but there were three people in that office, and they all talked at once. There was no quota, no possibility.

"It's this Kumbh Mela nonsense, you see," one of them said following me to the door. "They come like locusts."

"I would have thought by now that most of the crowd would be coming back down this way."

"Oh, coming is also bad. And going is also bad. And two weeks ago it was horrible. People were climbing in the windows and on the tops of the cars and they would not come down. Many police we had here every day. Look, you do one thing. You put up here a few days and then you come daily, and one time we will have a chance to squeeze you in third class. That way you take your chances, you see."

"I'll have to go back to Kanpur and try some other way. I can't pay for a hotel here day after day—"

"You mean money?"

"Yes."

"Now, you see, that makes the difference. You mention money, you see how costly it is to wait here and wanting to save your money and all. Then it's only a matter of a little tipping. That will save you in the long run, you see."

I took my cue. "Yes, that's a wonderful idea."

"Ah, yes. Now we're coming to our senses, you see? How much are you prepared to pay?"

"Twenty rupees?" I wished Singh were here.

His face lit up. "Oh, wonderful, this will solve all problems. You just wait here, I will arrange it." In a moment he returned with another man, and the two paged through some papers as they walked. "Ah, yes. Lucky chances, lucky chances. Here, surprisingly, we have a sudden cancellation. You say another is with you? Just right, just right. Here we have two berths exactly. One upper, one lower, first-class coach."

"Whom do I—"

He stopped me and took me aside. "Of course the tip goes to this other gentleman, as I am only helping here, but he's too sensitive, you see? You hand it to me just now because I don't mind. I am only helping you, you see."

Darkness came as our train arrived. Singh and I sat safely inside our coach sipping cold orange sodas while we waited for the departure whistle. The other two in our four-man compartment were elderly gentlemen in white kurtas and pajamas who sat across from us. One was fat and the other thin; the thin man stared at me through his thick glasses. Since we had not yet started, the bare light bulbs on the ceiling were barely glowing, so he leaned forward to peer at me more closely and remained that way—motionless and expressionless. But I was accustomed to such staring. Once on a bus in Korea, when I had suddenly become fed up with all the endless blank stares, I blurted out to a scholarly-looking old man who I was sure could understand, "This head will not turn into a pumpkin or do anything at all entertaining, so if you are expecting something interesting, you might be disappointed." He looked startled and hurt. I was immediately sorry. My words had been more impolite than his staring. From that time on I accepted the stares. So now I looked at the thin man across from me and gave him a genuine smile.

He returned my smile and he spoke. "Once we are moving

the lights will come up more brightly and these fans will turn. You are from . . . ?"

"U.S.A."

"And for what purpose you have come?"

"I'm just visiting."

"You are perhaps interested in our vast religion?"

"Yes, I'm interested in yoga philosophy."

"You see, this is also very vast. You have to look at it widely. There are so many methods. But they lead to the same goal. All the worships and all the practices lead to the same goal, to freedom from this, this, you see, this nonsense."

The whistle sounded, and the train began to move slowly through the station. I looked out at the people on the platform. Some of the younger vendors ran alongside the train trying to get back empty bottles through the windows or to sell a few last oranges and bananas. Some of them had just finished their day and had already laid down on newspapers and old blankets for the night.

The old man continued. "You see, our object is to be free from this world. This world is only illusion—you people may not understand that fact—and it is only pain for us, you see, for everyone." The lights came up bright and the fans began to turn, just as he had said, but now he did not seem to notice. "I am not an expert in this yoga business. I am not making any such claim. But so far as I understand the general truth of it, it is to withdraw from this, you see, this external *maya*. The only true happiness is to be found within, when you reach that divine source which you have forgotten."

We passed by a temple that was so close to the tracks I could look from my window right down on the statue of the deity. It was painted a shiny green, but I could not identify the deity. The flames flickered as the train went by. I wondered how anyone could sit before an altar that was only a few feet from a railroad track; perhaps it was placed there for the passers-by on the train.

"Who is there among us who can say he is happy?" the

thin man asked, still leaning forward, still peering through his glasses. No one answered. The fat man took a big gulp from his water bottle and belched loudly. "No one can say he is happy. We all try to say it, but of course, it is not true. You see, we are all liars. No one is happy. And who can say he speaks the truth? No one can say he speaks the truth unless he is again lying. The mothers are always telling 'Speak the truth.' Ask yourself at the end of this day or at the end of any day: 'Have I spoken the truth this day?' No, you have not."

I kept smiling and glanced at him occasionally, but I did not want to nod. Outside the window were the lights of a village, and as we passed I shaded my eyes with my hands to see more clearly. The soft oil lamps of village huts and farm houses have always enchanted me. Singh pressed the switch to turn off the big incandescent bulb, and then there was only the purple night lamp. I could see dark silhouettes in the fields. The fat man stood up, let down the berth over the thin man's head and began to lay out his bedroll.

"So we are all here, caught in this world, going here and there on trains and planes as though we had something important to do, and it is all useless. The truth be known, we are all unhappy liars, all helpless souls, you see, caught up in this illusion and ignorance. But yoga says we are not helpless. I think this is the idea of yoga. With discipline and with great effort we can escape this miserable existence. We join with the one highest God, and we are free from this cycle of births and deaths. This is the only happiness."

Singh unstrapped his own bedroll and handed me some blankets to spread out on the lower seat, and the fat man, having prepared his bed, climbed awkwardly into his upper berth.

"Well, it is time to say good night." The thin man took off his glasses and placed them on the shelf under the window. "We ought to close these windows against the dust."

I turned off the purple night light and lay back and folded my arms under my head. I was comfortably stretched across the seat where Singh and I had been sitting. The fan blew a steady soft breeze across my body, and the train purred along the tracks with a constant clicking, rocking gently from side to side. I felt sleep coming on, and I would be arriving in Hardwar in the morning, just as I had done once before. I was happy. I did not believe I was a liar. I was happy and that was the truth.

fifteen

Ram Panjwani was a large man with a round belly, a round face, and even a round smile. He seemed immediately and genuinely friendly. He only glanced at the letter I had carried from Kanpur. "It is arranged," he said.

The letter was from Mr. Shukla, Mr. Dudeja's friend, requesting accommodations for me and my companion. There had been letters sent, even a telegram, but the letter we now carried was in case previous communications had not gone through. Fortunately, Mr. Panjwani had been expecting us and was holding his finest room at his Sindh Panchwati Dharmashala.

On our way to the dharmshala, Singh and I walked through a large vacant lot where there must have been nearly a dozen big tents set up and nearly four times as many men in orange cloth and long beards. "Are these people all swamis?"

"Well, they are all sadhus, all renunciates. Anyway, that is what they are claiming, as you can see. Many will call themselves swami and others will call them swami, so we also may call them swami if we like."

Hardwar seemed far more crowded than when I had been here in November, even though a considerable portion of pilgrims and sadhus who had come for the Mela had left after April thirteen. We had already seen dozens of sadhus dressed in orange among the crowds of pilgrims along the main street, and there had also been many wearing only breechcloths or pieces of burlap exposing most of their dark skin, which was usually covered with ashes. Two or three sadhus wore absolutely nothing. All the rooms on the three floors of our dharmshala were occupied with pilgrims—some with large groups. Our room had two beds, two closets, two tables, two chairs, and even a bathroom with a Western toilet and an air conditioner; but most rooms were only empty space. Singh said this was an advantage for the pilgrims because they could cover every inch of floor with ten or twelve bedrolls. I assumed that every inn, ashram, dharmshala, and hotel was still full to overflowing.

"If you have already been to the Choti Walla Restaurant," said Singh as we walked up to the main street, "let us then try this place called the Cellar. We should at least check it out."

I had been in the Hardwar's Choti Walla on my first visit here, but I had not known about the Cellar. It was a cellar indeed, but it was too dark to "check out." As we started down the stairs, I had to feel my way along the wall. Inside only a few dim light bulbs were glowing, and coming in from under the bright sun we could barely see the tables and chairs, but it felt cooling to be out of the sun and there was a ceiling fan over every table.

Singh could read the menu before I could—probably because he was more familiar with the strange transliterations that named the varieties of vegetables and curries—and at my insistence he ordered enough for a meal and a half for both of us.

"You told me to call you Singh. Isn't that your family name?"

"Yes."

"Then are you Sikh?" I knew that Singh was the family name, or part of the family name, of every Sikh. But this Singh had no turban.

"No, I am Singh of another caste."

"What do your friends call you? Can't I call you something besides your family name?"

"My first name is Hridaya. You can call me Hridaya." He

pronounced it "Hree-day" and he said it was Sanskrit for "heart."

"What did Ram Panjwani say to you in Hindi?"

"He just asked me some things about myself. And he also asked the same that he asked you about your purpose here and if he can do anything to help you." Hridaya paused a moment and then he added, "I think I do not yet understand your purpose."

"My purpose? Just to observe. By watching and talking— and listening."

"But if you tell me more exactly I can try to help you more."

"Let's say I don't know exactly, and that's why I have to observe. I think the best way to observe is not to anticipate too much beforehand. I know what I really want to see, but I can always find what I want to see. Now I am not looking for what I want to see. Now I am looking for whatever is here."

"You want to see what is this swami business, right? This is what you told me."

"Right."

"Why?"

"Because my country is becoming like your country. I think every country is now beginning a very great change. Someday we'll be doing this swami business, as you call it. Maybe it will be quite different, but it will be more like your past culture than like ours. That's what I mean by change. Our future is going to be more like your past than our past."

"The same thing is happening with us."

"Right. Your new people are attracted to the fascinations of electronics, salesmanship, business management, and all these things. And they feel a sense of cause about it, a sense of human evolution, a new awakening. In the same way our new people are attracted to yoga and meditation and to concepts of Eastern philosophy like karma and cosmic consciousness. Here's an example: most Americans would be uncomfortable here—so much so that they would feel angry—not so much because of the heat and the inconvenience but because of the way of life. They could stay in hotels in New Delhi or Bombay, but they would hate to spend a day here where there's no meat or fish or eggs or alcoholic beverages, and they would feel contempt for these pilgrims and sadhus, saying 'This is all nonsense.' On the other hand, thousands of new people living in our intellectual and cultural centers from New York to California would feel more at home here than there for a number of reasons. For one thing many of them prefer vegetarian diets, and that's much easier here than there."

The waiter arrived at our table with two big bowls of hot soup. "We are also having the same change," Hridaya said, picking up his spoon, "but it is going the other way. Most of our modern people have learned to eat eggs, fish, chicken, mutton, even beef. They think it sophisticated and progressive."

"Of course these examples are sort of superficial," I allowed. "The real significant change is on a psychic level— Easterners and Westerners are exchanging basic mental and emotional orientations."

"For what reason?"

"Do you mean because of what cause or for what end? I think it's caused by this new world-wide communication for one thing, but I think the main thing is that people are changing places. I believe that people's basic orientation comes partly from their past experiences and not entirely from a combination of inherited genes and early environment. Otherwise it seems to me that generation gaps would become always narrower and cultures would become stagnant. What must be happening is that Easterners are being born in the West and Westerners are being born in the East —I mean Easterners and Westerners with regard to where they lived their past lives. For what purpose? I don't know, but I think it's something the earth is trying to do—something to cause new opportunity or new growth for the earth.

Some may say it's good, some may say it's bad. In any case, it's the present reality."

"Anyway, what do you want to do here? Haven't you got any plans?"

"Yes, for one thing I'd like to contact Swami Sivananda-puri. He may be in Rishikesh, but he may be in Hardwar. We met him in Rishikesh when our group was there last year. At that time he gave me a Hardwar address, and I have it in my book. Then he wrote to me at my place in California and said he was staying in a cave up in the mountains with Tat Walla Baba."

"Tat Walla Baba?"

"Right, I hope we'll be meeting him."

"What's the swami's Hardwar address?"

"The Sanyas Ashram."

"Ram Panjwani suggested we should go to visit Manasa Devi at the top of the hill. This is the temple of the goddess of desire. This is very famous for our pilgrims."

"I know, I heard him talk about it. Okay, let's visit the temple and the Sanyas Ashram both tomorrow, and today let's just walk around."

Walk around we did, for the rest of the day and all the next day too, because I wanted to look at the bazaar and the *ghats* and all the places I had seen here before. I wanted to take my time watching all the people.

I showed Hridaya the crowded bazaar, where perhaps a hundred shops sold everything from carpets and garments to sandalwood carvings and incense, and the *ghats*, where the river flowed as a canal and dozens of men, women, and children were now immersing. Hridaya showed me details that I might not otherwise have noticed or understood. For example, I assumed that all the people in the Ganges were pilgrims taking their holy dips, but the river was full of bathers, and it didn't seem proper to watch them closely.

"But look, some of them are diving for money. They make their living this way. See, that one got something!" Hridaya pointed to a young man in the river who just at that moment put something in his mouth and disappeared under the water. "Now, watch." The man came up holding his hands cupped together. He had scooped up a handful of the river bottom and let the dirt filter slowly through his fingers back into the water. "Nothing that time." Again he went under, head first, and for a moment his feet appeared above the surface. Unlike the pilgrims who stood in the river and ducked, he was not dipping, he was diving. "When he finds a coin he puts it in his mouth and when his mouth is full of coins he will probably go spend it. Maybe he will buy food or bidis, but you can't buy much for a mouthful of small coins."

We made an interesting combination of mutual guides: I led Hridaya around because I had been here before, knew what was here and where I wanted to look; but he was the one who understood the language, the menus, the money, and the customs, so he was the interpreter, arranger, and explainer. This was the way it was for the duration here and in Rishikesh.

I showed Hridaya the Hari Ka Charan, the most famous *ghat* in this famous city of pilgrimage. The *ghat* was situated on the right bank of the Holy Ganges to face the rising sun. Across from the *ghat* in the middle of the river was an island on which a tall clock tower called Birla Tower was built as a monument to Mahatma Gandhi after his ashes were scattered over the Ganges. Pilgrims were here in unbelievable numbers when I visited this *ghat* in November; now the crowd was many times greater as it crossed the bridge to the island and back again in a constant stream. Some waited patiently and others struggled to get to the river's edge to take their baths, to feed the sacred fish, and to fill their metal *lotas* with the holy water. Several temporary bridges had been constructed for the Kumbh Mela to accommodate these streams of people crossing to the island or to the opposite bank. Rope nets were hung from the bridges and anchored in the water in case any bathers were overcome by the holy current and swept helplessly downstream. We saw about a hundred special policemen lined up along the banks, the

bridges, and on the island to keep order among the enthusi-
astic throngs.

Ceremonies at sunrise and sunset were performed daily,
and on the evening of our second day we returned at seven
o'clock for the sunset ceremony. We stood on the island and
gazed back over the water at the shrine on the right bank
where the devotees sang their daily praise to Shiva. Of all
the chants that I had heard in the ashrams and temples, this
one was the most beautiful to me. The blending of so many
voices with the sound of the river made it especially enchanting. Six or more of the devotees who stood on the lowest step
of the right bank held burning torches over the water; the
flaming light danced in the ripples of the flowing river. The
chanting continued for twenty or thirty minutes, and when
it stopped pilgrims on both banks and edges of the island
put dozens of little leaf boats to float carrying flowers and
tiny flames of kerosene which flickered over the current
down the river, through the net, under the bridge, and out of
sight. Then the pilgrims began to bathe again, walking down
the steps into the river. Hridaya and I found a quiet place
along the right bank downriver from the *ghat* where we
could sit for a silent hour before walking back through the
crowded bazaar.

On the morning of the third day we set out for Manasa
Devi on a rickshaw to where the alleyway led down through
the bazaar to the *ghats*. There we crossed the road on foot
and started up the hill on a long, hot walk. At the start—for
a hundred yards or more—there were concrete stairs to ease
the climb up the steep slope between buildings and above
their rooftops, but past that point there was the familiar dirt
path, sometimes treacherously slippery and sometimes enhanced by steps of stone. All the way up the path we could
see the white temple shining in the sun on the hilltop
above us.

We were not the only ones scrambling up the mountainside in the intense midday sun. We met people on their way
down and passed others on their way up who were proceed-

ing even more slowly than we. Most of the pilgrims were elderly, and if there were any young ones they were with their families. Hridaya could identify them by their clothing and their speech. "I don't know what they said," he would tell me, "but they talk like they are from Madras." Or, "Did you see what they were wearing? They were villagers from Rajistan." Once an old man coming down very slowly stopped to talk to Hridaya. He pointed at me and asked questions in a loud voice, but Hridaya only tipped his head from side to side in the typical Indian gesture that means "Of course. Who knows? So what? Why not? Me too." So the old man looked at me and said, "Good! You go up and see God!"

"What did he say?" I asked Hridaya.

"I don't really know. I only understood what he said to you."

The sculpted image of the deity was in back of the temple buildings where the path reached the top of the hill. We had to take off our shoes and walk across the hot concrete barefoot. She was in the center of a number of other deities who were cast on a smaller scale and set into the wall surrounding her in a semicircle. People stopped on the stone floor in front of the goddess to bow to her and make their wishes. Hridaya and I also knelt and gave a long look at the goddess of fulfillment. We followed the others around the circle to pay the Indian gesture of respect to all the deities in turn and walked outside the shrine where a number of beggars sat— some of whom I supposed must have been carried up this hill—and looked over Hardwar and the Ganges. When everyone paid their respects to the goddess, I went back to make my wish.

"I like it here," I said to Hridaya as we sat in the Cellar for our evening meal.

"You mean in this Cellar? In this country?"

"In this world. There may be problems, but this world has got potential. I know I'm going to be around here for a lot more lifetimes and I'm glad. I want to see what happens. I think there's going to be a whole lot of spiritual evolution right in the world, right here on the surface of the earth. That's what excites me."

"Why do you say this?"

"I don't know. I just feel good. Let's go to the Sanyas Ashram."

It was dark now on the streets of Hardwar, and somewhat more silent, but hundreds of seekers and sanyasis still shuffled along carrying begging bowls and various belongings; occasionally there was a family from the city looking very dressed up and touristlike. The lights in the shops and the flickering oil lamps of the vendor's carts shone softly on the faces in the street, and I watched them as we passed, just as they watched me. Frequently in these crowds I saw a face that I longed to know. Usually it was an old and venerable face or a fresh, young face with a look of sensitive awareness. I had only to look at these faces and think about what caused distances between people and what caused the longing. Hridaya had learned the way to the Sanyas Ashram and we rode a rickshaw in a direction opposite to our usual and crossed a low, wide bridge far downriver from the *ghats*. With only a few pedestrians on the bridge it was dark and quiet. We could hear the river rushing and see the ripples in the water. At the end of the bridge we turned right on to a road that followed the river downstream. Eventually we turned left from the river and down a dark, narrow road that sloped slightly, allowing the rickshaw to coast. Now the only sound was the whisper of the wheels against the hard dirt, and the only light was the faint rays emanating through the cracks of tall shutters behind second-floor balconies. From a distant building came a soft, yellow glow and the sound of chanting voices.

The driver pointed. "That's the Sanyas Ashram." He braked to a slow stop and we got out.

We stood at the entrance to the ashram and looked in at the coutryard that was surrounded by the large building. The entire courtyard was a garden, and in the center under a graceful tree stood a table and five or six empty chairs.

There was a wide veranda around the inside of the building about three feet above the ground, and there were many doors leading into first-floor rooms. Around the upper level was a balcony, and even more doors and a narrow stairway went up from every corner of the garden.

I wondered where the chanting was coming from. It filled the courtyard and echoed off the inside walls of the building. There was no one in sight.

"Wait a minute," I said as Hridaya started through the entrance. These sounds, wherever they were coming from, seemed a perfect blending of voices and melodic tones, and as we stood in the calm night looking in on the garden softly aglow with yellow lights it felt as though it would be insensitive to just go walking in. "Let's stand right here and listen."

Two small boys came around the outside of the building. They stopped about a foot in front of me and stared blankly. They were both smoking bidis. Hridaya talked to them in Hindi.

"They live here," he told me.

"They look pretty young to be smoking."

"No, no. They're just cleaning boys, it's all right. They say they have never heard of Swami Sivanandapuri, but the *puja* will be finished soon and we can make inquiry." The boys smiled at me and pointed inside. "They say there's an altar just inside in this front corner. If we go inside we can watch the *puja*."

As soon as we stepped through the entrance we saw the chanters. They were fifteen or twenty robed figures seated lotus-posture on a raised platform. Most had shaven heads and their robes shone golden under the lights, making them look more like Buddhist monks than Hindu swamis. Hridaya started toward the chairs in the center of the courtyard, but I sat on a stone ledge just inside the entrance. Hridaya quickly moved back to where I was.

"Are these people all swamis?"

"I don't know, I suppose so. Why not? I think they will all
say that they are swamis. We just call them all swamis for
respect."

I assumed this was a daily affair that probably began at
seven every evening like the ceremony at Hari Ka Charan,
but probably lasted longer. I would be happy to listen for
hours. It was not likely, I thought, that Swami Sivanandapuri
would be here, but there was no way to tell by looking at all
the "swamis" sitting on the platform. Everyone in the ashram
was here, no doubt; this was probably a required activity.
But why would they all be swamis? Swamis are adepts, not
aspirants. Where would the aspirants be? Were there no
disciples? Don't think all these thoughts, I told myself. Just
listen.

The chanting went on, and Hridaya and I sat quietly leaning against the wall; I closed my eyes.

At this moment another chant was being repeated while
torches burned at Hari Ka Charan, and as the Holy Ganges
flowed south, devotees were singing their chants mile after
mile all down the river. To the north, in the high peaks of the
Himalayas, the songs of countless saints and sages echoed in
their caves, and across the vast oceans there was chanting in
corridors and chambers of Catholic cathedrals, and choirs
sang in churches, synagogues, and temples. All across the
globe the chanting went on in a variety of tones and tongues.
So it had been forever.

This activity is not confined to the earth, I thought. It is
an eternal thing, a part of every place and every time. These
sounds are a duplicating of sounds from deeper in the universe. One can sit in the silence and listen until one hears
that place where these sounds are so constant and so real
one knows they have never started and will never stop. But
even these sounds are a duplication—a constant surface reflection of a deeper essence. What I was hearing now was an
evening *puja* in north India. It was not an illusion—it was
real—and what made it so painfully beautiful was that it was

reminiscent of that eternal sound out of which it was created and for which (in those intermittent moments when it is briefly remembered) there is great longing.

I opened my eyes when the chanting stopped, and all the swamis on the platform stood up. They began to touch one another's feet as we sat there watching. It seemed that every one of them touched everyone else's feet, and sometimes two or more of them bent down at the same time, nearly bumping heads. When the first of them stepped off the platform and started across the courtyard, Hridaya approached him and I stood up. I looked at all the swamis' faces as they passed, but none of them looked at me. Hridaya talked to three or four of them as they walked across the courtyard; he had to follow as he talked because they did not stop walking. Finally he walked back to the platform and talked to the last robed man, who was just stepping into his sandals; then he returned to where I was standing.

"None of them have even heard of Swami Sivanandapuri. One of them told me that if he had ever been here at all he surely would have heard of him. But that last man said that countless swamis come and go, staying for only a few hours at a time, and no one can say that they should not give this ashram as their address. Most swamis have no particular permanent place."

"Well, it's a good thing I wrote to him in care of Tat Walla Baba as he told me to do in his letter. If I'd written him here, he never would have gotten it. But I still can't imagine how any mail could ever reach Tat Walla Baba's cave."

"Why not? They will get their mail the same as they get their food. Someone has to go down and pick it up."

We hiked up the quiet road in the darkness.

"What are you planning to do now?"

"My plan." I thought for a moment as we walked. "I would like to go to Rishikesh."

"When?"

"First thing in the morning."

*   *   *

We shared a crowded taxi with two elderly couples for the
ride from Hardwar to Rishikesh. It was as beautiful a ride
in the early April morning as it had been that autumn afternoon when I had last come this way. The real difference was
that now it all felt familiar, and I knew what was ahead. I
remembered having passed the impressive lumberyards
along this road before, but now the signs "Ram Panjwani
Lumber Company" caught my eye.

Because we planned to return to Hardwar at the end of the
day, Hridaya and I carried only our water bottle, some halazone pills, and a supply of rupees. We decided to keep our
room at the dharmshala until we arranged accommodations
in Rishikesh—hopefully at the Tourist Bungalow. I felt that
anyone I really wanted to talk to would be in Rishikesh. We
had arrived in Hardwar after the main day of the Kumbh
Mela—which I regretted only a little—and now there was
only the great crowd of pilgrims who stayed on to make the
most of their long journeys or to wait for seats on trains. I
knew Hardwar was an important holy city in the history and
culture of India, but it had much more of a frenzied, marketplace feeling than Rishikesh, much more of what Swami
Sivanandapuri might have called "circus."

From the Koffee Korner we took a tonga a couple of miles
up the road to Muni Ki Reti, and then walked up the hill to
the Tourist Bungalow. It was good to see familiar faces. We
reserved a fine room for the first day of May—four days
hence—and walked back into Rishikesh as I had done so
often the previous autumn. I found my Sikh friend, Mr.
Tirath Singh—whom Harvey, Tom, and I used to call the
Food King—at his Neelam Restaurant. This tall, gentle Sikh
had overseen all the meals of "Dr. Green and party" while
we had lived at the Tourist Bungalow.

"Your friend, Uma Dutt, will be glad to know you came
back," Mr. Singh said as we sat down for breakfast. "He was

asking about you. You should go to see him." Uma was a young aspirant who had lived at Swami Rama's ashram since childhood. He had spent several days with our party here in Rishikesh, teaching us practical Hindi sentences and singing chants for us. Our entire party liked him, and I called him brother. "He is staying with Mahantji at the guesthouse at Bharat Mandir."

"I was planning to look up Uma right after we finish eating," I said. "But I had thought he would be at the ashram."

"Swami Rama is now in India, you know, and you should contact him before he returns to America. He brought a couple of hundred followers from America for the days of Kumbh Mela, but many of them have left for home. Uma doesn't stay at Swami Rama's any more." As usual, the Food King could be depended upon for the latest information. The only thing he did not know was where Swami Sivanandapuri might be found.

Hridaya and I were standing waiting at Mahantji's guesthouse in the shade of the largest tree in the driveway near the gate when Uma came riding in. I introduced him to Hridaya, and Uma led us through the pilgrims around to the back of the building. The grounds of the guesthouse were so crowded with pilgrims who had remained after the Kumbh Mela that it was nearly impossible to move about. They all looked impoverished sitting cross-legged on the dirt, crouched over small fires to cook bread or rice, or stretched out to sleep unprotected from the hot sun. When we reached his room Uma spoke in a manner that sounded like he might have said, "Must you even sit crowded around my door like this when you can see that I am bringing guests?" We sat on the cot in Uma's room. "I think you should talk to Swami Rama," he said. "Swami will be returning to America before you shift to the Tourist Bungalow. You can call from Mahantji's office and tell him you would like to see him. But don't tell him I'm here. Don't tell him I'm not, but don't tell him I am."

At four o'clock Hridaya and I rode in a tonga along the

highway to the Ram Nagar turnoff and down the country road of Swami Rama's gate. I had expected the ashram to be buzzing with people, but it seemed nearly deserted. Not a soul was to be seen as we walked from the front gate down the driveway and through the ashram yard and the grove to the river's edge. I drank lukewarm halazone water from the thermos as the blue water of the holy river sparkled around the bend and flowed cold over my feet. I looked back toward the ashram. There was the veranda at the top of the building where I had stood months ago to see the bend in the river, and there on the other side of the wall Swami Rama sat in meditation in his private room. I recalled the time in the lobby of the Lodhi Hotel on my first day in India when Swami had said to me, "You are my brother and you have come to my country." For a moment I looked at the building. It seemed so silent and still. Somehow I knew I would not see Swami Rama this day. That would be all right; I had come to this place and that was enough. I waded out to a large, round boulder only a few feet from the edge and poured several handfuls of water over my head and face. Each time I held my cupped hands full of water toward the bright, yellow sun descending slowly toward the water just a way downriver. I sat on the rock with my feet in the water and made my mind and body still.

At five o'clock we approached the building and stood looking at the cacti until one of the ashram guards came out and asked us to sit near the dining-room door. He then informed us that the swami was still in meditation. He usually sat till six or six-thirty. At five-fifteen I wrote a brief note to Swami Rama and left it with the guard, and Hridaya and I started up the driveway toward the waiting tonga.

"We should not be leaving," Hridaya protested, "we had better go back. Swami Rama will be angry."

"He won't be angry. Why should he be angry? He made the appointment for five and then we were told that he would be occupied for another hour and a half. So I wrote I'd see him another time."

"I think the guard was surprised when you simply wrote a note. The swami expects everyone to wait for him."

"If so, it is a wrong expectation."

"But these people think of him as master. You told me that."

"There is the master in him the same as in you and me, and we should all be thoughtful of one another. Swami Rama is not my guru, you know; he's my friend and he broke our appointment, so why should he be angry if we don't have time to wait indefinitely?"

"But I know he won't understand. He expects everyone to wait for him. The custom has developed."

"Sometimes waiting is part of a sacred ritual, and it's wrong to make mockery of it in a pretentious way. I'll wait for any swami anytime when it's part of my training or devotional duty. But we should not imitate that situation when it does not exist. It cheapens the real thing."

"How can you know when it is real?"

"Well, for one thing, there won't be a horse and driver waiting and wondering under a hot sun. Our tonga driver may be a saint. Why should we keep *him* waiting?"

"What would you like to do here in these few days before we shift to Rishikesh?" Hridaya asked as we waited for our breakfast in the Cellar.

"We'll just walk around. I'd like to carry the camera today and take a few pictures of Hardwar. Let's follow our steps of day before yesterday, only this time with the camera and recorder."

There was one *ghat* just downriver from the permanent bridge that was always crowded with local young people who seemed to have no home other than this *ghat*. Many of them sold souvenir postcards or pictures of famous gods and goddesses, and some asked for donations for ashrams or orphans or whatever they could think of; some of them just

begged. Along the river there was a row of ten or twelve
burlap-covered stalls whose owners waited inside, usually
asleep, for visitors willing to pay rupees for their soothsay-
ings and oracular advice. As we walked through this *ghat* on
our way to the water we passed a group of boys standing in
a circle talking enthusiastically. I wondered how they managed to stay alive.

"Good morning!" one of them shouted as his eyes met
mine.

"Good afternoon," I answered, and the others laughed.

As we walked on to the river he followed alone a few feet
behind us, and when we sat down on the masonry embank-
ment and took off our shoes to suspend our feet in the water,
he did the same—only he had no shoes to take off. He
seemed to be about fourteen or fifteen, and I assumed he was
probably two or three years older than he appeared. He was
thin and dark and had large brilliant teeth that looked
healthy and beautiful when he smiled, and he smiled often
because he knew I could not speak his language. Hridaya
spoke to him eventually, very cautiously at first, either because he wanted to maintain an appropriate distance or
because he was not sure about the boy's language. But the
boy was fluent in Hindi and spoke with such charm and
sincerity that Hridaya soon found himself engaged in lively
discussion. They talked about the Kumbh Mela and about
some of the people who had come here, about the new hy-
droelectric station whose sign could be seen a mile away on
the other side of the river, and they talked about him. Occasionally Hridaya repeated their words in English and our
friend smiled at me and nodded, satisfied that I was understanding. He had come from some farming village in the
south, but he had grown up alone, managing to live from
day to day, mostly in Bombay around the Gateway of India
near the rich Hotel Taj Mahal and for the past year or so in
Hardwar. When he first arrived here he got a job in a small
hotel, but that had only lasted a few weeks.

"What's his name?" I asked Hridaya.

"Raju," the boy answered. He said it several times slowly as though he thought I might have trouble getting it right.

People like him have such pure, open-eyed faces, I thought to myself. "Raju," I said aloud.

One of Raju's colleagues came up and watched us for a moment. He had one very thin deformed leg which he kept hooked around a walking stick that looked like a broken broom handle. He held his stick in both hands when he walked and leaned his chin on it when he stood. His smile was just as striking as Raju's. As soon as he had a chance to interrupt he asked Raju for a bidi, and when he had lit his bidi he hobbled off.

We spent a few hours with Raju and we could have spent a few hours more, but Hridaya and I remembered that we wanted to arrive at the Sanyas Ashram well in advance of the *puja* to arrange for the recording, and we had no idea when the *puja* began.

"We'll come back," I told Raju, and Hridaya translated.

The Sanyas Ashram, or at least the road down the hill in front of it, felt quite different in the daytime. The flat, heavy, painted walls of concrete looked harsh under the hot sun, making the atmosphere in the ashram yard less enchanting at this hour. All the swamis, if they were swamis, shuffled slowly back and forth in diagonal lines across the courtyard or sat lazily on the verandas with their bellies sticking out.

Hridaya spoke to the first man who noticed us as he passed. I wanted to see if we could record the chanting this evening. Hridaya pointed to my cassette recorder as he talked, and the man stared at it with a frown. Then he smiled. I never learned what Hridaya said to him, but he gave me a cordial look and told Hridaya that he would like to sit on the veranda and chat with me. He thought it would be quite all right for us to record the chanting.

The swami led us to the veranda and arranged three chairs
in a triangle. He and Hridaya talked in Hindi. "He has asked
me your native place and I have already answered," Hridaya
interpreted, "and he has just now asked if you have any questions for him or any point of curiosity."

"I would like to know something about the chanting we
heard at the *puja* here two nights ago." I watched him while
I waited for his answer. He was a young-looking swami with
a round, bald head and a broad, gentle face, who looked at
me with a calm and open expression. A sharp voice came
from a corner of the veranda.

"Why? Why? What do you want?"

Hridaya and I looked toward the voice, but the young
swami did not turn his head.

"What is your purpose here? For what purpose have you
come?"

The swami in the corner did not look young and monklike.
Neither did he look old and dignified like the ones with long,
white hair and flowing beards. This one had short gray hair
and a prickly-looking beard, and he glared at me through his
old-fashioned, frameless spectacles. "For what purpose have
you come here?"

Perhaps he wondered why I hesitated. It was not that I
was startled or disturbed, for I had become used to the
harshest of tones. The cold aloofness and harsh formality of
the Indians—especially in the north—is such an ingrained
custom that I was beginning to suppose there must be humor
in it. I hesitated only because I wanted to think of a new
response to an old question. They would never tire of the
question. Hundreds of them could ask me one time each, but
there was only one of me and I was getting tired of the
answer.

"Do you mean my purpose right here or my purpose in
India?" But that was my usual response.

"Yes! Yes! Yes!"

Maybe he was actually angry. If so, it was his own idea.

"What do you wish to know?" I asked again, so quietly that he leaned forward slightly to hear me. "Do you wish to know why I have come to this ashram or why I have come to this country?"

"I am asking you for what you have come. For what you are going here and there and hither and thither searching, searching, searching?"

He peered at me over the top of his glasses, and I said nothing. "You are rushing about on jet planes, spending money, searching, searching, searching. Search within yourself! Don't search far and near."

Still looking into his lap, the younger swami grimaced slightly, stood up, stepped off the veranda, and walked slowly across the courtyard without even glancing at the impetuous swami.

"This is no search. You must do searches within. You are searching outward—these are the stones, these are the trees, these are the ashrams, these are the asanas, these are the men—are you not a man? Have you got not the conscience?"

Still I said nothing. He may have been upset, but I was not disturbed. I was not sure how he felt. I knew about within and without, and I knew about the search of which he was speaking.

"You think you have got everything?" He paused. "Still you think you want something?" He paused again and then he shouted, "Still no peace within!" His voice echoed off the wall on the other side of the garden. From various points in the ashram yard many eyes turned our way. Struggling to get his foot out from under him, the disgruntled swami shifted in his chair and began to rub the foot with his hands. "You will go to New Zealand, you will go to Siberia, you will come to India—go here, go there, search and search—"

I smiled and nodded my head and said "Hmmmmm, yes, yes."

"You wander here and there, but you find nothing, only materials. You see a mountain, 'Oh, look at this, what is this?

Oh, this is a mountain.' But this is nothing—only sightseeing. So then you search information from others. Still it is useless. Search within yourself! Do not search from me."

"Perhaps you are part of my within."

He looked shocked. "What?"

"Perhaps you are a part of my within," I repeated.

"No, no, no, no, I am not such a man."

"Do you feel that you know whether I am searching within or whether I am not searching within?"

"I know," he said. "I know."

"What do you know?"

"This is no search, you are searching outward."

"How do you know?"

"Because I have searched outward." He shouted a long list of place names—places, I supposed, where he had traveled in this lifetime, and I did not recognize any of them until at the end of the list he said, "Himalayas." He frowned at me and shook his head. "Nothing! So is the case with you. You are wandering and searching outward. What is that you are searching?"

"You know that I have come here. But do you know whether I am searching within?"

"I don't know. This depends upon you. You have got the eyes for seeing, nose for smelling, teeth for taking—but what do you take, what happens in you? Have you searched that?"

"I am."

"What?"

"I am."

"Oh, then it is good. Search and search. Search and search. Search—"

"Suppose I want to get something from you—from your search," Hridaya interrupted.

"No, no. I am not such a man. I have got nothing with me."

"Suppose I think so. Then?"

"I don't know," he began, and he went on for a long time at such a speed that neither of us could understand him.

Hridaya wanted to end it. "We have had a very nice talk with you." He put his arms on his chair and began to stand up.

But the swami snapped his fingers. "Now I come to the point!"

The younger swami returned to his chair and whispered something in Hridaya's ear. For a moment the older swami waited, leaning forward in his chair, pointing a finger, and looking as though he was holding his breath.

"No, I will tell you," he went on. "Now I come upon the point." He paused to give me the chance to ask him to continue, and then he spoke in the quieter tones appropriate for profound words: "A man in a cave in the Himalayas—he will live more happily than in any of these palacious buildings in the United States or anywhere. So are they fools? Are they fools? They do more work in this world than all the pious preachers. There is something in this atmosphere. And where it is not received, there is no receiver. Where there is a receiver, it is received. So go and search with confidence."

He unfolded his legs and leaned far forward in his chair so that his glasses nearly touched his knees and hoisted up his robes with his hands so that he could see his feet as he slipped into his sandals. He stood slowly and limped away as though his feet were asleep.

I did not want to stay here for the rest of the day. I had the memory of the chanting from the previous *puja*, and now all these gratuitous words of advice. That was enough from this Sanyas Ashram.

"That other swami came back and spoke something just a minute ago," Hridaya told me. "He suggested that some of these swamis might feel disturbed if they see us recording."

"I was thinking the same thing. Maybe some day we will come to this ashram again. I guess it doesn't matter. As our swami friend would say, it's just another external place."

We walked up the road, over the bridge, along the main street past our dharmshala, and through the bazaar. It was dark when we reached the *ghat* where we spent the early afternoon. It was good to see Raju's shiny smile in the darkness when he found us sitting on a concrete bench in his *ghat*.

We continued our conversation about the strange swami whom we called the angry swami, later changing it to the outspoken swami because neither of us was sure whether he was angry or not. I mentioned I would rather have talked with the younger swami, who had a sincere interest in conversing with me.

"You know, it's humorous," I said as the three of us stared into the flowing river. "I think that swami was a little confused. He must have thought there was some value and importance in all his advice to me, or he would not have put so much energy into it without my even asking. Yet he also insisted that there was nothing of value or importance to be found in an external search. So I suggested he might be part of my within, and he really disliked that idea. Twice he said he was not such a man and he had nothing to contribute. But I don't think he wanted us to believe that. In any case, it was useful as well as fun. It was useful for my internal search— it was part of my internal search, in fact. But it was also useful for my work—for the purpose for which I go hither and thither."

"How was it useful for your purpose?"

"Because it was what was. And that's what I'm observing. Suppose a man goes to a great and famous saint in a cave to ask some questions, to get from him some ideas or information or valuable quotes or whatever. Suppose the man asks and asks and the sage remains silent, and then the man waits patiently for long hours and still the sage is silent. Then at last he gives up. He is disappointed because he got only silence and thinks he has nothing to report. But the truth is that he has something interesting to report. He got silence, and there's a lot of meaning in that. I went to the Sanyas Ashram neither for sightseeing nor for information; I did not desire to ask any questions. And without asking I got a lot of emotional, dramatic opinions about myself and my motives and my country that were merely thoughtless speculations, and there's a lot of meaning in that. You remember what I said to you the first day in the Cellar? I said I knew what I *wanted* to see, and I could always find what I wanted to see. I told you that I came here now to look for whatever is here."

"I know. You are observing this swami business."

"Swami Rama once said to me that there are very few real swamis—only a handful in the whole world. I'm beginning to realize that the word swami has two meanings. One meaning is master or master of self. The other meaning is dropout."

"What is a dropout?"

"A dropout is someone who stops participating in the economic and political systems, one who stops working in the usual sense. But I don't think dropping out is necessarily related to spirituality or spiritual growth. A bridge builder can reach sainthood while continuing to build bridges, and a fool who drops out will continue to be a fool."

"We call them renunciates."

"No, that's just the point. A renunciate is something else. Renunciates don't depend upon ashrams. Renunciates don't live on handouts. Renunciates don't depend upon orange clothing or any other image. Renunciates are workers in the world—or wherever they are; they are workers on every level. They work and work and work, and they renounce the fruits of their labor. Renunciates are those who have reached the point where they no longer need the fruits of their labors for their spiritual work. But there's no such thing as a person so saintly that he no longer needs to work and yet needs to live off the fruits of other people's labor."

Raju sat quietly for a long while, not understanding this strange-sounding language. But now he felt that it was his turn, and he pointed at the lighted leaves that were just beginning to float down the river and spoke enthusiastically in Hindi.

Hridaya listened, but then he said to me, "Anyway, you really did like the chanting at the Sanyas Ashram."

"The chanting was a kind of useful, meaningful work. And one of the beautiful and spiritual things about it is that it would have sounded the same if those swamis had not been swamis. They could have been merchants or beggars. They could have been wearing neckties and cuff links or motorcycle jackets and helmets. Their chanting was a spiritual thing that had nothing to do with their orange robes or their titles. And something else interesting today—after all that swami said, his final point, his main point, was about the guys in the caves in the Himalayas and about how they are working in the world. But we're far from those guys in the Himalayas—you and me and the swamis—so we have to find another way to do our share." I looked at Raju who had once again been left out of the conversation. "It would be good if we could be like ashram swamis or temple monks when it is time to do chanting, and if we could be like Mr. Dudeja or Mr. Panjwani when it is time to be organized and efficient, when as people, it is time to share in people's business. And then it would be good if we could all the time be humble and genuine—like Raju here—and smile a lot."

sixteen

Within an hour after we had settled in our room at the
Tourist Bungalow in Muni Ki Reti, Hridaya and I encountered Swami Sivanandapuri on the path above the boat
landing. He was standing in front of the swami institute near
the Gita Temple leaning on the fence that surrounded the
stone images of the deities, and he was looking down the
path in our direction. As we approached he put his hands
together and raised them high above his head. At first I did
not recognize him because his face was thinner and he wore
dark glasses and a few weeks' growth of beard. But when we
were close enough, he called my name.

"Swami Sivanandapuri, how great to see you! What a
lucky chance that we met you just now!" Hridaya and I were
on our way to Tat Walla Baba's, I explained, and I had just
told Hridaya that I was not sure I could find the place without the swami's help.

"Lucky indeed," said Swami Sivanandapuri. "I've been
staying at this swami institute ashram for some months now,
and if I had not been standing here you would have missed
me. But it was not by chance!" He reached into his pocket.
"Look," he said, "here is your letter of nearly four months
back. Last month I expected to see or hear from you, but
since I did not, I decided you had changed your mind about
coming back. Only a few moments ago your face came before me and I began to think of you. So I took out your letter
and read it again. Then I put it in my pocket and came out
here to watch the passers-by. You see? I didn't know it myself, but I was actually waiting for you!"

The path was crowded with pilgrims and noisy with voices, so we entered the ashram grounds and sat on a stone bench under the shade of a large tree. A variety of flowers bloomed in the rock gardens, dozens of birds sang in the trees, and the morning sun cast sharp shadows on the ground.

"It's beautiful here," I remarked.

"It's pleasant at the moment. But it is not usually so. Usually it's like a circus ground. Crowds of pilgrims pushing, shouting, preaching, making noise day and night, speakers blaring—" He stopped and studied my face for a moment. "I have not been well." Then he fell silent again.

"This is Hridaya Singh, a friend of mine from Kanpur. He's traveling with me."

They exchanged greetings in English.

"After you left I have not been well," the swami said again. "For a long time my condition has not been good. I moved to Tat Walla Baba's place, as I told you. I tried to live in my cave through the winter, but I could not endure the cold. Past times I would have been all right. I think I am going through some internal changes. My body grew weak and I actually got pneumonia. I left my cave, and they were kind enough to give me a room at this ashram. With my meditation and my breathing practices I improved. But then the Kumbh Mela came, and it was like a circus. Still it is like a circus." He shook his head thoughtfully. "Were you here for the Kumbh Mela?" he asked. "Did you see the Kumbh Mela?"

"I was in Hardwar, but not for the main day. I arrived here after the main day of the Mela."

"Good! It was God's blessing. Your god is always watching you. Had you been in Hardwar for the main day you would only have been caught in the crowds like everyone else. It was rude and grotesque—I was there. It was a competitive thing, and some were even hurt. People stood so close they could not breathe properly. For six or eight hours no one could move to have a drink or to relieve himself or to sit down to rest his feet. You were not here, and that was a blessing. Where are you staying? I think you are put up at the Bungalow, isn't it? Please let me stay with you."

Somehow I had known that he would ask that, but I was not ready to answer. It would be useful to have the swami available for guiding and interpreting. On the other hand, it seemed important to keep my private quarters private—to have a place to retreat from swamis and all their words.

I changed the subject. "Shall we go to the Choti Walla for a cold lemon squash?"

"Ah! Very good!" He looked at Hridaya. "Always he is having a wonderful suggestion. Yes, it is a wonderful idea!"

Could it be boredom, I wondered to myself, that could cause a renunciate to be so elated at the thought of a cold lemon squash? But then I recalled how amiable and easy-mannered this swami was. He was simply being accommodating. This was part of his *sadhana*—part of being at home with Westerners. I had met a lot of swamis since I last saw this one, and among them I had found many rare and interesting characters. Swami Sivanandapuri may have been less scholarly and authoritarian than most, but he was definitely the most benign of all the swamis I had met; in that category all the others fell somewhere between him and Swami Rama, who sat at the opposite end of the spectrum. Therefore, I decided, there should be no problem in having Swami Sivanandapuri join us at the Bungalow. Though I had intended to avoid the issue for today, I would bring it up as soon as we were seated at our table at the Choti Walla.

"I'd be willing to engage another room at the Tourist Bungalow," I began, "and we've arranged to have our food brought up from the Neelam, so you could join us for meals. But that would cost many rupees, and I have a limited budget. Maybe it would be best for me to just give that amount of money to you?"

"If I can have my choice, I would rather have the room than the money. I can live free of cost where I am now, but if you don't mind I would rather be at the Bungalow. I don't need the money. And when you are finished here, I'll just shift back to this side."

"I'll have to talk to the tourist officer," I said. "There are still a lot of pilgrims coming and going and most of the rooms are reserved." That was a fact, but it was also a convenient justification for whatever decision I should wish to make.

"So shall I come to inquire this evening?"

"No, let's decide tomorrow. How about meeting in the morning and going to see Tat Walla Baba?"

"Good. And we ought to start out at eight to be in time for Baba's morning schedule. I'll arrive at your room at seven-thirty."

"There's no reason for you to go all that way and back again. Let's meet over here."

"Then I shall be at the boat landing at eight o'clock. Anyway, I must say that it is not for your convenience but for mine that I want to stay over there. I really must have some escape, even if it is only a few days."

"He is really insisting to stay with us," Hridaya noted as we went back across the river. "I don't understand why. These swamis can stay freely at these ashrams. I think you should just give him the money."

To Hridaya I explained my belief that the swami really needed the change and the rest that he could get by staying at the Bungalow, and to the tourist officer in the Bungalow office (who insisted that "these government facilities are not really for these local swamis," and that "swamis should not be engaged in the guide business") I explained that my work in Rishikesh would be facilitated by having the swami nearby and always available. So it was allowed and arranged, and Room 11 (with private bath) was to be occupied by the swami beginning the following day.

At eight o'clock the following morning Swami Sivananda-puri was waiting down by the Ganges just as he had promised.

"Oh, wonderful. You are in good time. We shall arrive at

Baba's cave by ten o'clock without difficulties. Perhaps you want to have a cold lemon squash before starting up the mountain."

I agreed.

"Oh, wonderful idea!" and just as I had seen him do some months before, he hoisted his robes to above his knees and clomped gingerly up the concrete stairs.

"I saw a snap of Dr. Green which appeared in your *Time* magazine about two months ago," Swami reported as he sipped his lemon squash. "It showed him with that nails baba sitting on his nails. Did you see it?"

I had seen it. In November Tom had taken that photograph for Elda Hartley's work when the Greens were wiring up that little man on his bed of nails at Swami Rama's ashram. It appeared in the March 1974 issue of *Time* as part of the cover story on psychics.

"Well, I'll tell you how I saw it," the swami went on. "A young lady from Europe carried it all the way from her country. You know, that magazine is sold all over the world. She bought the magazine, and when she saw the snap of that little baba she became a seeker. Can you imagine that? I don't know how she found me, but that was only a few days ago. She told me she had been searching all over India for nearly six weeks. You know, there was no hint of the location of that scene except that one could guess it was near the Ganges. When she had been a few days in Rishikesh we met and talked, because as you know I am always talking to Westerners. She showed me the snap of this little nails fellow and said she knew in her heart that he was to be her guru. A strange girl she was, so anxious and emotional about it. So I had to take her to see him. You remember where he sits? Right under that big tree up there on the path." He pointed through the back wall of the Choti Walla where we were drinking our cold lemon squash. Then he laughed. "Do you want to see him today? We can easily stop by to pay our respects before we start up the hill to cross the streams."

"What happened when the European girl saw him?" I asked.

His smile quickly left his face. "It was sad," he said. "It was sad. At first she only looked. She must have stared at him for nearly a half-hour. I could not bring myself to ask if she wished to put some questions to the funny fellow, so I just stood beside her and said nothing. At last she turned to me and said, 'I'm not impressed. Let's go away from here.' But then I could see that she wanted to cry and at the same time she wanted to conceal her sad disappointment from me. She looked as though all her guru dreams had been broken. We sat down on one of the benches along the path, and I consoled her. I told her that if she realized that her relationship with her guru was already well established, just as it is with every human being, she could give up this silly, useless guru-hunt business. I told her that it is foolish to pay attention to those who are making spiritual claims for themselves, and it is also foolish to make exotic claims or assumptions about others who do not deserve or desire such identities. Only because a man is strange and does uncommon things, should we call him guru? So I told her there was no need for disappointment. She had not lost a guru. She had only lost her mistaken idea of guru. But now that she was in India, I told her, she could get some practical spiritual knowledge from some practical spiritual teachers."

He looked at us as if waiting for some reaction to his words, and Hridaya and I tilted our heads from side to side in agreement.

I thought to myself that if Swami had met even one such seeker inspired by that photograph, perhaps dozens of Westerners may have come from across the seas to find this "guru" on his bed of nails begging coins from passers-by along the path to Laxman Jhula. Disappointment was inevitable for those who failed to find him and for those who succeeded.

We did take the time to climb a few extra steps up the path to watch the nails baba for a moment before starting through the mango orchard and up the mountainside. The nails baba squatted on his haunches with only the soles of his feet resting on the points of the nails. This day there was a woman with him. She sat on her haunches in the dirt, staring at him as he stared at the sky. She looked gypsylike with her bright ragged clothes, her jewelry and her makeup. There was a small monkey tied on a rope that was attached to the tree, and he ran back and forth between the two squatting figures. Many times he jumped on the nails baba's shoulders and tugged at his long, matted hair, but nothing disturbed or distracted the little man. I wondered if he always kept himself in a semitrance.

"Is that woman his wife?" Hridaya asked the swami.

"I don't know," the swami laughed. "I really doubt he has a wife. Maybe she's his sister."

I began to feel self-conscious standing on the path staring at the two strange-looking people and discussing them within range of their hearing. So I contributed a few coins and suggested we leave; and as we walked in the shade of the mango trees I thought to myself about this strange little man whom I had either seen or discussed four or five times. Was he a trickster who cheated the gullible Indians out of their money? It was not quite that simple. At Times Square or Hollywood and Vine he would fail to make a living because the clever Westerners would arrive at some conclusions about the relationship of the sharpness of the nails and the distance between them, and he would be "discovered" to be a "hoax"; but it was obvious that the Indian pilgrims either admired or enjoyed him enough to support him financially. In the eyes of his public he was a religious man—no more so for his bed of nails than for his holy pictures, candles, incense, and the ashes that covered his hair and skin to help prevent physical desires. To spend his days and nights on those nails (and I observed that they were not extremely dull or close together) took a measure of practice and endurance. His presence on that path was interpreted as another example of renunciation and devotion, and these things are

meaningful in India. The spiritual implications notwith-
standing, I could not think that he was any less useful to his
fellow-man than an army general or an oil corporation
executive.

It was a familiar walk through the orchard, into the woods,
across the streams, and up the steep mountain paths. Following this path, I realized that I could have found my way
alone. But I was glad that our swami was with us. Besides
making everything more interesting, I needed an interpreter
if I was to speak or listen to Tat Walla Baba.

Swami spent a few moments inside the cave of the Sleeping Baba, whose corrugated tin door was open on this day,
while Hridaya and I waited on the path above; when he
emerged he reported that the Sleeping Baba was sound
asleep as expected and was likely to remain that way for a
long, long time.

We strolled along the path a way beyond Tat Walla Baba's
cave to have a look at his tree. I looked at the empty ground
under the tree and remembered Harvey and the European
lady and the words that were spoken there last winter.

"That's where Baba sits in the wintertime. He sits an hour
or more every morning and afternoon under that tree,"
Swami explained to Hridaya, "but now it is far too hot. Not
for Baba, but for the comfort of his visitors. So he sits inside
over there where it is cooler. Come. We are a little early, but
let us wait inside."

I had not guessed that visitors were allowed to enter that
wooden pole and burlap structure with its corrugated tin
roof that Baba's disciples had built for him against his mountain, and I was eager to see inside. We left our sandals in the
doorway and stepped down on to a hard dirt floor that was
smooth and swept clean. I felt a rush of relief immediately.
Even the morning sun had been bright and harsh and far too
hot for mountain-climbing, and the air inside here was cool
and refreshing. An old man was sitting on a folded carpet in
front of a low, heavy wooden table or bench, and when we
came in he jumped to his feet and greeted us and made a

sign for us to sit down on the carpet. We sat and he went to get us some water. This place was like a scene from Never-Never Land or from some enchanting storybook. My eyes followed the old man to where the water cans were kept, and I could see that either man or nature had carved far into the mountain, making a cone-shaped cave that narrowed into darkness where there seemed to be some sort of altar made of stone. The mouth of this cave was nearly as high as the roof that came up tight against the side of the mountain. There were steps carved out of rock that led up the mountain wall, and the wooden beams and metal were cut away where the steps met the roof so that Tat Walla Baba could pass to and from his private cave above. Now for the first time I saw the entrance to his cave in the stone cliff wall above our heads and for the first time I knew how he was able to reach it.

The old man brought the water, cold and sparkling in shiny metal bowls, and Hridaya and the swami drank without hesitation, tipping the bowls above their heads and pouring into their open mouths so not to touch their lips to the vessels. For an instant I thought about my halazone pills, and then I decided that I would drink Tat Walla Baba's water without hesitation. I imitated the proper drinking procedure as best I could.

A young Sikh and his wife and their little daughter came through the door, and the old man and the swami had us stand up off the carpet while they unfolded it to make a place for the additional visitors. Then we all sat quietly on the carpet watching the wooden platform where Tat Walla Baba would sit.

When he appeared at the mouth of his cave above our heads, we all jumped to our feet, but he quickly descended his stairs and walked straight out the door, pausing only a second or two to show us his wide smile and urge us to be seated. He was carrying a towel and a bar of soap.

"He will go first to the stream and then he will come and sit," the swami explained in English.

After about fifteen or twenty minutes he reappeared in the doorway and everyone jumped up again. The old man rolled out the mat on the wooden bench and Tat Walla Baba took his place. Beginning with our swami and then the old man, all the visitors prostrated themselves before him and touched his feet. The young Sikh gave a bag of fruit as an offering.

"You may go forward and touch his feet," Hridaya whispered in my ear. But I did not. This baba seemed a straightforward and unassuming man in spite of his unbelievably long hair and his tiger eyes. He sat so calmly and naturally through these formalities that one would think he failed to notice everyone was touching his feet. If I could touch the feet of anyone, I could touch the feet of this baba—but later. This was serious business in my mind—not the sort of thing one does to go along with the crowd.

The Sikh and the baba did all the talking—probably in Punjabi—and no interpreter was needed. I had been told that Tat Walla Baba spoke his own mixture of Hindi and Punjabi, and probably that was why he alone always sounded like a recording playing backward. I simply sat there, trying neither to listen nor to think, but only to be still and to be. I had told Swami on the way up that I would like someday soon to carry my recorder and have an interview with Tat Walla Baba, but that this day I wanted only to sit quietly through his morning hour. So I was happy with the way it was.

The room that was separated from this sitting room by the dividing wall behind Baba's back was a kitchen. I knew that when, as Baba talked, I began to notice the sounds and smells of cooking. A few minutes before the cooking began, a tall, gentle-looking man came from the other side of that wall to divide and pass out all the fruit that had been given as an offering; Tat Walla Baba was the only one who did not eat. Now I looked at Baba's large body and big, round stomach and hoped that the tall man was preparing him a hearty and delicious meal. But that was not the way it turned out. When Baba's visiting time had expired, he said something to the swami, who announced in English that Baba had offered his food as *prasad.*

Eight of us sat on burlap mats in the hole in the mountain and ate bowls of rice and cooked vegetables while Tat Walla Baba watched. When we had all finished, he let down his hair and ascended the stairway to his cave, with his long, matted braids trailing on the steps behind him.

When Hridaya and I returned to the Bungalow, there was a swami in the office.

"This is Swami Kaivalyananda from the Sivananda Ashram," said the tourist officer. "He is one of the swamis who knows something. He has deeply studied the Upanishads and Gita, and he is an authority on all the epics and scriptures, and he properly speaks English. I think you will enjoy talking to him."

I had seen this man before. He had come several times to visit someone who was staying at the Bungalow when our party was here in November, but none of us had spoken to him. He was a tall man and he wore a cloth wrapped high on his head, making him look even taller. The turbanlike cloth and his long garment were so immaculately laundered and so light in color that they looked more pink than orange. From that first meeting I often thought of him as the pink-robed swami. His dark skin contrasted strikingly with his bleach-bright clothes, and his teeth were large and shiny bright. It was apparent he was from the south.

His English was excellent indeed and easy to understand. Instead of the usual harsh tones and clipped accent, he had developed a somewhat Americanized British accent that was flowing and smooth—probably the result of long and studious practice.

"So you have come again to India. I have just now been hearing about you. You were one of Dr. Green's party here this past winter. In fact, I may have seen you. I know I saw Dr. Green, and it seems to me I have seen you also. Dr.

Green has been much spoken of and written about here and
there for his research and his lectures in our country. I am
sorry I did not talk to him. But I understand you are come
alone this time. And you are wanting to speak with some
teachers, isn't it? This is a continuation of the same research?"

"Well, in a way."

"Sit down, sit down here and be comfortable, and tell me
all about this research—and what is the purpose of this research. I think it is some sort of science? You have a laboratory and all."

The tourist officer, my new swami friend, Hridaya, and I
all sat down while I offered a few sentences about the equipment that measured brain waves, heart rate, skin temperature, respiration, and so forth, and about how we had
observed psychophysiological correlates of a number of individuals who were proficient in various types of yoga and
meditation. I felt hot and tired and hardly in the mood for a
spur-of-the-moment discussion that might well last for hours.
But then I had come a long way to hear whatever there was
to hear, and I could only hear it by sitting and listening.

"Of course, all this science is well and good. This is all
science." He waved his arm through the air. "The explanation of the universe and the process of evolution can be
handled as a science. But this that you are talking, this is
very limited. All these instruments, this is only body science.
You are not studying yoga and meditation, you are studying
the body."

"Well, the body and the mind. The mind-body relationship."

"You see, meditation is not a function of the mind."

"Yes, but at least the mind is involved, isn't it? When you
speak about the quieting of the mind—"

"You would call this the involvement of the mind? I would
call this the noninvolvement of the mind. This is just my
point. In meditation the mind is not involved."

"But couldn't we say that the appropriate functioning of
mind is important for achieving a state of meditation?"

"Perhaps for the beginner this may be said. This is also true for the body. The beginner must learn to sit quietly or he will never proceed to the next step. But the goal is to reach that higher state—beyond body and beyond mind—and then the state of the body and mind becomes unimportant. So you cannot measure meditation with these instruments."

"Anyway, I think we're aware of that. We aren't trying to measure meditation."

"You said you were examining these yogis and meditators."

"But not the state of meditation—the psychophysiological correlates—the degree of self-regulation of mind and body that they have achieved in the process of their training. We can measure, for example, the level of activity of the brain—"

"You see, the brain and the mind are not one and the same."

"Wouldn't you say that the activity of the brain reflects the activity of the mind?" I asked.

"I would say that if the brain becomes less active the mind becomes more active. The activity of thinking may be decreased, but that is only the surface. The mind is just like an iceberg. Do you know the iceberg? Only a small portion may be seen above the surface. That may be compared to the small part of the mind that is functioning in the external world—the intellect, the thoughts, and the sensations. The unconscious mind, the internal mind, is much more vast. But even the deepest depth of mind is not the essential part of man. Mind and the self are not one and the same. The way to understand mind is to first understand man's essential nature. Then we can clearly evaluate these external functions."

"I think most Western scientists believe that the external functions are all that exist."

"These external functions are not without existence. But by themselves they cannot be understood at all. One must realize that God-self within him, and then he can understand that these outer forms are mere reflections."

"If you mention the God-self where I come from, you're

talking about religion and not science. Science wants to confine itself to physical substance, to the properties of matter—at least science in America. And as far as the study of man is concerned, science goes as far as the body chemistry and the brain and that's it. Everything else is religion, according to the Western view, whether it concerns the mind, the soul, man's true nature, spiritual evolution, or whatever. The two never get anywhere because they never come together, even in the same man. Many intelligent people think they should be kept apart, that they have nothing to do with each other. And many intelligent people live dual existences, like Dr. Jekyll and Mr. Hyde, like some sort of split personality. They have one way of looking at things in church, maybe heaven and hell and the devil and all that, and then they go to their science labs and instantly assume an entirely different viewpoint and adopt an entirely different set of thoughts about the nature of the universe and the meaning of life."

"This sort of dualism is unhealthy, and it makes no sense," the swami retorted. "This dualism should be denounced—even if it means denouncing religion. The whole knowledge—the whole truth about the universe must be recognized as science. From the physical level to the spiritual level, all the knowledge is science and it is all pursued as science—as a scientific effort."

"That's what I think," I said. "And that's why in the West we have to approach it from the physical level. Because in the West that's as far as science has developed. In your sense of the word science, we're an underdeveloped nation and we have to start within our limitations. We have to begin by observing and measuring the physical reflections with physical instruments."

"Then it is good. And this dualism should be denounced. This is unsafe, you see. You know, it is said that no honorable person can go to a church nowadays—because he will be insulted the very first moment. They will call him a sinner. No respectable person can go to a church. Because nobody is born in sin." (Had I said that myself, I'd have put it a bit differently; but it was interesting to hear a swami speak of the churchly concept of sin.) "Everybody is born in God. The great prophets have said that the basic defect in man is ignorance. All the evils come from ignorance only, because in his ignorance man does not know what he is. In a state of ignorance he identifies himself with the physical world and the physical body. Then all the prophets and all the gods he worships will not be able to give him liberation. Man himself is the maker of himself. It is up to him to wake up to the wisdom of the saints. Everyone who has discovered the truth is a savior. There are as many prophets in this world as there are human beings, because every human being has in him the son of God. He is actually the Christ—the truth—but we have to realize that Christ consciousness within us.

"But we can usefully denounce these religions. All the religions are made by man. We can denounce them. If they can deliver us from this dualism we can accept them, but if they create dualism they are as bad as anything we can find in this world. A materialist can be very good—better than a man who is religious. A materialist can be very unselfish, even though he may not believe in God. But a man who is religious can be very sectarian. A pure scientist can see that the whole universe may be understood by science. But a scientist who is caught by his religion—he has fear of discovering certain truths. He has fear that something may not fit with his religion. Therefore, out of his fear, he insists on keeping his science limited to an area that does not approach his religion. If he could denounce his religion, his science could move on. Otherwise he will have a dual consciousness, and in that way he can hate others. He can hate other beliefs and other ideas, and he can hate people who think differently. And that hate will become a bondage.

"In one sense, each man has to become a materialist to some extent in this world because the human psyche is polluted by so many conceptions, and all the religions are there to trap him and to brainwash him. These religious beliefs have to be removed. And in order to remove them each man

has to become a materialist—like a clear slate—and then he
can proceed from that point. This does not mean that he
should denounce God. But he should not believe in a God
that he cannot see, that he cannot conceive of. Because, you
see, his religion wants him to believe in a certain god—a
certain god of their conception. This is false. We must understand and believe everything with a scientific philosophy.
You see, there are many common religious theories in your
Western world about the process of creation and evolution
that have been disproved by science. So that religion must
be denounced. And there are certain laws of the universe—
physical laws and spiritual laws. If religion does not agree
with these laws, it is the fault of religion and not the fault of
the laws. It is better to be a materialist for some time and
then to go from there to the spiritual knowledge, the true
knowledge. Then one will not feel that it is religion. Spiritual
knowledge is not religion."

As he was talking Swami Sivanandapuri was walking up
the road carrying what was no doubt the sum total of his
worldly possessions in an orange cloth bundle with a big
knot for a handle. He had stood out on the road at the gate
watching us for a few minutes. I realized that he was afraid
of disturbing us, but I let him stand there. I was very much
interested in what Swami Kaivalayananda was saying, and I
thought it was insightful and pertinent. I was also amazed
at the fluidity with which he spoke English. Nevertheless, I
was tired and it was getting late, so I waited for Swami
Kaivalayananda to pause long enough for me to use Swami
Sivanandapuri's patience as an excuse for leaving. After all,
he was standing under the hot sun and was no doubt anxious
to get settled in his room. But Hridaya had the same idea:
he quietly stood up and walked off while Swami Kaivalyananda was still talking and took Swami Sivanandapuri to
Room 11.

Hridaya went to Room 5, where he waited alone for me
until it was almost too late for dinner. I had seen the boys
from the Neelam Restaurant arrive with large cans of rice

and vegetables, bottled soft drinks, and even ice, which I knew they went to the trouble to carry up the hill as a special favor to me. Some time after that the sky had gradually darkened, and still we sat and talked. The whole while he was talking, Swami Kaivalyananda seemed to be right in the middle of the point he was trying to make, and that made it impossible for me to find an appropriate moment to say thank you and goodbye. I was hoping that Hridaya would come for me, but he did not.

At last there came a point in which I imagined a way to bring that day's lesson to a graceful close. "That's something I wanted to ask you about," I slipped in quickly. "Again you've used that word *atman*. Could you tell me the meaning of *atman*?" That was an important word. I had seen it used in a lot of literature and Swami Rama had used it often. I supposed one could learn a great deal just by traveling around India asking a variety of individuals to explain *atman*.

"*Atman*," he began.

"But maybe I shouldn't retain you even longer by asking questions," I interrupted again. "I've taken a lot of your time and I've made you very late. Also, I think they are waiting for me. But if you could take only one more moment to explain *atman* . . ."

"*Atman* is the self in us. *At–ma*—it comes from its root words. *At* means that which holds. There is something that holds the psychophysiological organism. It is something that sustains this body. This body has come from food, is sustained by food, and it should go into food. But something greater than food or matter is energy. Food and substance is converted from energy. And that something which holds energy is mind. Energy is converted from mind. But there is something else that holds mind or the psyche itself, this nucleus of the psyche. And that is called *atman*. So *atman* means that which is imperishable and that which holds everything. That is the inmost self in us. Without that, these outer forms of being cannot be held, cannot exist. For example, we move in this space and the body has got its being in this space. Space is the medium in which all physical existence is existing. But where do our thoughts exist? In what space? Where do our emotions, our mental activities, our intellections, and our beliefs and conceptions exist? In what space? That is also a space—akin to this space—and we call that the space of consciousness. And the spiritual reality, the spiritual plane which transcends all this—this we can call the real dimension. This is the dimension which transcends the whole of the universe. But this is the dimension that is the existence within which all of these spaces— physical and conscious spaces—are held. So we call it infinite. We call it unknown. We call it unthinkable. But it is the unthought thought in us, the unseen seer in us, the unheard hearer in us. Without that we cannot think. Without that we cannot see. It is the same thing that sees in the eyes, it is said.

"This self in us, this root consciousness, though it identifies with the psychophysiological organism, though it is very subtle like an atom, it is infinite at the same time. So long as we identify with the body, with the mind, with the intellect, and with the ego, we have that understanding that is nourished and tutored by the different knowledges of the world, then we will not be able to realize that plane or that dimension which is infinite. But the moment we cease identifying ourselves with these things, you see, that exposes us to the spiritual knowledge. We realize immediately our atomicity— that we are almost like atoms. Immediately we realize, simultaneously we realize that we are infinite. This truth is the root truth. Here we realize the inconceivable, unthinkable truth, that is the thing. Then we become perfect in this world.

"The other world is not somewhere hidden in the clouds or hidden in the stars. It is in us. Every day we go into the other world, and we come back from it without knowing it. We come back from it without knowing what it is. You see, this is a defect. And how can a man realize what he is? If there is a God, he must be in man. He must be the root being in man. God is not what we conceive him as. A God conceived is no God, a God spoken of is no God. A God we can think of is no God—because we can think of him. God must be unthinkable by man. If we can understand God by mind, that means we are understanding only that mental form of him. He must be in our understanding—but beyond our finite understanding. So we are one with that infinity and we cannot even conceive of ourselves by the use of the mind. Jesus Christ himself said, 'Seek ye first the kingdom of Heaven and all these things shall be delivered unto you.' The Kingdom of Heaven is within us. Man is made in the image of God. God himself has come into the universe. God himself is man."

Hridaya and Swami Sivanandapuri had carried a table and some chairs from the dining room and were sitting out in the gravel yard under the stars. "Where have you been?" they asked. "Your supper has been a long time ready, and we ourselves have been waiting."

"I've been right here in the universe," I answered. "There's no place else to be."

Swami Sivanandapuri laughed. "Yes, but sooner or later you must come to eat!"

The boys from Neelam carried food to our outdoor table, and Swami Sivanandapuri chanted his usual grace. We ate mostly in silence, and the words of Swami Kaivalyananda ran again through my mind. I had heard all those words before, and I knew I was to hear them again. But as I sat in the still, warm night air, I concluded to myself that those words alone were worth my trip to the other side of the globe. Any trip that I could make would be another step on the journey within.

seventeen

May 6 was the anniversary of the Buddha's enlightenment, and the same evening of 1974 was the night of the full moon. I knew a place in the mountains that could be reached by taxi in half a day, so I decided to go there for a closer look at the moon. It would be a day of rest and recuperation away from all the swamis and extreme temperature. I had a head cold that had built up over the past week from the heat, but I had become psychologically adjusted to the high temperatures so that, except for my stuffy head, I was quite comfortable. I thought that if I could get away from the scorching heat, even briefly, my head would clear up for good.

So Hridaya and I left early in the morning. We walked into Rishikesh and hired a taxi to Dehra Dun, forty-two kilometers to the north. From there we shared a taxi with two wealthy businessmen, and for twenty-five rupees each we made the three-hour climb up the steep mountain road to Mussoorie. Early in the afternoon we checked in at the Savoy Hotel. I remembered this place because I had come here in the winter with "Dr. Green and party." Then it had been quite cold, and the southernmost range of the Himalayas had been covered with snow. Now it was just pleasantly cool and I was comfortable in my cotton kurta. But it felt cold to Hridaya—it felt rather like his Kanpur winters—and he had to wear a sweater. After a late lunch we hired a four-man rickshaw and rode into Happy Valley. This was a Tibetan settlement just across the valley from the foothills of the Himalayas. It included a home and school for orphaned children, many of whom decided to begin the lifelong training to become lamas.

Riding in the rickshaw made Hridaya laugh, and his laughing made me laugh too. The rickshaws were like little wooden-box trailers with two big wheels and T-shaped tongues and big, heavy seats wide enough for two or three passengers. Normally the rickshaws were operated by two men in front, one pushing on each side of the T; but it was easier for four drivers to push two adults up the steep road out of the valley. There was always a row of these rickshaws parked along the main street of Mussoorie waiting for customers. I supposed that no more than half of them could get work even on the busiest day, so apparently the men had agreed to split each job four ways. It felt ludicrous to sit in the two-wheeled box on a big comfortable chair (probably once the rear seat of an old British luxury automobile) and be pushed down the road by four old men.

Hridaya laughed out of embarrassment. "My country is such a place!" he exclaimed. "It's ridiculous. Men pushing men! Suppose we push and they ride? What then? They should have to pay and they cannot because they have nothing—barely enough for food. They are pushing because they have nothing, and they have nothing because they are pushing."

"In my country it's the same thing exactly," I said.

"No, you have not such rickshaws, I know it."

"Not rickshaws, but we have the same situation. We have the same conditions, only on a much grander scale."

But that night we rode a rickshaw again. When we had finished supper at the Savoy Hotel, we went out to be under the moon; we decided it would be pleasant to ride along the road in a silent rickshaw. The main road ran along a ridge beyond which the mountainside plunged down into a huge valley. Motor vehicles were not allowed beyond the bus and taxi stations a mile or so below this ridge, and it was always quiet in Mussoorie. Our four drivers wheeled us easily along this level road, and we overcame our self-consciousness

enough to have them push us back and forth many times.
The full moon was a brilliant gold, and it hung out over the
valley almost close enough to touch, either to the right or left
of us, depending on which direction we were being pushed.

At one point along the road there was a rest station with
large concrete benches; we asked our drivers to stop for a
rest. They would not use any of the benches but insisted on
sitting in their rickshaw. Hridaya and I sat in a small pavilion
that hung out over the edge of the ridge with fat concrete
poles supporting it. It had a couple of benches and a railing,
and sitting with our backs to the road we could see only the
moon, the stars, and a distant range of mountains on the
other side of the valley.

"Look!" I said. "There's a fire over there. See it? Is that
part of a celebration?" Happy Valley was around the other
side of our mountain, in the direction of the Himalayas, but
maybe there was a Buddhist temple or a monastery in those
distant hills.

"I noticed that some time back," Hridaya answered. "I
think it is likely to be a forest fire because there are no roads
or dwellings on that mountain. Forest fires sometimes start
like that, especially in the midsummer months. If there is no
access by road there is no way to fight them and they just go
on burning."

"Let's just sit here for a while, okay? I really wanted to
stop here for a few minutes of silence."

But after only a moment, I spoke again. "You know, there
are a lot of world-wide meditation groups that have a special
program of meditation for this night, and hundreds of temples and ashrams . . . think of all the thousands of people
who'll be sitting in silence at this very moment."

We sat without talking for a long while. From this vantage
point it seemed we could see to infinity. The peaks of the
Himalayas reached high above our heads behind us, and we
could look right over the tops of the lower mountain ranges
toward the south. Far below us and way in the distance, even
the lights of Dehra Dun twinkled in the night. Beyond the

golden moon that was rising now right past our faces and up over our heads, we could see forever into the luminescent sky. For a moment I felt as though we were sitting at the top of our world. We were tiny specks on a huge globe that was itself only a dot in a vast universe. But something from that universe was looking out through our eyes, or perhaps it was looking in. We were the universe looking at itself . . .

"I think I told you about Rolling Thunder?" I asked, breaking the silence again.

"I remember. What do you call those people?"

"We call them Indians too because when Columbus—"

"No, no, this I know. We ourselves call them Indians—American Indians or red Indians—just like you do. But what did you call Rolling Thunder? Something like swami, you told me."

"Oh, medicine man. I guess I did tell you that a medicine man was something like a swami. But you or someone said a swami had to be a renunciate. Rolling Thunder's hardly a renunciate, except maybe for the money he renounces that he could get for being a healer. He's very much involved with the world, and that's why I was thinking about him just now. One day when I was in his house in Nevada he talked to me about the earth in such a way that I could feel it—I mean the earth itself. I could feel the being that the earth really is. And just now I could feel it again. In fact, I could almost feel more than that—I could almost sense the feeling and the movement of this whole thing that's under us and all around us. Whatever it is, it's a living being and it's conscious—self-conscious—I can feel it. Sometimes I can almost participate in it. Haven't you ever felt your own consciousness almost get away from you, from your personal self-awareness, and sort of draw out, like it's starting to blend with some much wider consciousness?"

Hridaya sat silently and watched the sky. "Maybe," he said. "Maybe sometimes. I guess that's what these swamis are telling you about, isn't it?"

"I'm not sure," I said. "That's what I want to find out.

Because what I'm talking about is not withdrawal. It's not searching within and it's not nonattachment. I don't think it conflicts with these things, but it's something different to me. What I'm talking about is nonseparateness—nonindividuality. That's what interests me, that's what I think is important. Selflessness. But that might be what Swami Kaivalyananda meant when he said, 'When we are exposed to the spiritual knowledge we realize our atomicity—that we are just like atoms. But immediately and simultaneously we realize that we are infinite.' And he said, 'This truth is the root truth.' So it boils down to the same thing: to realize the Kingdom of Heaven within—to realize the true self—is to achieve selflessness. I can get a feeling of the whole world sitting here with the moon so close, and all this space around us, and the entire earth curving under us. It seems like the full moon always appears right at the horizon and moves up fast. It's easy to see how it's moving around the earth and how the earth itself is turning. Did you know, there are those who say that the moon is the dead body, the discarded body, of the being that is now earth?"

"I may have heard it, I don't recall. Do you believe this?"

"I don't know. I guess I neither believe nor disbelieve it. Anyway, all the while that we were silent I was just thinking about these rickshaw guys and about Raju and his friends at the Hardwar *ghat* and about people in Kanpur and Calcutta —and Kansas."

"Why?"

"I don't know. Because of sitting here, I guess. But I wasn't thinking really—I mean, I wasn't carrying on a conversation with myself. It just all flashed through my mind. All the humans are one person—or a part of one person. I'll bet that's what's really meant by self-realization. It means realizing what the heck the self is in the first place, realizing that the self is us. That's the transpersonal self, the whole self. You remember in the story of the Buddha how his whole trip was motivated by compassion? And you remember how he fasted for a while and then realized that he would fail if he didn't eat? That was to symbolize that there's a wrong kind of renunciation. Buddha renounced denial. He gave up denying the existence of the physical world and all the related practicalities. And when he reached nirvana, he could have simply faded away, right? I mean physically faded away. But he didn't. He got up from under his tree and started walking. Why? Because he wanted to meet people. I think the way to enlightenment is through awareness of the earth—caring about the condition of the world. It seems to me that a personal desire for personal liberation is a lowering of the consciousness to the selfish domain. The spiritual path is raising the consciousness to transpersonal levels. Self-consciousness, group consciousness, community consciousness, social consciousness, humankind consciousness, planetary consciousness, cosmic consciousness: it seems to me that these are the logical steps to enlightenment—not the increasing self-interest of the individual person. Buddha didn't gain enlightenment just sitting under that tree. He must have had dozens of lifetimes of study, service, and sacrifice, following his eightfold path—compassion and right action and all that."

"Yes, we can see depictions of the many incarnations of the Buddha," Hridaya said. "But I am not so familiar with the whole thing. Just what he was doing in all his lifetimes, I have no idea."

Again we fell silent and watched the sky. The moon had climbed higher now, and it looked smaller and farther away. After only a moment Hridaya spoke again. "Either we should return to the rickshaw or we should pay them and let them go."

"Let's go," I said. "I'd like to ride one more time down to the end of the road and back. It might be a long time before I can be on a mountain ridge like this again—on a full moon night in the clear, quiet air below the Himalayas."

The four drivers smiled. They would be happy to make one more trip back and forth along the ridge. They looked healthy; at least they had the advantage of not living in a dusty, crowded city. I told Hridaya that I would enjoy living here myself.

"Originally I had supposed you came up here to relieve your head cold," he said as we climbed into the rickshaw.

"That's right," I answered, "and I think it worked. I feel almost normal."

"But actually you have come to think about Buddha, isn't it? Those are Hindu temples along the Ganges. The *pujas* are devoted to Krishna, Rama, Siva. And the swamis and sadhus talk about the Vedas. This is the day of Buddha's enlightenment, so actually you came to meet the Tibetans and to devote your thoughts to the Buddha, isn't it?"

"That's interesting. It's a coincidence. It just worked out that way. If Happy Valley was not here, I would still have come to get away from the heat, and to see the full moon from the mountain."

"And you offered silent prayers to the Buddha, and then you have been speaking of him, mainly."

"No, that's not the way it was. In fact, I wasn't even thinking about Buddha's enlightenment then. I just automatically used Buddha as an example."

"Example of what?"

"Of what I was talking about. About awareness of the earth, caring about the condition of the world. What the swamis say about the spiritual potential—or God in man, or whatever—makes me feel more hopeful about everything, even about the condition of life on earth."

"This is why you came to India, right? You told me some time back that you had some idea the world is trying to do something."

"I want to help communicate because that's what I think it's trying to do. I think humanity is trying to communicate with itself. That's the spiritual growth that lies ahead, I believe. But the only way I can imagine it working out is through a massive international humanitarian endeavor. From where we're at now, which is on the planet, our spiritual work is to work on the planet. When swamis or yogis say, 'Search within,' and 'Work on yourself,' I would like to know what they mean. Those are easy words to misunderstand and to use as an excuse for inaction. Do they mean develop a nice personality? Do they mean do asanas and work on your figure? Do they mean avoid all work that's not self-serving? Do they mean sit in the corner a few hours a day and say mantras and burn incense? Do they mean go into meditation and withdraw and let the nonseekers feed you? I don't think *personal* self-awareness and *personal* growth means much at all. The self is not just you or me, it's mankind. Mankind has to become aware of itself—on a down-to-earth, whole-world, international level. A few days ago Swami Kaivalyananda said: 'The other world is not somewhere hidden in the clouds or hidden in the stars. It is us. Man is made in the image of God. God himself has come into the universe. God himself is man.' And Swami Rama has said the same thing exactly. I think that means a lot. Those are important words. We belong to the life of the world. And the world belongs to the Kingdom of Heaven. Look at this light shining on us and on all the trees and everything. It's coming from the sun, and it's being reflected by the moon. We're supposed to be moons. We're supposed to be shining."

It was hard to leave Mussoorie, especially since even my body felt so much better there in the mountains. We stayed an extra day, but I would have liked to have stayed an extra month or two. On the afternoon of May 8 we got back to Dehra Dun, Rishikesh, and on to our room at Muni Ki Reti by a combination of bus, jitney, tonga, and our own feet.

Swami Sivanandapuri was waiting on the step in front of the dining room. "Ah, you are returned! And how did you enjoy your wonderful vacation?"

"It was beautiful. I only wished I could stay longer."

"And where is our Mr. Hridaya? Supper is now under preparation."

"He'll be coming in a minute."

"I also have not taken my evening meal. I saw that you had returned, so I am just now waiting."

"I hope they've been feeding you while we've been gone."

"Yes, yes. I have been fine in all respects, and I have not had such peace in months. This has been most helpful for me, you'll never know. Recently I had been much disturbed. I did not tell you, actually, but this religion business disturbs me more and more. And then especially because of the Kumbh Mela I have been deeply troubled."

I sat down on the step beside him. "Why is that?"

"You see, I believe this is wrong . . ." He paused for a long moment as though considering how to be accurate and just with his words. "Don't you feel that this is exploiting?"

"You mean the Kumbh Mela?"

"The ideas and philosophies are good, but they are used to exploit people. Not only Kumbh Mela, all these festivities and these so-called divine places. They are used to attract people. And here, you see, people easily fall for these attractions. They come from far and near. By the thousands they came—by the millions—to the Kumbh Mela. Large crowds of people mean large sums of donations, and all these temples and ashrams fall into the nonsense of competing with one another. Have you not heard the spiteful loudspeakers blaring all along the Holy Ganges? It is a shameful thing. They are competing in this manner, you see? And they go on increasing their output until it becomes an unbearable thing. In the place where I was staying there was a loudspeaker war with the Geeta Bhawan just beside; and they went on, each trying to outdo the other. It created a terrible distortion. I had been in my cave near Tat Walla Baba, and I came down only because I had fallen ill. Still I had wanted peace, but there was no peace at all. And there is no peace for all these people. We are not doing right by these masses. Either the swamis should withdraw entirely from the people or they should do something helpful."

"What do all these masses think?" I asked. "Do they expect to achieve *moksha* in their lifetimes?"

"This is the point. They are led to believe they have only to come and pray and give what they can and they will receive *moksha*. These days many do these things for money, even the wealthy. And it is the same notion. They believe they have only to give to the deity and double or triple the amount will be coming to them in the future. There may be some truth in it, but we are misleading the people. This is what troubles me. I feel that we are misleading and exploiting the people in the name of religion. I saw the masses of people crowding and shoving, racing to get into the Ganges, even stepping on one another. And this rich man who pretends to be seven or eight years younger than his true age—that one who calls himself a master in your country—his followers are hostile, particularly his Western followers. They have come to the Mela and had been hostile toward the others. Even the police had to be called. This is not a spiritual thing." Swami called him by his Indian name, but I knew he was talking about "Sat-Guru" Maharaj Ji, and Hridaya confirmed it.

Hridaya arrived and our table was set. This night we went inside to eat under the harsh fluorescent lights and the ceiling fan. Three Westerners sat at another table talking over tea, and they greeted us when we went in. They were two young ladies from Canada who were on a sightseeing vacation and an American student who had traveled to India by himself to study Transcendental Meditation. They had all arrived at the Tourist Bungalow some days before Hridaya and I left for our trip to Mussoorie and they had made friends with Swami Sivanandapuri in our absence. "You have taken your supper?" the swami asked.

"Yes," answered one of the girls. "And without you. You refused to eat with us today."

"Because I was waiting for my friends."

"Swami! You mean we are not your friends?"

"You are all my friends!" He laughed.

They sat silently while Swami sang the chant, and they

listened to our conversation as we ate. I wanted to pursue this subject of *moksha* because I wanted to know what it meant. I knew how it was defined, or supposed that I did. *Moksha* was liberation—liberation from the wheel of births and deaths—and therefore enlightenment. In Hindu philosophy the masters were those who had achieved such enlightenment, and if they appeared on the earth in physical form, it was by their own choice. Achieving *moksha*, I thought, meant becoming a buddha or master. But I wondered what it meant to the masses of people about whom swamis and others were telling me: "They spend their life savings and journey far and wide on these pilgrimages in search of *moksha*." The same questions remained with me: Did these millions of Indian pilgrims and worshipers hope and expect that their present lifetimes would be their last? Did they believe that *moksha*, as I thought of *moksha*, could be achieved by some meaningful pilgrimage or by some sincere gesture of devotion?

"What you're actually talking about," the American interrupted, "is self-realization."

"Well, I guess so," I said. "I guess that's another word for the same thing."

"Well," he said, "that's what TM is all about."

"The goal of Transcendental Meditation is self-realization? Is that the way they say it? Of course I guess that's the goal of all these pursuits." I had not really talked to this man except for a brief conversation in which we exchanged names and hometowns and I learned that he was a TM student. In fact, I had not really talked to a TM student at any length before. It was interesting, I thought to myself, that I should be asking an American in India about Transcendental Meditation when there must be many times more members of this group in the Western world.

"That's what they tell us. I think TM is supposed to be the most efficient system so far worked out for achieving self-realization—at least the best system for modern people."

"I thought they emphasized more worldly things like developing a sharp mind, learning to relax, and getting along with others."

"But that's supposed to be only the beginning. It's supposed to take five or ten years to reach self-realization."

"Five to ten years? You must be thinking of it differently, because that's not the way I think of it."

"You mean Transcendental Meditation?"

"No, self-realization," I said. "If self-realization is used to mean *moksha*, how can we use it to mean something else also? And I think *moksha* means enlightenment—nirvana, Buddhahood."

"Well, that's what they mean," the American replied. "Or they call it cosmic consciousness. It is the same thing, isn't it? Cosmic consciousness?"

"But I don't think it's just a glimpse or a fleeting experience of cosmic consciousness, I think it's a permanent state of being."

"Yeah, but if you get there once you can get there again just by repeating the same method. If we do the practice like we're taught, we are supposed to attain cosmic consciousness in—I think they say, for most people, six or eight years approximately. Of course a lot of people don't stick with it that long. Or even if they stick with it they still miss a lot of times. You're supposed to do mantra at least twenty minutes every day, and I think if you miss enough times, you lose everything."

"What do all these people do after their six or eight or ten years? Do they just carry on in the same way as realized beings, and go on saying their mantra at least twenty minutes a day?"

"I don't really know. I don't think I've met any of those people. See, I haven't really been involved with TM very long at all."

"I don't know either," I said. "I don't think I've ever talked about cosmic consciousness with anyone in TM—you're the first one. It just seems like all these words mean different things to different people, and probably none of us can really understand the meaning of self-realization. That is, until we've reached it. To me self-realization, *moksha*, liberation, nirvana, enlightenment, cosmic consciousness, Buddhahood, and Christ consciousness all refer to the same state of being, whatever it is. But I don't think I can achieve it in ten, twenty, or thirty years whatever I do. There may be a handful of near-masters on this planet; but I think almost every one of us has countless years of being and countless years of doing between here and cosmic consciousness or *moksha* or whatever we call it. On the other hand, it's an inevitable eventuality for everyone. So I'm more interested in the immediate tasks than in the final goal, and I think it involves meditations and mantras and a whole lot more."

"I am always thinking the same thing exactly," Swami Sivanandapuri remarked as he wiped his plate with his last piece of *japati*. "Why do we not take tea?"

One evening Hridaya and I walked up the road to the Sivananda Ashram to call on Swami Kaivalyananda. We had not seen him for several days. He had come twice to the Tourist Bungalow since we had returned from Mussoorie, but the first time we had been at the bank in Rishikesh and the second time I was asleep under the fan in my room, sheltered from the hot afternoon sun. Hridaya had met him in the reception office and promised that we would visit his room at the ashram. We had decided to awaken early and to sleep late each day and to be as lazy as possible in the hot afternoons.

We could hear chanting in the night as we walked up the long stairway to the ashram gate. There were nearly fifty ashram members and guests performing an evening *puja* in the garden. We had to pass close to them to get up the path to the rooms on the hill above. So we walked carefully around in front of them, trying to be little noticed and at the same time to see whether Swami Kaivalyananda's dark, hooded face was among them. He was neither among the worshipers nor anywhere else on the grounds; he did not answer his door though we knocked several times.

"I thought it was room twelve," Hridaya said. "Suppose we have the wrong room?"

"I don't know, I wouldn't know which other door to knock on." Room 12 was in the middle of a long row of rooms on the upper floor of the building. "I sure don't want to disturb some other swami."

"Why not? It might be a good way to meet another swami."

A robed figure appeared at the top of the stairs as we walked along the veranda. "May I help you?"

"Which is the room of Swami Kaivalyananda?" Hridaya asked. "Is it not room twelve?"

"Yes."

"But he does not answer."

"So you should try again."

"I don't want to disturb him if he's in meditation," I said.

"No, no, he is always in meditation. You should try again. It's all right."

We knocked several times again, and Swami Kaivalyananda opened his door. "Oh, it is you, sorry," he said, pulling the string to turn on the one bare light bulb on the ceiling. "Please, come inside."

"We don't want to disturb you."

"No, it is all right. Please come in."

We took off our shoes and sat down on the hard cement floor. There was a small table fan in one corner of the room, and the swami turned it to point in our direction. "Let me offer you some lemon squash." We watched as he dipped water from a covered bucket on the floor, cut several lemons and squeezed the juice into the water. From a brown paper bag he sprinkled out some sugar, and he mixed the contents by pouring it back and forth from one vessel to another. His room was like a concrete prison cell without windows. The walls looked dark and cheerless in the light from the bare bulb that hung from the ceiling, and there was no furniture, not even a bed, a mat, or a cushion.

"I have a cot," the swami said, seeing me glance about the room, "but sometimes I keep it outside. I like to sleep out of doors."

We drank our lukewarm lemon squash from metal cups and carried on a spontaneous conversation about the weather, the Sivananda Ashram and our trip to Mussoorie. Apparently I was still thinking about the meaning of self-realization, because without my knowing how it happened, we were discussing the subject of *moksha*, self-realization, cosmic consciousness.

I told the swami that I had been wondering about the meaning of those words. I was sure that people had various ideas of what they meant—I was not sure what they meant to me. But particularly I wondered about the process. It seemed to me that everyone was on the path to the highest consciousness. What other path or destination could there be? Yet obviously great numbers of people were doing all sorts of specialized things to hasten the process for themselves. I wanted to believe that the process could not be a personal one, I told him. I wanted to believe that the only way was through sharing and giving. I could not believe that it was possible to race along this path, or that it was important to reach the end in a minimum number of years. I could not believe in a quest for cosmic consciousness, which was simply a more spiritual form of a personal ambition to get ahead.

"That highest truth, that highest state, is not a thing to quest for," the swami answered. "It is not a thing we can be ambitious after. We cannot gain it through any exertion, we cannot externalize it. All that we can do in the form of *sadhana* is to remove that ignorance. There is no instrument to cognize the highest truth. If there is that instrument, then anybody can take that instrument and go. You see? What in the form of *sadhana* we can do is we can remove the ignorance which prevents us from seeing this."

"I've wondered about all the throngs of people who flocked to the Ganges," I said. "They went without food and sleep, they got diseased from the river water, many of them died, thousands of them nearly did, and they all risked their lives. What part of them benefited from that holy dip? Did they really get closer to *moksha* by nearly stampeding one another in this spiritual competition than they would have by staying home and spending some energy for their neighbors or their community? Now in America there are all sorts of new systems, all kinds of yogas and meditations. Soon there will be millions involved, just like it is here. Maybe some of these people are aiming for self-realization, but I think most of them are just working on their bodies and their personalities. In any case they don't seem to be working on life or on the condition of the world. Many of these pursuits seem to decrease people's natural gregariousness and their capacity to care because they increase the illusion of individuality."

Swami Kaivalyananda took our empty cups and set them by the water bucket, opened his door wide to let in the night air, sat down again, and crossed his legs. "There are some who want physical beauty, some who seek long life, some who seek material things, wealth, various successes, and so forth. Yoga is not for these things. There are various types of yoga, people have said, and they have called these things yoga. But these things are not yoga—what we call these asanas and all. One may develop one's physical beauty and personality and more symmetry. They practice this for that. But this has nothing to do with spirituality at all. And then again, there are people who want clairvoyance and clairaudience and all that. This also has nothing to do with spirituality. Actually, if they develop a sense which is not useful to them normally, and over which they have not complete control, they will go mad after some time. They will not be able to live an appropriate social life. When you have clairvoyance and you go on seeing things connected with the other world, that knowledge is useless to you. Unless we have great virtue and understanding it is not useful to see these things, and it is not required. If we develop these faculties and these insights, they do harm rather than good. They do definite harm to us. But if you know the highest reality and highest truth, then all these lower aspects and visions, they are with you and you can utilize them in a proper way. They are known in a total awareness sense. The highest spiritual knowledge is very rare. It is only once in a thousand years one gets total realization—once in a thousand years among saints. In the Bhagavad Gita it is said that among thousands of people only one man even strives for perfection."

"But there are a lot of people, it seems to me, who believe they can achieve total realization—cosmic consciousness or whatever you call it—by doing their thing for a number of years. For example, I heard that TM people believe they can achieve realization in six or eight years. By saying their special mantra over the years, I believe they are told, they can become realized beings."

"No mantra can lead us to that!" the swami said slowly, shaking his head. "Mantra utilizes the sound element. It is of the lower energy. These mantras and meditations they are teaching—they are only a mental act. They are dealing only with the lower energy. Even the great philosopher, Shankaracharya, the great teacher of all times, has said that. And he is the teacher of this Maharishi Mahesh Yogi. He cannot go against that. Shankaracharya has said that these things are mere mental acts. Either you have a conception of an object externally, or an idea inwardly, which is unreal, and you contemplate on that and you get a kind of mental state just like a trance. Just like a trance, which Shankaracharya has compared to sleep. And this is not real. Any mantra which exists at all exists in the lower world, which is the world of energy. That cannot lead us to the highest truth. It can reveal to us the world of energy. One of the greatest rishis, who was supposed to be the incarnation of the three godheads, has given us these words, I will tell you."

The swami stared thoughtfully at the ceiling for a moment, and then he spoke in Sanskrit. From a pocket in his robes he pulled out a small pack of crumpled bidis. He took one, straightened it with his fingers, and lit it with a wooden match which he struck against the concrete floor. "This means that none of the mantras can lead to the truth. None of the mantras can reveal it. Nor can the tantras reveal it. Meditation on the mantras is only a mental state, a modification of the mind. This activity can be useful to acquire certain powers, but it can destroy us also. If one is not sufficiently purified, if one does not have a certain purity of mind, and yet one repeats the mantra, it becomes a destructive power. These mantras, under certain conditions, can be a step toward a higher step, but that in itself can never lead us to a higher realization." He lit his bidi and shook out the match. "Unless one has spiritual guidance and unless one has developed a great purity of mind, the mantras are not useful in themselves. In any case, they are related only to a mental state. Also, one needs much previous and preliminary training on how to utilize that mantra energy. Otherwise it is dangerous. Absolute realization is a different process, developed and demonstrated by the rishis, which consists of the knowledge of the Upanishads. Here the process is this: an aspirant develops certain qualifications. He must have definite qualifications such as dispassion and discrimination and the sixfold virtues. When he has got these qualifications and a burning aspiration for the reality, he must go and sit in the presence of a guru who is himself established in the truth and who is well-versed in the scriptures of knowledge. And the process is hearing. He must hear about it. And he must reflect, use the intellect, and contemplate on what he has heard. What he has heard is knowledge, and he must consider it, reason about it, use his power of reason, which he has highly developed. He must think about it and reason with himself. So hearing, reflection, and consideration—this is the process. This is the process which leads us beyond knowledge, to the point where we have no need for knowledge. Then even the Upanishads are not needed. They are only useful to help eliminate wrong knowledge. So this is the process—eliminate wrong knowledge, and when wrong knowledge has been removed, this process also goes."

"Sometime I would like to talk to you about the meaning of the word 'guru,' " I said. "This word has new popularity in America, and it seems to me its real meaning is not even slightly understood."

"No, you see, there is confusion. Because you have got all these pseudo-gurus misleading your people. I shall come to talk to you tomorrow."

"Tomorrow we shall be spending the full day on the other side," Hridaya told him.

"Across the Ganga?"

"Yes, we shall spend the time morning and afternoon with Tat Walla Baba. Do you know him?" Hridaya asked.

"Yes, I know that baba. He lives with the trees."

"Well, he lives in a cave up there," I said.

"He has always lived and walked among the trees, they say. He is a friend of trees. And some have told that this fellow pulls trees from the ground at times. He has done it with his own hands, pulled them easily from the ground, roots and all, by the willingness of the trees. They are all his friends, they say."

Hridaya looked at me. "Shall we make a move? We shall take our leave, Swami, we have disturbed so much of your time."

"No, no, it's all right," the swami said, walking out onto the veranda. "I wanted you to come. Look! Come look here at the fire!"

We had noticed it before. High on the mountain and far upriver, there was the golden light of a distant forest fire, just as we had seen from the ridge in Mussoorie.

"We have been seeing these fires," Hridaya said. "Are they not caused by the extreme heat?"

"Yes, the heat and the dryness. It often happens. Spontaneous combustion. They will do something about it. They will not let it go on in that manner or it may burn off the entire mountain."

"What do you think can be done to stop the fire?" I asked Hridaya, as we descended the many stairs from the ashram gate to the road.

"I don't know," he answered. "I think there are no roads to that point. Anyway, there is no equipment, and there is no water to fight such a fire."

Swami Sivanandapuri was also looking at those distant hills. When we reached the Tourist Bungalow he was standing on the road in front of the office. "That fire on the mountain can be seen clearly in the darkness. It appears closer than it was the previous night. Have you noticed?"

"We were just now talking about it only a few moments back," Hridaya answered.

"Are there caves or people up there where that fire is?" I asked.

"Not just there," Swami said. "But in time it may approach the German Baba's cave and come on down. It may be moving this way. Before that time they will have to stop the fire. That is what I'm thinking just now."

"Then let these old babas make rain by some supernatural means," Hridaya laughed.

"Not supernatural," Swami said seriously. "It will be natural. It is the only way."

eighteen

Swami Sivanandapuri, Hridaya, and I started out in the early morning for our day's expedition across the Ganges. I packed my camera and recorder and we filled a thermos with ice water from the dining room.

"It would be nice if it would stay this temperature all day," I remarked as we started down the hill. "This is plenty hot enough for me." When we reached the main road at the bottom of the hill, I paused to see if there might be an empty tonga coming our way.

"This is a day of walking," Swami said. "Let us not begin by waiting for a ride." But then, remembering that he was not one to make suggestions, he added "Don't you think this is correct?" So we walked to the boat landing.

There was the usual large crowd at the boat landing. "Look!" said the swami. "Today is a blessed day indeed! Today they have formed a queue at the boat landing. Spontaneously, it appears, they have decided to put some order into things, rather than trample one another on the way to the temples." We got into the boat much faster than if there had been no queue, because when the crowds were shoving I always felt self-conscious as a foreigner and hesitated about being sufficiently aggressive.

Every boat crossing was so much the same I felt as though I were experiencing déjà vu. It was difficult to believe there were a different thirty or forty people in the boat every time. In each boat were people from many provinces, people speaking many languages, yet they all gave the same united cry as the boat pushed off from shore. One would have thought they had rehearsed it. They threw coins into the water, filled their brass vessels, sipped water from their cupped hands, splashed their faces, and urged their young-sters to do the same. And always the youngsters simply sat with their arms over the side, feeling the current against their hands. Because of my recent contemplations and con-versations with swamis, I found myself thinking, as I watched these people now, how good it would be if they could do their hoping and praying for everyone—at least for every-one who was in the same boat. Why did they not wet one another's foreheads and lift water to the lips of one another?

Hridaya brought me out of my thoughts: "Now remember what I told you and get ready to jump. The boat hits the sandbags once and then bounces back."

The three of us stood up on our seats and leaped to the ground as the boat hit against its sandbag mooring.

The plan for the day called for hiking twice up the hill to Tat Walla Baba's cave. We wanted to spend both the morn-ing and the afternoon sessions with Tat Walla Baba, and we planned to spend the time in between at the Maharishi Mahesh Yogi Ashram, which was on the same side of the river. The ashram was nearly deserted, according to our swami guide, but the site itself was supposed to be worth seeing. "It's a beautiful ashram and grounds," he had told us. "You will be impressed."

We reached Tat Walla Baba's cave at just the right time. He was coming down his stairs as we were stepping out of our sandals and into the cool air of his burlap lean-to. "Are you going to put questions this morning?" Swami whispered in my ear after I had given my offering and he had touched the baba's feet.

"No, later," I whispered back. "This afternoon."

My original intention had been to sit and listen during the morning session and to ask my questions in the afternoon. Besides, the atmosphere in Tat Walla Baba's dwelling just now seemed more relaxed and congenial than ever, and I wouldn't have spoiled it by talking. Perhaps it was my own feeling. Perhaps he was beginning to feel familiar to me. Hridaya and I were the only ones here who could be called visitors, and we had not come seeking anything in particular. No one would be asking any questions. Tat Walla Baba seemed very informal. Not that he changed his bearing in any way or sat in a different manner—he just projected that feeling. He chatted with the man who had been working in the kitchen on our previous visit, and it was apparent that they were both amused. No doubt this man was a close disciple. Though the baba's unusual mixture of Hindi and Punjabi was strange to the ear, he had a pleasing, melodic tone of voice and a natural, open laugh that made one feel at ease. He laughed especially cheerfully when an old burlap-covered figure who looked like a friend and a fellow cave person popped in to share some snapshots. The old man left as abruptly as he entered, merely giving Tat Walla Baba a careless wave, and I could hear him laughing far down the path. I wondered what sort of funny photographs an old renunciate like that might be carrying about. No one else had been offered a look.

Tat Walla Baba glanced at me and spoke to his disciple. "Those were snaps of these babas," the disciple said to me in English, "which had been taken some months back by an American lady just as you intend to do today. They were delivered to the name of that gentleman just now, sent from your country by post." That was the first I had heard this man speak English—somehow it always surprised me the first time. I nodded my head in response because I did not want to thank him for answering my question.

For a while no one spoke and we just sat there. This felt to me like the ultimate in relaxation. We were not trying to be silent, to meditate, to maintain any posture or state of mind, to think or not to think, or even to rest. We were just sitting there. Tat Walla Baba sat with one foot on his bench and his forearm resting on his knee. He slowly moved his head back and forth as though he were almost unconsciously observing the people around him, but when our eyes met I felt that strong penetration even in his casual glance. Tat Walla Baba did indeed have a presence. I knew it did not come from any affectation or pose, nor from anything he said or did, but I might have wondered whether my imagination was enhanced by his impressive appearance and this romantic setting. He sat before us with his long hair rolled around his head like a turban, and his strong frame and very large stomach made him look incredibly solid and stable.

To our left as we faced him was the rock wall of his mountain that had been carved to form the cool, dark alcove on the ground level and the stairway that led up the sheer cliff to the mouth of his cave. To our right were the endless miles of sky and forest and even a distant glimpse of the River Ganges that could be seen when the burlaps were rolled up against the poles. And the birds were always singing. It seemed one could count nearly a dozen varieties of bird songs in one sitting. Perhaps the nature that was around him partly accounted for his own nature, but I knew whence came the presence that I felt in him. It was his stillness and his sense of serenity. I could not think that he had achieved perfect wisdom, but I could believe that he had achieved perfect poise.

I reflected about the first time that I saw him, the time in the previous autumn when Swami Sivanandapuri guided Harvey and me up this mountain and we sat with him under his tree. That had been the day we had spent with the European lady who belonged to the Self-Realization Fellowship in Los Angeles. I had not seen her since she received her initiation from Tat Walla Baba, and I wondered whether she had changed in any way. I remembered the strange and uncomfortable conversation I had experienced with that lady when I had mentioned Martin Luther King. What is the use of far-out spiritual pursuits, I wondered to myself, before we have cleared away the ignorance so close at hand?

Tat Walla Baba leaned over and said something to his disciple, and the disciple, who seemed to have been drawn from some deep concentration, looked at me and cleared his throat. "Baba says your Martin Luther King is a true saint."

In my surprise I said, "What?"

"Baba says your Martin Luther King is a true saint."

"I believe it," I answered. "That was what I thought."

Almost immediately my thinking, recalling, and verbalizing stopped as though those last remarks, spoken aloud, were the end car on my train of thoughts. I believe I went on hearing the birds, but for a long time I was not aware of my sitting. The disciple divided the fruit and passed some out to everyone, and I supposed it was a sign that this time was coming to a close. I had no watch to look at, but judging from the usual length of Tat Walla Baba's sessions, I could guess I had received about an hour of timelessness. I had also received a rare and magnificent tranquillity, a part of which remained with me throughout the day.

Without waiting for gestures or courtesies from anyone, Baba stood up abruptly and walked out the door and over the hill into the sunshine beyond. As we were putting on our sandals, the swami told the baba's disciple that we would be back in the afternoon.

Strolling down the mountain path, I thought about the silent sitting. The presence of Tat Walla Baba's stillness was a real entity, and being in that presence had a real effect. Just now I could sit down on the path where we walked or on a rock overlooking the valley and easily regain that state of absolute peace in which I was engaged only a few minutes ago. For that matter, I could do it in the river boat or in a jogging tonga or even on a noisy corner of Rishikesh—if only I could do it now before even the memory faded. But the feeling would soon pass, and I would need someone like Tat Walla Baba to restore that feeling of serenity. Not only had I observed the existence of presence, but I had experienced the use of it as well. This had been an adequate indication of the meaning of presence, I thought as I followed the swami and Hridaya, who were now conversing rapidly

in Hindi, down the steep slope. This had been an example of
why pilgrims travel, why seekers sit in the presence of saints,
and why devotees seek *darsana*. The stillness that I now
could only remember is a state to be longed for, because
only in the pure peace of that state is one closer to one's true
nature. But as we went through our day, the outside distractions would once again close in around us, and that ever-
present silence would be covered up by all the sounds on the
surface of our beings. I knew that even the longing could be
lost, but it would not slip away from me. Thousands upon
thousands had lost their longing, especially in my country
and in the rest of the busy, modern world; still there were
thousands and thousands of pilgrims, seekers, and aspirants
who were enough aware of themselves not to forget their
longing. Tat Walla Baba was a good example of a spiritual
presence because he was constant enough in his stillness that
it was always there. The peace within him was so real and so
closely visible that it reminded me of the forgotten peace
within myself. But there was more than a reminding: there
was also a direct causation. People vibrate—on all the levels
of their being—just as surely as a violin string or a tuning
fork vibrate. Part of the purpose of sitting in the presence of
a venerable human being is to discover some sympathetic
vibrations. When we met the road that came from Laxman
Jhula I could see the roof of the Tourist Bungalow on the
hill way across the river. This was the furthest downriver
I had ever been on this side of the Ganges.

"Now we reach the road," announced Swami, "the same
road we have used to walk to Laxman Jhula. You see? It's
easy to come here. So many times I have urged that you
should visit this ashram grounds. From the boats one has
simply to reach this road and then turn down instead of up.
Maharishi Mahesh takes this road by jeep, I think I told you.
They drive him all the way up to Laxman Jhula, across the
bridge and down the road, making a circle. He's the only one
who could do something like that. It's actually not allowed.
It's a matter of wealth, you see, after the Beatles and all. But

nowadays he doesn't come. We have at last nearly reached. It's not far from this point."

We followed the road and walked for a quarter of an hour directly under the hot sun. This was one of the hottest days yet, and the only help was that the air was very dry. At a point where the road crossed a stream and went up over a hill there was a patch of shade provided by a group of trees, and we stopped there for a sip of ice water from the thermos. "The gate is just upon that hill," Swami said. "Soon you will see. Do you know, some time back there was a television just where we are standing."

"A television? What do you mean?"

"Well, the television itself was just down there," he answered, pointing. "That was the part that one watches. And the camera was up here on the road. They had a particular camera, one especially suited for television, and some girls were dancing up here. Anyone could stand up here before the camera and one's exact image should simultaneously appear below on the television."

"Closed-circuit television," I said.

"That was exactly what they named it!"

"What was it doing up here?" I had not seen television in this country except at the best hotels in the largest cities.

"It was a kind of advertising, so it seemed. It created a spectacle. At that time they planned for this place to be the world headquarters for Transcendental Meditation. They wanted it to be a popularity, a kind of fashion. So they had films and televisions and one could see how Maharishi Mahesh Yogi had appeared on television here and there. They tried many curiosities to entice the crowds, you see, but they could not achieve such popularity as they desired. After that they concentrated their efforts in foreign countries. Here there are so many genuine sages and highly developed yogis, many, many beside whom this Maharishi Mahesh is not so learned. It was a problem here to make such a great and powerful movement as they dreamed of."

The ashram did look abandoned. The buildings that would

no doubt have been the most impressive were not even finished and were now beginning to fall apart, and the swami told me about other buildings that had been planned and not even started. At times I wondered where our swami obtained all his facts, if facts they were, but I supposed he got around in this guide business and he had been doing it for a long time.

"It looks like there's no one here," I said.

"As I mentioned, I believe this place has been nearly forgotten now."

"I'd expected at least a small crowd. In fact, I thought there would be quite a few Westerners here. Our friend in the Tourist Bungalow came all the way from America to study TM here."

"He is the only such case I have encountered. I had wanted to show you this beautiful location and all the fine gardens but if you should like to meet people, perhaps we can find someone in the office."

"No, that's all right. I was just surprised, that's all."

But we were walking toward the building with the sign that read "Office" and Swami thought we ought to say hello before walking about, if there was anyone to say hello to. We walked past a row of apparently empty cottages, which Swami informed us had been intended to be the living quarters of permanent students and teachers. A young man came running in our direction and reached the front door of the office at the same time we did. He was smiling and friendly. "Come in. Welcome, welcome."

He unlocked the door and led us inside, and with a magazine or pamphlet he slapped the dust off of the wooden bench in front of the desk. We sat down on the bench and he sat down behind the desk.

"This American friend would like to ask some questions about Transcendental Meditation," the swami told him.

"That will be all right," the young man said. "I myself am trained as a teacher." He got up and turned some knobs and switches on an electric air conditioner in the window, but nothing happened, so he blew hard on the panel. Dust flew, he coughed, and yet he continued playing with the knobs. He even gave it a couple of gentle hits with the heel of his hand. "We have an air conditioner from United States here, but just now it is in need of repair."

"That's all right," I said, though actually I had been watching with hopeful anticipation. This would have been quite a fancy place if all the TM dreams could have been fulfilled in India.

"And just now we have no supplies to serve tea in the office. I could fetch it, actually." He looked at the swami with a questioning look. "Do you have some time free?"

But Swami looked at me. "Oh, we really came just to walk around the grounds," I said, and then I felt sorry for voicing that desire. There was not much else to talk about, since we wanted to roam the gardens and I did not really want tea or desire to ask questions about Transcendental Meditation. But he looked disappointed, as though he hoped I had come for TM. I might have become a member, or I might have been able to study here. I might even have become his student. One thing about joining something is that it creates happiness: it creates a kind of fellowship between the joiner and the joined.

"I see you have some printed matter here," I said. "Maybe I could take some of that along with me?"

He selected a few papers for me and explained that this was a significant time for the TM movement because at this very moment there was an important meeting in Great Britain at which Maharishi Mahesh Yogi himself was present, and the purpose of that meeting was to launch a great new world-wide campaign. The ambitious plan included a schedule for distributing initiators over the entire globe at a ratio of one for every so many of the population. According to this young Indian, it was all being worked out on a world map according to population densities so that first the required trainers could be trained and stationed and eventually the whole human race could be initiated.

Hearing that, I could have asked some questions about TM. I could have asked whether TM students were taught that this was the only way to self-realization. What did it mean to be an initiate? And were initiates eventually required to initiate others? How would all the noninitiates in the world be reached? How were they to be convinced? Might they ever resort to the use of force? What is it that the TM movement is trying to spread? Or does one have to become a part of that spreading in order to know? I might have tried a more customary question, like "How did you happen to become interested in Transcendental Meditation?" But all I wanted to do was to walk around, not to ask questions. I would read the papers he gave me. There were thousands of TM practitioners in America whom I could question at some future date. We thanked him for welcoming us and allowing us to see the grounds, and we started out on the path around the garden.

The living, growing things were well maintained. There were healthy trees and flowers and a variety of plants in appealing arrangements; there were irrigation ditches, sprinklers, and fountains, and even ponds with fishes.

"You see? I told you you would be impressed," said the swami many times. He also said, "I hope you will buy this place," which I took to be a joke. But he repeated those words many times too, and eventually I realized he was serious. "He has given up to make this his headquarters, I am sure. His interests are abroad now, I'm sure he will sell. If they do spread around the world, they will prevail lastly in India, and then first in the larger cities. That is their contemporary plan. Originally they hoped to draw the people to them. Now they are going directly to the people. In any case, you should ask him. I'm sure he will sell."

"I don't have money to buy any place," I responded. "Hridaya, why don't you purchase it?" Hridaya reported he had been considering purchasing the entire Ganges.

"No, no," the swami laughed. "Actually I am trying to urge

you seriously. This is why I have been wanting you to see this place."

"But really it's impossible, you know. Besides, if this place were to be sold, it should be sold to an institute or ashram here—not to some foreigner."

We walked halfway around the perimeter of the grounds, cut through the middle of the garden on a path between the irrigation ditches, and now stood on the porch of the main house which was near the riverbank high above the water. It offered a magnificent view of Ganges because one could see a great length of the river and its opposite bank in a single perspective. This had no doubt been the sometime residence of Maharishi Mahesh Yogi. For all I knew, he could be coming back tomorrow.

"I did not mean that you should take it for yourself alone as your personal property. It would of course be an institute or ashram, as you think correct for it. But you could easily get the money in your country where there is an abundance of wealth. You could interest some Westerners of means, because there is great interest in this yoga and philosophy among your people. Otherwise I am afraid if this place should be abandoned entirely, it might become too late. This beautiful potential might be wasted."

"Do you think it could be wasted?" I asked. "This is a beautiful place. I don't think it could be wasted no matter how it is used. Maybe there need not be anything here."

"Suppose there would be some power plant or factory here?" Hridaya asked me. "What then?"

"You've got a point; but I doubt that could happen."

We headed back toward the gate. "My point is," Swami added, "that this should be taken as a chance. Indians go to the West and the Westerners are so eager to meet them. They gather in great crowds, we are told. So why not Westerners to India? Not for their personal journey, but to work with our people. Our people can learn from you as well. This friendship is so important. You know I am always thinking this thing. What a wonderful chance is this place here for a joining of East and West!"

When we were back on the road leading to Laxman Jhula and once again under the glare and heat of the direct sun, we did not speak again until we reached the shade of the mango trees. I guessed the temperature was over one hundred, even in the shade; but compared to being right under the sun, it felt cool inside the orchard. I began to hum some melody from Swami Sivanandapuri's repertoire of devotional songs, remembering the days many months ago when he used to sit around the Tourist Bungalow playing the harmonium.

"Oh, you are so much at home walking on these paths," Swami exclaimed. "You are just like one of us. How many times in previous lives you must have walked in just these places? I did not mention it, but several times during this day I felt as though the three of us had been together before. Perhaps we are repeating something?"

"Well it's an interesting idea," I said. "I've heard such things have happened. If I was around here a hundred years or so ago, it would be interesting if I could remember it."

"You can definitely remember if you want and if you try. But you have to completely forget your body and your outer nature, because you were not having this body and all these habits and tastes. The subconscious memory remains, and you can recall it if you want."

"You were just talking about the joining of East and West," I said. "How do you think such a thing is going to happen?"

"You see, the two of us are having the same interest exactly. Would it not be wonderful for many people to travel just as you are doing, and many of our people to travel over there? They should not try to be teachers or moneymakers or founders of large movements, but pure seekers. They should be seeking each other, seeking to share, seeking to make something whole out of the two parts. Do you think it can happen?"

"I think it is bound to happen," I answered. "I think it is inevitable. What I believe is that Easterners are being reborn in the West and Westerners are being reborn in the East. I've seen young people all over Asia who have nothing Eastern about them but their skins. And there are a lot of new Americans who can't possibly be Westerners. This can't be dismissed as the nonconformity of the younger generation or the influence of the media—it's only partly that. We can find people growing up in the same societies with completely opposite social orientations. And this is happening all over, East and West. Still, these opposite qualities always clash, always conflict, whether it's across the globe, across the country, or across the generation gap. But what has to happen is a blending of the two opposite qualities. It's exactly what you said—making something whole out of two parts. It can't help but happen."

"He has spoken this thing many times before," Hridaya reported.

"It is a happy thing to hear," the swami said. "A wonderful thing to hear."

We reached the Choti Walla Restaurant hungry and thirsty and at the appropriate time in our schedule. We could have a good, leisurely lunch, walk slowly up the hill, and reach Tat Walla Baba's cave some minutes before he came out for his afternoon session.

"Today you are having your camera," Hridaya said. "You should definitely take some snaps of the Choti Walla."

Swami laughed. "And you can show your friends that you have visited two highly respected wallas in these hills: Tat Walla and Choti Walla."

Hridaya and the swami offered some explanations, as we were having our lunch, about these "wallas" and the meaning of their names. Even the Choti Walla was a religious symbol. He was so called because of the "choti" of hair that protruded from the back of his head. There was a time when this hair style could be seen among certain Hindus, and the small, almost unnoticed pigtails of hair that many men wore nearly hidden against their heads was a remnant of this Hindu practice. I had thought the Choti Walla was just a young local boy who was willing to sit around the restaurant all day with his skin painted pink and take whatever salary it produced home to his poor parents. But his was a lifelong identity, I learned, which he had inherited from his father and which would be passed on to his first son. It had become sort of like a copyrighted trademark: this fat, young boy was the living Choti Walla, and no one could use him or his name but by his leave and for whatever compensation he demanded. I had thought "walla" meant vendor, seller of goods and services, because there was the banana walla, the tea walla, the rickshaw walla, and so on. But "walla," I was told, meant "one who" or "one of." The Choti Walla was not so-called because he was selling something but because he was "the man of the choti." What then, I wondered, was Tat Walla Baba—"the man of the tat"? Yes, indeed. Tat was burlap, or actually, the jute from which it was made. And since Tat Walla Baba was first seen in his youth wandering through the snowy forests wearing nothing but burlap, his only identity was "Tat Walla" or "Boy of Jute." Later he became Tat Walla Baba, the respected old man of jute. Now that he had his permanent dwelling farther south along the Ganges (as a result of the desires of his disciples), he had no need for burlap and spent his summers and winters in his loincloth.

"Don't forget to take some snaps of Choti Walla," Hridaya reminded me as we got up from the table; and Choti Walla, who managed somehow to maintain a constant but genuine smile, was most obliging. We went on our way, once again over the Laxman Jhula road, through the mango trees, and up Tat Walla Baba's mountain in the hottest part of the day.

"Ah, today is lady's day, it seems," remarked the swami, looking in through the door of Tat Walla Baba's lean-to. Hridaya and I took off our sandals and stepped into the welcome cool air. Baba was already on his bench with his English-speaking disciple beside him. Also present was the

old man who had served us water when we had come some
days before, and there were nearly a dozen visitors. Most of
the visitors were elderly ladies. Maybe they were traveling
on some sort of package-tour–pilgrimage, of which there had
been especially many during and after the Kumbh Mela.
These ladies appeared nearly overcome with exhaustion. They
gasped and sighed and called the names of the gods and
goddesses. Again and again they touched the baba's feet as
though expecting to get from him the strength they so desperately needed; and he only sat motionless with an indifferent
expression, staring out through his door into the sunlight.

"Now you are wanting to record Baba's voice, isn't it?" the
disciple asked. "This morning you told you have camera and
recorder." I supposed I did want to record if it were still possible. In the morning we three had been the only visitors, and
now I wondered if I should have done it then. But this
morning, I remembered, had been best the way it was. The
disciple and the baba had a brief conversation, and I was
informed that I was welcome to record.

"Will you take snaps now?"

"Anytime," I answered.

"Baba wants that you will take snaps just now, before
beginning."

Hridaya handed me the shoulder bag and I took out the
camera and opened its case. When Tat Walla Baba saw the
camera he immediately stood up, walked quickly out the
door, and unfastened his hair, letting it fall to the ground
around his feet. I took several shots and we went back inside.
The old ladies were walking restlessly about inside, fanning
their faces with their hands and saying, "Ram, Ram, Sita,
Ram!" and when he sat down they prostrated themselves
again, one after the other, touching first his feet and then
their foreheads. This baba projected the same attitude toward everything, the questions, the picture-taking, the touching of his feet: he neither enjoyed it nor minded it a bit.

"Please wait some minutes before you record," the disciple
said, "and let Baba have some talks with these people."

So Baba talked while his visitors listened. I had no way of knowing how much they understood—Swami had told me his manner of speaking took a great deal of getting used to— but at least they were calmed down, and they listened politely. His voice and his manner were quieting, and I did not doubt that he was having some therapeutic effect upon his visitors.

There was a brief silence, and then Tat Walla Baba looked at me and spoke in his own language. "All right," the disciple said, "why do you not record?" I also had been listening attentively, though I had not understood a word, and had neither prepared the recorder nor thought of what I wished to ask. I had purposely not rehearsed any questions; but I realized, as I plugged in the batteries, mike, and cassette, that I would now need to know what I wished to ask. Tat Walla Baba was watching me as I handled the machine. I supposed he had seen a number of cameras and recorders in his current circumstances, but I wondered what he thought about such things. That, I realized, was my first question. I would ask what he thought not only about these modern tools, but also about this particular use of them, about people coming from the West, and about the means now available to facilitate world-wide communication.

"Now you will first put your questions, right?"

"Right."

"And then he replies and you record it. Otherwise it is difficult for him to speak like a man who is preaching or giving lectures. He is not in practice to preach or give lectures. But if you have some questions on spiritual aspects, go on asking and he will go on replying. Any type of questions you want to ask, you just put him and he will reply."

So I asked my first question, speaking in English to the disciple, and I left my recorder running throughout the four steps of the process from the question to the answer. There was my question, the Hindi translation, Tat Walla Baba's response, and the translation back to English. The baba gave a long answer to my first question, and the disciple, who did his best to remember everything Baba had said, gave nearly as long a translation. But I learned later that my question had not been interpreted in the sense I had meant it. I had wanted to hear Tat Walla Baba's thoughts in the category of international communication, particularly East-West communication. I thought that with the question of the tools of communication I had an appropriate way to begin, because here I was in this quiet cave with a camera and a recorder. My intention, or at least my hope, was to arrive at the questions of brotherhood and world consciousness, especially since this baba had called Martin Luther King a saint and seemed himself to represent the quality of peace. But the interpreter had asked Tat Walla Baba to say what he thought of Westerners possessing so many material luxuries.

What Tat Walla Baba had replied, in the words of the interpreter, was that we Westerners do indeed have a life mingled with materialistic luxuries; but all such luxuries, including the camera and recorder that I had mentioned, are not permanent but perishable, and this fact leads those who are attached to material things always to desire more. "Today you are having this tape, but in the near future you will be desiring a better tape. And if you get a million dollars you will later be thinking that perhaps God may make you a multimillionaire."

I had heard that philosophy before and would no doubt be hearing it many times again, and I accepted the importance and truth of those words. But I did not accept them as an answer to my question, simply because I had asked a different question. I had not used the words luxury or material; but since the interpreter had used them in his answer I supposed he had used them in his translation of my question. In any case, I had not arranged my thoughts carefully and had not put the first question very well at all, and now I was feeling peculiar about the focus of the interview. The disciple-interpreter was doing his best and I liked him. I liked his manner and his way of speaking.

"I think so many points I am forgetting," he concluded,

after his long translation, "because it was too lengthy, but the main aspects of his speech are this: that you must not be blind after these luxuries—you must be open-minded. Know who you are and know yourself. That is the main point."

"It is not necessary for me to say so, but for my own feeling I would like to say that this is not my own tape recorder or camera. I have no tape recorder, I have no camera, I have no wrist watch, I have no automobile, I have no radio or record player, and I will probably never own any of these things nor have any desire for these things. However, I sometimes use things. I can drive an automobile and I can operate a tape recorder and I learned how to operate this borrowed camera just enough, I hope, to take these pictures—and I hope they come out because these things are useful. I'm using these things not out of desire for the things but out of—"

"I should say without any attachment."

Maybe, but I could not claim nonattachment. "I would like to separate my question from the question of attachment," I said. "I was wanting to know whether these or any objects can be useful as tools. That is, tools for some purpose—without regard to attachment or nonattachment. Does anything in the physical world, or the world itself, have any use? Can anything be useful for the purpose of humanity?"

We were never able, in ninety minutes of recording, to detach ourselves from the issue of the great wealth of Westerners and their great attachment to material luxuries. Either that was all the interpreter wanted to talk about, or that was all Tat Walla Baba wanted to talk about, or that is the only issue that there is.

"I see."

The disciple and the baba conferred for another many minutes, and the disciple translated again: "Baba says he cannot agree that you Westerners can live in all these luxuries and still realize nonattachment. I will give you an example: suppose you are living in electricity. You remember, in the United States there was one power failure—"

"In New York, yes."

"For twelve hours in New York. What was the condition?
So you may say that you are unattached, that it does not
capture your mind—but once it is out of order, your mind
will be out of order."

Though we had not begun to deal with the questions I had
really wanted to cover, we had at least approached them,
and I knew by the end of our discussion that we had approached them in the only way possible. If I had simply
asked Tat Walla Baba to talk about brotherhood and peace,
he would have spoken of that peace which exists eternally in
the spiritual realm. Once I achieved liberation, I would have
been told, I could get that eternal peace. I was interested in
peace on earth—the peace the angels sang about. It was not
that I dreamed of any worldly utopia or believed that the
ultimate spiritual condition of man was to be realized in the
condition of life on earth. But my immediate interest and
concern was the planet itself and the physical life that in-
habited it, from the point of view of the earth as a being and
from the point of view of the earth as the physical arena for
incarnate man's spiritual endeavors. The only time I had
seen Martin Luther King in person was once in 1960 when
I was temporarily back from Korea, and the words that were
still most vivid in my memory were man's need "to learn to
live in dialogue and not in monologue." Some years later, in
a booklet from a world-wide group called Meditation Group
for a New Age, I had read the words: "This is the age of
group endeavor." These were the kinds of thoughts that stuck
with me, and these were the things I had wanted to talk
about. So there still were the questions of doing things and
using things. Perhaps my first question should have been
whether there was anything to be done on the physical plane
other than to try to leave it, and whether world problems
exist in any sense or are entirely illusions. I could not believe
that the only real problem was the problem of attachment.
If that problem was real, the other problems must be equally
real and equally in need of solution. The way to liberation,

it seemed to me, was through the clearing away of the problems on all levels.

I believed that I needed more than ninety minutes with Tat Walla Baba. I would have liked to have talked for ninety days. But this day's session was at its end. He would be leaving us and we would be going down the mountain. It was likely that I might never see him again, but if ever I could spend ninety days with Tat Walla Baba, I supposed I would prefer not to talk at all. I had climbed up this mountain partly to hear his words, his thoughts, and his viewpoint; but what I had liked in him, what I would remember about him, was his pure stillness. It was not even the man—the unusual voice, eyes, hair—it was the peace about him that had been good for me. This time, before we left, I touched his feet.

"That was nice," Hridaya remarked, on the way down the mountain. "Baba did so much talking for your recording. But actually I could not entirely understand his speech."

"I could follow," Swami Sivanandapuri said, "because I am accustomed to hearing him. Are you satisfied? I think it was not going exactly according to your idea."

I explained how I had felt that the answers I got were only indirectly related to the questions I had intended to ask.

"No, no, no, I know," said the swami. "Because we have talked about these things and I know your mind. I am sorry I could not do the translations. I was wanting to say something even as we sat there, but the man is his steady disciple, you see, and he was there functioning as the interpreter. With the proper translation you could have put your questions to Baba. On the other hand, if I had interfered he might have felt—"

"No, of course I understand," I said. "I had sensed that the difficulty was partly in the translation process. Did Baba give all those examples about Westerners and materialism, like about the power failure in New York?"

"No, no. Baba has not mentioned those things. That fellow created his own examples. He made his own points in the translation, and he made his own *sense* of the questions. It was all influenced by his own viewpoints."

"Well, I suppose renunciation and the giving up of worldly things must be one of Tat Walla Baba's pet subjects—and I can relate to that issue. But I had wanted to consider something more than that."

"Baba could have understood your interest," Swami said, "and he is willing to discuss anything. Renunciation is the natural way with Baba because it has been an automatic thing for him. I think that other fellow might be preoccupied with that question entirely. Perhaps he has come from some modern city and struggles to withdraw from the outside world."

"I think this is the case with nearly all these swamis and sadhus," Hridaya declared. "Not you, Swami, but most of these others. Doug and I have discussed this thing. They are thinking only of themselves and their liberation and nothing else. And if you ask them they say, 'We don't care. Do not care. Do not care for these things!' Therefore they themselves have not considered deeply, because they don't care. They have escaped the question. Suppose all the people of the world decide to try for instant liberation and they drop everything? What then?"

"Ah, you have made a good point," Swami replied.

"Right," I said. "The real point is that if all of humanity could achieve liberation in this manner, all the worldly issues would cease to exist—maybe even the earth itself. But since that's not the case, the question of meaningful human endeavor is important."

"Ha! See whom we have met on the road," Swami exclaimed as we reached the bottom of the hill. Someone was walking in our direction, but I did not recognize him. "Choti Walla! Come, come, we want to talk to you!"

The Choti Walla was on his way home; he looked like a schoolboy on his way home from a class play. It looked as though he had scrubbed his skin until it was painfully raw, and his matted, oily hair hung down the back of his neck. He was wearing jeans and a short-sleeve shirt.

"Why have you left your duty?" the swami went on. "We are just now on our way. We were prepared to put some questions. Now your public sitting is over, but we are in need of advice."

The boy looked at the swami with puzzled eyes, but his habitual smile remained on his face. Swami seemed to be making fun of the boy and Tat Walla Baba at the same time. Fortunately, I thought, the boy would not understand his English and would merely think the swami was greeting him enthusiastically.

"This man is in search of answers," the swami said, pointing to me. "And he has come a long way. Please give your reply to his question of questions. What is the means for living in the world? By what means can we serve the purpose of human affairs?" He stepped aside and gestured dramatically toward me.

For a moment the boy and I only smiled at each other. Then he said in a loud, cheerful voice, "Advertising!"

"Ah-ha!" The swami laughed. "There is some meaning in it!" The boy gave us an informal wave and went on his way, and Swami Sivanandapuri was delighted with himself. "Now we feel satisfied and light-hearted! And we shall go to the Choti Walla for a cold lemon squash, isn't it?"

nineteen

The day after our visit to Tat Walla Baba and the Maharishi Mahesh Yogi Ashram, we returned to our afternoon siesta schedule and stayed inside under the fan during the heat of the day. Just before sunset, Swami Sivanandapuri came around to our room and reported that it was now cool enough to be outside. "In fact," he said, "I believe it is actually cooler out than in. And the air is somewhat pleasant. Why do you not bring out your chairs and sit?" The swami's room had no furniture except for his bed, but we had three comfortable rattan chairs and our room faced the gravel yard at the rear of the Bungalow. It was pleasant outside. There was even a gentle breeze that swayed the trees along the fence.

We had not been sitting long before Swami Kaivalyananda appeared from around the corner of the building. "Ah, here you are, my friends! Good evening! I had been sitting in the office, you did not know. But I have been informed about your afternoon resting, so I did not want to disturb you. I am accustomed to this heat, you see. For me it is all right." Hridaya stood up to give him his chair. "No, no, it is all right. Where will you sit? I don't make people get up—I'm not like that, you see." But Hridaya excused himself, explaining that he had business with the receptionist. He and the receptionist had become good friends. They had the same family name, and Hridaya had supposed the receptionist was of the same caste, though he had not wanted to ask. I knew Hridaya would rather sit in the office and chat with him than listen to the philosophy of the swamis.

We had arranged to have supper as late as possible to give

us a chance to get cool enough to get hungry, so I was left with two swamis to talk to and about two hours' time for talking. There was one thing I particularly wanted to talk about—I had been thinking about it since we were running up the hill soaking wet the night before.

It had rained suddenly and furiously last night, catching Swami Sivanandapuri, Hridaya, and me before we could reach the Tourist Bungalow, thoroughly soaking the three of us. We had been late getting back across the river because we had lingered too long over lemon squashes, missed the last boat, and spent a long while finding a boat driver who could be pursuaded to make a special trip for a handful of rupees. If we had not been late we would have been safely in our rooms when the rain turned on. As it was, we had been forced to run for shelter to a little roadside shack and squeeze in with a half-dozen others. Everyone had seemed uncommonly surprised (except Swami Sivanandapuri, who kept saying, "This is good, I might have known it!"), and one young man even held his hands together and moved his lips in prayer. To me it had been more thrilling than surprising. The sudden sound and smell of rain was exciting, and I knew it was a timely and purposeful thing. All day, as we had walked in the hills across the river or sat in silence in Tat Walla Baba's cave, the steady fires that we had seen by night had been burning down the mountainside—invisible in the hot sun, but coming dangerously close. I knew that Tat Walla Baba had *intended* this rain, even as we had sat in his calm presence. Otherwise common sense would have sent him and his followers scurrying down the stony path with at least their lives and a few sacred objects. Last night I had asked Hridaya about it as we were getting out of our wet clothes back at the Bungalow—about whether he thought Tat Walla Baba had himself caused the rain. Hridaya had guessed it was not Tat Walla Baba alone who had done it but he and his colleagues together. Hridaya had called it a "cooperative group effort."

Today as we sat in the gravel yard behind the Bungalow,

the sky was hot and clear as always. The rivers were full, the ground was wet under the surface, and no fires burned on the mountain.

"What brought that rain last night?" I asked.

"It was the weather," Swami Kaivalyananda replied, sounding as though the answer were self-evident. "By the forces of nature it rained, that's all. And it was a fortunate thing."

"Indeed, it was a wonderful thing," Swami Sivanandapuri added.

"I had thought maybe it was intentionally brought about. It seemed to be, because of the timing and the way it had been discussed and everything." I had been thinking for some time that such things were possible. Almost everyone well-acquainted with traditional American Indians has reported witnessing purposeful rainmaking. Shintoists in Korea believed in such a possibility and so did Swami Rama. And I had seen the medicine man named Rolling Thunder appear to influence the weather in so many instances that it would have been irrational for me to deny the possibility. "It seems to me that things like that are really possible," I said.

"Possible!" exclaimed Swami Kaivalyananda. "Of course possible! It is the only way things happen. Everything is intentionally brought about. You are already knowing this. Only a fool thinks things occur by chance."

"Right!" inserted the other swami in a cheerful voice.

"Nature does not move by chance," Swami Kaivalyananda continued. "Nature does not move in some haphazard manner. What would be the purpose in it? And there must be a force behind it. It cannot move on its own. Material things are blind qualities. Physical matter and energy and all the elements are only potentials, blind potentials. They cannot possibly be self-actuating forces. What is the power that controls all the processes of nature? There is a power, maybe unseen, that is behind every moment, every occurrence. There must be a mover of mind, energy, and matter. There must be an intelligent principle. Without a purposeful evocation, no eventuality can be born. Nothing happens by some chance movement of blind matter and blind energy. These outward movements that we see, these natural occurrences, are only outpourings of that intelligent will. No phenomenon can proceed from an unintelligent principle. It is the intelligent movement of a power inherent in the Absolute which brings out these phenomena."

"Very good," agreed Swami Sivanandapuri, leaning back in his chair and looking at the sky. "Very good."

Those words stimulated me. I marveled at the way Swami Kaivalyananda had put them together, and I marveled at the meaning behind them. I had heard the same meaning communicated by Rolling Thunder, Swami Rama, and others, and I was looking forward to hearing the same meaning many times again from many people—from many locations and cultures. These words were the key words. They were the truth in a nutshell about the nature of the universe.

I recalled something Swami Rama had said nearly four years earlier in Topeka, Kansas. He had talked up the idea of a journey to India from the time of his arrival, and once he spoke enticingly about the prospect of seeing the great sages who live in isolation in the heights of the Himalayas. "If you should ever enter the cave of one of those great saints," he had said, "you can put the question 'Why do you sit here in isolation? Why do you not come out into the world, you who are having such knowledge and power, and do some useful thing where there may be need?'" Swami Rama had then paused and smiled at me, knowing I would consider that a most interesting and important question; and then he had leaned close to my face and almost shouted the words, "The rivers would not go on flowing nor the moon go on circling but for those great ones whose powerful will on earth carries out the plans of the Masters of the universe! You have never imagined! All the functions of the worlds are delegated and carried out in a practical manner!"

But there were questions that remained, and though I had not dwelled upon them constantly, they still remained four years later. There was the endless question of suffering. What about natural disasters, plagues, starvation, and war? If all conditions and occurrences come forth from or are carried out by some purposeful, intelligent will—whether it be God, the Spiritual Hierarchy, the Lord, the Government of the World, or the saintly delegates in their Himalayan caves—why the suffering? Why all the tragedies and obstacles? Out of what higher force was human misery created, and why was it even allowed? I thought of questioning my two swamis who now sat quietly looking at the sky, but I could not ask these things now. These questions were too much to throw out just like that—too much to properly consider on a casual evening sitting in our chairs. I realized this because I already knew some part of the answers, and even what I knew was a big job to verbalize.

The answers to these questions involved the whole story of evolution, of the seemingly painful struggle for awakening. There was the matter of the law of karma, the law of opposing forces. There was the matter of *maya*, or illusion, and of the battle against ignorance. There was the proposition that our tragedies and ill fortunes appear quite differently to the saints and sages. And there was the complicated concept of the manifesting power of the image-making faculty, the idea that all the turmoil and commotion of our earthly lives is simply our viewing of our own descriptions. That would be a great deal to have to cover in the yard here before supper. But there was no need to entirely avoid these issues. Perhaps I could go on asking about the weather and lightly touch on some small aspect of these big questions. "Why didn't it rain before?" I asked. "If all these occurrences are brought about by purposeful intelligence, as you called it, why couldn't it have rained days or weeks ago, before it got dry enough for fires to start?"

"Ah, you have a good point," Swami Sivanandapuri admitted.

"But you have answered it yourself," said Swami Kaivalyananda. "You yourself have called it timing. Suppose it had rained and the forest had not become dry. Where would be the need? But you have seen how things developed. So the need appeared and it was answered. Power is applied properly by virtue of the need."

"I think I get it," I said. "At least a little bit. I know an American Indian medicine man in Nevada and I've seen him make rain—or at lease I believe I have. He's told me many times that there's a right time and place for everything. He says the right time includes having a reason for everything. The need must be there. And my understanding from him is that this is the key to power—a sense of the reason, an awareness of fulfilling a need. But still it seems to me that the need for rain existed as soon as the air was dry, or at least when the trees began to dry out."

"The need existed when the condition resulted in the consequences. If it had rained earlier, there would have been no need for rain last night. Soon you will eat because you are hungry. Suppose you have already eaten? Then there is no need to eat. How else can it be explained? Those who speak about the right time and the right place, they are conscious of this timing. They are conscious of the need for the need. You are speaking of the precluding of the need and we are speaking of the appearance of the need."

"That's right," I said. "Now I've got it completely. At least if I don't think about it too hard."

"No, no. I know what you're thinking. You are thinking of prevention, preventing tragedy. Otherwise, you think, it is too late. These medicine men and yogis do not control the order of all these forces and counterforces. Why? Because, as you have quoted, there are a proper time and a reason for everything. Here, you see, there is not perfection. Perfection exists in the highest reality. There there is a single unified will, one movement in one direction. But here there are all directions, and in all directions move the forces and counterforces."

"Ahhh!" commented Swami Sivanandapuri, crossing his legs.

Swami Kaivalyananda continued: "Those who use power properly are always attentive to proper time and place. They do not dictate decisions, but they participate in them. They do not arrange the order of things, but they participate in that order, they play a part in the arrangement. Yet many people think themselves helpless because they see that everything is arranged, they see that everything develops according to a certain order. They do not realize their participation. Here, you see, is the confusion. So many people consider themselves helpless because everything is arranged, and they passively follow that. Others, on the other hand, are passive because they are believing things happen by chance, so they are the helpless victims of chance. It is an absurd thing, you see? And there are those who develop some powers without the proper understanding and misuse them. So this proper understanding becomes an important thing. One must understand that intelligent principle and work with that. One must work in harmony with that.

"And there is another way—another level of power, another level of participation. That is what you call prayer. In my country, you see, in my province where I come from in the south, there is a ritual for this rainmaking. And it is a common, common thing. There is a well-known practice among the villagers, and it may still be used, according to the proper method. This is a complicated ritual and I will not tell it, all the steps. But I may say that it is a very complicated and exact thing involving twelve maidens, twelve virgins, you see, *gopis*. They are true devotees. And then there are twelve vessels of milk, and it goes on through all the details. It is an exact thing. And the purpose of ritual is that it is devotion. So here they can bring about the result, they can bring rain. This is for agriculture. There is no emergency, there is no fire, but here they have made their request. This is what you call invocation, what you call prayer. So there are such rituals.

"And there are rituals that are bad—very bad and very harmful. Those rituals that are carried out for greedy, selfish purposes will be harmful in themselves. The rituals themselves will be cruel and harmful. One example I will tell you, and this is a known thing, a well-known thing among certain people. There is a cruel ritual for the power of clairvoyance. There is a preparation which may be made by taking the eyes of numerous animals, certain animals, and it must be done in a certain manner. And the one who makes and uses this preparation has the definite and clear power of clairvoyance. But how cruel it is—without killing these animals, you extract the eyes, you see? Birds, snakes, monkeys, cats—"

"He is telling it!" blurted Swami Sivanadapuri, suddenly sitting up in his chair. "He is telling about—" and in a lower voice he pronounced the word in Hindi as though it were forbidden to say it.

"—and you make a preparation with these eyes, according to the proper method. It becomes a liquid, like a kind of oil, and this you can place upon a certain leaf."

Swami Sivanandapuri shook his head and looked uncomfortable.

"Yes, it is a cruel thing," continued Swami Kaivalyananda. And my point is only to show how such powers are achieved at such great cost. It is unspeakable cruelty. And the perpetrator of such cruelty brings all the consequences upon himself. He experiences unbelievable madness and unbelievable anguish. So the rituals which are carried out for an improper end are in themselves harmful.

"At the same time, rituals that are harmful or dangerous should be seen to serve an improper end. So many means by which people attain psychic powers and experiences are dangerous. They may have unwanted side effects, and they may be harmful to the body. This is not simply that there are some disadvantages in the methods. It is that such methods serve an unfit purpose, a misuse of human endeavor. There is no way, absolutely no way, to achieve clairvoyance or any of these psychic powers that is not wrong and harmful unless they come automatically. There is no good way or safe way except through spiritual development and spiritual awakening to the point where these psychic perceptions are naturally included as a part of the total awareness."

As often happened after such discussions, we fell into a long silence. Swami Sivanandapuri settled comfortably again, and Swami Kaivalyananda lit a bidi which he found in his robes. I leaned back in my chair with my arms behind my head and looked into the sky and thought over all the things that Swami Kaivalyananda had said. The sky was growing darker now, and stars were beginning to appear. The swamis and I were sitting silently when Hridaya came back from the office. Uma was with him. We had not seen Uma for some days because he had been sent out of town on some errand for the Mahant.

"Are you deep in meditation?" questioned Uma in a playful voice, "Or are you weak from hunger that you cannot . . ." He interrupted himself to perform the proper greeting: "*Namaskara*, Swami, *Namaskara*, Swami, excuse me. Why do you not take meals? Food is waiting."

Swami Kaivalyananda stood up. "Oh, I am keeping you from your supper."

"Please join us, Swami," Hridaya offered. "Let us all join together."

"Thank you, but I must return. My meal is also arranged, and I myself am late. Tomorrow I shall come again. In the late afternoon as usual."

"I would still like to talk to you about gurus as we began to discuss the other day," I said, "and also about something else you nearly mentioned today—drugs. Gurus and drugs."

"All right. I take my leave then. *Namaskara*."

"I will answer you anything you want," Uma said, still feeling playful as we walked toward the dining room. "Just put your questions, any questions. You will be amazed such answers you will get!"

"All right." Swami Sivanandapuri laughed. "Be prepared. You will be amazed such questions you will get!"

Uma had already eaten, and he took only a small bowl of curd so that he could keep us company at the table. When he had finished his curd he sat quietly for a few minutes watching us eat, and then he began to sing. Uma was a Rishikesh person. He knew almost all local swamis and they knew him. They knew he had lived for years at Swami Rama's ashram and they knew he worked for Mahantji Sharma. And some of them knew he was an accomplished singer of devotional songs. He had learned entire epics such as the *Ramayana* and the *Mahabharata*, and he sang the songs from memory, one after the other, in a clear and beautiful voice. Now as he sang at our table, Swami Sivanandapuri was so moved he could hardly finish his meal. Hridaya, who had studied the tabla, used his fingertips and the heels of his hands to approach the tabla's sound on the top of our dinner table. The swami closed his eyes and swayed back and forth in his chair, and every time Uma stopped singing, the swami urged him to continue. "Oh, this is wonderful!" he would say. "I am in—what you call—seventh heaven!" We had sat for over an hour in the dining room listening to Uma's songs when the boys who served our food suggested we might carry on as well outside and let them close up.

Swami Sivanandapuri said good night as we stepped out of the dining room. "I want to hear more," he said, "but next chance. Now I will get my sleep and awaken early. Oh, and let me tell you one thing. I must thank you for all the hospitality for me here. I cannot express my appreciation. I think I shall be shifting in a day or two, so I just wanted to thank you in this opportunity."

"Where will you go? Do you have a place?"

"Oh, I can easily return to the same place on the other side. It will be quieter there now and I feel up to it. These days have been good for me, and I feel well recuperated now."

"Anyway, I'll see you before you leave here."

"Before I shift, after I shift, and many years hence, we shall be meeting again."

The following afternoon we took a tonga into town and that evening we had supper at the Neelam Restaurant. The receptionist from the Tourist Bungalow was sitting at one of the tables, about halfway through his evening meal, when we arrived at the Neelam. "Well, Swami Sivanandapuri moved out of his room at the Bungalow while you were gone," he informed us. "And he left a message for you that you should visit him when you can. Do you know the place?"

"Approximately," I answered. "He has a room in the institute over there. Do you know his room?"

"I know only as much as you," the receptionist said. "But tomorrow I may cross over with you, if you like, and I will help you locate him."

When we had finished our supper and were leaving the restaurant, I suggested to the others that we take a tonga back to the Tourist Bungalow. But as I expected, we walked in spite of my suggestion. So I walked as fast as possible, in order to be done with it as soon as possible, and the others had a difficult time keeping up with me. I really enjoyed walking, and everybody knew it. But the unspoken truth was that I did not like the road from Rishikesh to Muni Ki Reti because it seemed to me that it was unnecessarily unpleasant. Taxis, trucks, tongas, buses, horses, starving dogs and cows and people, both coming and going, used the same narrow road, and the road was covered with dust, grease, soot, litter, waste, and bad smells. Riding in a tonga, one could ignore the whole scene because the buggies were high off the road on their large wheels and moved fast enough to create a slight breeze. Riding in a tonga, one could close one's eyes or look at the sky. But whenever I walked along this road I could not help thinking about it—not so much that it was unpleasant as that it was unnecessary. This street was trying to tell people something. The filth and bad smells were miserable for everyone whether they were resigned to the situation or not, and the miserable condition prevailed because the majority of the local population was too holy to do anything about it. It was not the filth I was thinking about, it was the question of renunciation. Was this renunciation business simply an escape? Was it simply an avoiding of physical effort and all worldly endeavor? This place was dusty and dingy, and in the smoke and fumes it seemed like some low-level astral existence. Was there no one who wanted to clean, if not beautify, this place? Or would that be impossible, owing to the fact that this was all *maya*?

Every time we went from Rishikesh to Muni Ki Reti we passed the sadhu's mess hall where renunciates flocked by the hundreds to be fed. It was obvious they had not transcended worldly things entirely. Most of the movement along this road was to satisfy the needs of the belly. If all this world was *maya* to these people, why did they spend so many of their waking hours walking to the mess hall and back and waiting in line for food? Why did they ask tourists for money as they went to and fro along the road? Why did they cough and choke in the dust and smoke and cup their hands over their noses and mouths?

Maybe, I thought, these conditions are purposedly allowed in order to promote the practice of withdrawal. Whether it was intentional or not, this was the way it was working out. It was as though people were saying, "Let us ignore the conditions in which our bodies live so that we can attend to that far-off place in which our souls live." Was this supposed to be the process of nonattachment? It appeared to me that by virtue of necessity, these people were extremely preoccupied with the things of the world—the satisfying of hunger, the safety of their bodies as they moved along the street, even the importance of where they put their feet. Could it be possible that they were hardly conscious in this earthly realm, that as they walked they maintained an awareness of a higher bliss? I could not believe it. I believed these people were as much distracted by their physical environment as any people I had ever seen. I believed that the physical environment was part of the spiritual realm, not somehow apart from it. I believed that where incarnate beings had their bodies was where they happened to have their souls—not that the body was the soul, but that all of the body was within the soul.

Swami Rama had often talked about *maya* in Topeka, Kansas. Once he related an anecdote about a time his teacher gave him a demonstration on the meaning of *maya* in the Himalayan forest, and then he quoted his teacher as saying, "You think that this is *maya*? This is not *maya*! All this is God! To think that it is not God is *maya*!"

Anyway, I thought as we turned off the main road up the hill toward the Bungalow, if this is God, it's God even as it is. Still, we can do with our streets what we wish and what is best for us. To work on the street is just as spiritual as not to work on the street.

When the receptionist at the Tourist Bungalow got off work the next day he went with Hridaya and me to the swami institute, as he had promised, to help us locate Swami Sivanandapuri. He was certain that we could find his room, though we would likely have to ask many swamis. But the receptionist did ask many swamis—he even asked in the office of the institute—and he always got the same response. That "Sivanandapuri character" had no room anywhere, we were haughtily advised, he was just hanging around here and there operating his guide business. He certainly had no connection with this institute, one fat, bald swami insisted, and he certainly never lived here. I wanted to walk around for a while in case we might run into him "by chance" again, but at last we gave up.

At suppertime we met the Canadian ladies in the dining room. They reported that they had spent the whole day with our friend, Swami Sivanandapuri, and we reported that we had spent the whole day looking for him.

"That's why you didn't find him," they said. "Because he was with us all the time."

"That may be why we did not meet him," Hridaya said, "but we thought he was put up at that institute across the river. He told us that he was put up over there and that he could shift back to the same room. But all the swamis say he has never lived there."

The Canadian women were not surprised. "He has a room there. He really does. But nobody likes to tell where anybody is. We've had that happen all over. Whenever you ask one swami about another swami, you get some kind of a runaround.

"But he does have a room, it's right by the main hall. Anybody over there who knows him should know where his room is. They just didn't want to tell you. They don't like him."

"This is the case!" Hridaya exclaimed. "This is the explanation. They are all knowing and yet they are not telling because they don't like that swami. They are critical of his popularity." Hridaya liked Swami Sivanandapuri best among all the swamis because Swami Sivanandapuri was always so pleasant and agreeable. "But he is the only one who is not critical of the others," Hridaya continued, pointing his finger at me, "and you should definitely tell that point if you write about these swamis. You want to quote and tell about these swamis, is it not? So you should not exclude anything. Frankly, you should tell it how they criticize each other and put themselves first above all others. They may be knowing something which they studied and learned from their teachers, but for this they sacrificed their humanity. There is no cooperation among them. They will tell you they have developed these good qualities on a higher level which may not be apparent to us, but they will say it about themselves only and go on criticizing the others!"

Actually, Hridaya was nearly right. Some of the holy men we had talked to had been critical of some of the others, at least in comparison to themselves. And for some years now I had been hearing swamis and yogis say about one another that so-and-so really didn't know very much. This spiritual quest, if that's what it was, did seem to lead to a sense of competitiveness, to a sense of a race—a race against time or a race against someone or something, certainly to a sense of separateness and even isolation.

Swami Kaivalyananda and I arranged to spend an entire day together at the Tourist Bungalow. I knew it would be my last opportunity to talk with him because we planned to meet Swami Premvarni Balyogi, a friend of Uma's who had a small ashram near Laxman Jhula, and then to leave a day or two open for accounting and packing before departing for Kanpur. So when I got up and went to brush my teeth, I saw him walking about impatiently in the yard outside our door.

"Ah, there you are!" he said. "Why do you not hurry? You are wasting the finest part of the day. You have not had your breakfast, isn't it? I shall go to the kitchen and tell them to make haste with it."

After breakfast we sat outside while there were still some moments of relatively comfortable air, and Swami Kaivalyananda wasted no time or words getting from the trivial to the essential—from the unreal to the real. He made a few simple observations about the season, the sky, and the sun, and without waiting for me to comment, he began to talk about the birds, the trees, the rocks under our chairs and the spiritual meaning behind all this life and existence.

"For what is all this evolution?" he asked, not expecting a response. "What is the purpose in it? If there is no purpose in it, then all this is meaningless. If there is no spiritual design behind the movement of evolution, then evolution is meaningless. And what evolves? That which is nonpermanent only can evolve. The physical body, the mind, the sense —these are nonpermanent things." He reached over the side of his chair to pick up a stone from the ground. "In the minerals there is consciousness," he said. "There is life. This stone is moving toward senses. It is trying to get sense of life. The root thing is there, it is vibrant with energy, and it is trying to get life. Then from life it wants to get sensations.

Bacteria have got sensations. The bacteria have got a sense of touch. Trees and grass have got a sense of touch. They have got certain sensations—so, life and sensations. Then from there to conscious mind. Here comes the conscious level of animals. And then comes self-consciousness. You see? But even in the mineral condition, the absolute truth is the same. In the grass, trees, birds, and animals the absolute truth is the same. Because if there is not the absolute truth in all this life, what is the ground for it? What is the source of all this life?"

So we talked about evolution and nonevolution, about the movement of the nonpermanent toward the permanent, about the awakening of nonawareness into the nothing-but-awareness. And when the sun got hot, we moved our chairs inside.

"What is this word 'guru'?" I asked. "What is the meaning and the function of the guru?"

He began with the words I had hoped to hear. He said, "Guru is the self within." I had heard those words from Swami Rama and even before Swami Rama. That was the concept of guru that I had developed before the word became a part of Western vocabulary. I hoped that the original meaning of the word—the ancient meaning, the meaning that was intended when the word was first formed—was the meaning that still prevailed in India in spite of the efforts of so many businessgurus from India to misuse it in the West. Such public personalities as Americans liked to refer to as gurus were as far from gurus as it was possible to get, I was sure, according to the original definition of the word. It was my feeling that such public personalities were harmful individuals, not only because of their financial exploitations but also because they have contributed to the obscuring of the true meaning of guru and the true meaning of self-realization. When people in India, especially young people, asked me if I knew why Krishna Murti and others in the West had "spoken disapprovingly of the guru-chela relationship," as they put it, I had supposed I could guess the reason. The word guru seems to have been destroyed in the West. But I hoped that the word could be used and understood in my country. The interest in Eastern philosophy was more than a passing fancy, I was sure, and I knew that in order to understand the concepts, people would have to understand the real meanings of the terms.

Swami Kaivalyananda continued: "Guru and discipleship, this is very ancient. Guru is the personification of truth for the disciple and therefore one who can confer realization of this truth upon a fitting disciple. A fitting disciple is one who has achieved the proper discipline and who has that particular relationship to this guru. Only a rare person can be called guru, and only by his personal disciples, only by those few particular individuals with whom he has that intimate traditional relationship. No one is a guru for people in general. Even a true guru cannot be a guru for others who are not his intimate disciples. But in the true sense, beyond appearances, guru is yourself. Guru is your higher self appearing to be manifested in a different body." Swami Kaivalyananda pointed his finger at me and said very slowly, "*He is you.*"

He leaned back in his chair and folded his hands in his lap, and in the pause that followed I thought of a further question. I wanted to ask about those few popular figures from India who are called guru or sat-guru by thousands of Americans. The moment I took a breath to speak, he sat up and started talking as though he thought I might change the subject. He wanted me to have a clear and complete picture of the meaning of guru.

"Your guru knows you personally and intimately. He knows your mind, your intellect, your personality and your way of reasoning. Therefore he alone knows your confusions and how to dispel them. The guru knows the disciple more closely than mother knows child, husband knows wife, brother knows sister, and the relationship is a closer one, even in the worldly sense. This is why there cannot exist any public guru. There cannot be any guru who is available to whomever comes. There cannot be any guru who is sought and found by a disciple, however great the guru or however strong the disciple's desire. The guru always contacts the disciple. Otherwise he cannot be called guru. The guru is the one who goes to the disciple, because the disciple, you see, is blind. Though the guru knows the disciple, the disciple does not know who the guru is. But they do not choose one another. This is a prearranged thing. The guru knows this because he is established in the truth. He is the one in whom the disciple will see himself, and he has no other motives— no motives to teach, no motives to have disciples. He has crossed this formidable ocean of *samsara*. He can lead the disciple across because he himself has accomplished it. He leads the disciple as that part of his own being which has yet to cross. Because guru and disciple are one." Again he leaned back in his chair.

"We have this situation in the United States," I said, "where some people, particularly a few people from India, are claiming to be gurus for just anybody and everybody. Once before you talked about people posing as gurus in the West—"

"You see," he interrupted, "this is not the meaning of guru. These people cannot be gurus. There are no public gurus and there are no gurus who have such motives and methods as they have. If they call themselves gurus, they are pseudo-gurus. There were a few spiritual teachers who became known in your country and even honestly encouraged the collection of money to establish ashrams. There was Swami Vivekananda. There may be some genuine spiritual teachers in your country today—some who are not well known—but there are no public gurus. Actually speaking, the guru-disciple relationship is not an institutional thing. None of these institutions and organizations consist of gurus and disciples."

"But these people in the West are not only calling themselves gurus, they are also saying, 'I am the *only* guru. I am *the* guru, there is no other guru. Everybody should come to me.' "

Swami Kaivalyananda laughed and shook his head. "This cannot be. No guru can say, 'Come to me.' No guru can say, 'I am the guru.' The guru-disciple relationship is very rare in this world. In the spiritual sense we all have our gurus, but the meeting of guru and disciple on the physical plane is very rare. And in that relationship the guru teaches not as a teacher but by experience and by example. His life itself is an example. It's an historical fact. Jesus Christ had his disciples, and just see how they lived together. They lived like brothers, they lived like intimate friends, they lived like family. And there was love—human love and spiritual love. But now these pseudo-gurus live in the top stories of their buildings, and if a so-called disciple goes, he has to wait there like a slave; there may be a queue, queuing up, you see, and you have to get an appointment to see him. He does not know you, he does not even know who you are. These people who are making public advertisements and attracting the masses, they can call themselves lecturers or public speakers or organizational founders and heads, but not gurus. Gurus and disciples associate directly, like close friends. The guru knows the disciple like he knows his own self."

"But here's the problem," I said. "I think there are some real aspirants in the West, real aspirants with burning desires. They have spiritual orientations and are very different from the generations before them. These people have a craving for gurus, for guides, and they are actively searching for them. Where are the gurus for these people?"

"Every man gets exactly the guru he deserves. Every man gets a guru according to his understanding. All the gods and all the prophets that we worship will not be able to give us liberation unless we turn ourselves to the task. Man himself is the maker of himself. He is the owner of himself, he is the redeemer of himself. It is up to him. Everyone who has discovered the truth is a prophet, is a savior. He can help another. The highest truth is conferred upon a wise person as an act of grace—it is true—but this does not mean that only one prophet is there. There are as many prophets as there are human beings, because every human being has in himself the son of God and also the son of man. Everybody is, essentially, the Christ, the Truth, if we accurately interpret the word 'Christ.' But we have to realize that Christ consciousness in us. We cannot say that one prophet is the savior of this world. We cannot say that only a certain particular person can lead all of us to the truth. Because realization is not a condition in time and space or in any particular sphere. So the phenomena of prophets is a continuous phenomena. Throughout history they come and will continue to come, in every clime and time. And who are these prophets? They are humans only. Man himself is the prophet. Westerners will have to first give up these pseudo-gurus. Then they will have to learn the meaning of guru. Once they understand what the guru is, they may have their gurus. Once you can be loyal to your real guru, your guru will invite you. Most of these Westerners are perhaps not seeking the highest spiritual truth. Most of these Westerners may be seeking merely experiences."

Again I marveled at the way he had put these abstract philosophic concepts into foreign words. From what I had learned about this swami, I believed he spent most of his time alone, studying and writing. Yet he always managed to sound as though he had spent his lifetime explaining things to Westerners like me. This day he also marveled at it: "At times I speak freely and flowingly, just like an unobstructed wind or a flowing river."

While I napped that afternoon, Hridaya went with Uma for a dip in the Ganges; and when I awoke, hot and wet with perspiration, I wished that I were in the river with them. There was no running water at this hour, as the pump was broken, but we had two buckets of water stored in the shower. I dumped half a bucket of water over myself and checked over my dollars and rupees account until Hridaya and Uma came back.

"Swami Kaivalyananda has not told you he is here?"

"No, is he?"

"He's sitting in the chair outside, right by the door there."

I put on my kurta and went out to join him. "Sorry, I didn't know you were here."

"This morning while we were talking my government set off an atomic explosion."

I did not know how to respond to those words. They were surprising and unexpected. I was not sure what they meant or whether I had heard them right.

"It is true. It has been reported in the news. Experimentally they have done it. It was a test, but they have demonstrated India's capacity to produce the atom bomb. They are saying this thing was not a bomb which they tested. Our government has made a statement that this capacity has been developed for domestic purpose only and not for military use. Anyway, all our people and all other people have been startled by this."

"It's a surprising thing," I said. "It's frightening in a way. Yet in another way it could be reassuring, especially to the people of India. I mean, other countries have nuclear power."

"Yes, it may be a good thing in a way. Those who have had this power exclusively may not like it, and those who cannot have it may not like it, but it may be a hopeful and encouraging thing to our people. Actually, it is neither good or bad, you see. It is the same thing we have been talking. All these potentials already exist and may be used as powers. Anything can be misused. All these things—money, electricity, atomic power, psychic power, mantras and tantras—are at the same time both good and dangerous. The dangers are always there, and any development along any plane may increase the dangers unless there is upward movement toward higher levels of consciousness. The only safety is in that highest discipline and highest awareness. Let us go inside until the sun is below the mountains."

Swami Kaivalyananda wanted to tell Hridaya and Uma the news about the nuclear explosion. They also were surprised, and they seemed not to know whether to think it was a good thing or a bad thing. I temporarily forgot my other questions for the swami as the four of us talked about the meaning and implications of what had happened. We got into a discussion about India, economics, and international affairs.

One of the boys from the kitchen brought in four cups, two pots of tea, and some hot milk on a tray and set it on the table between the swami and me. Though I could not understand their words, I knew that Hridaya and Uma were telling him the news in Hindi.

"Let us talk about what you wanted," the swami suggested to me. "You wanted to put some questions about drugs or something."

"That's all right," I replied, "we can talk about anything."

"All right, talk about anything."

"Well, what I had wanted to ask you was whether you thought there was any spiritual significance in the experiences produced by drugs. Is there any benefit to be gained from the use of drugs like psychedelics?"

Swami Kaivalyananda was always eager to answer my questions. He took a deep breath, and again he was flowing like an "unobstructed wind" as he had done this morning.

"Drugs have been used in ancient times also. It is not a modern phenomenon. They have got some value, but the value is psychic value. They can give some psychic powers and some psychic insights, so they do have some meaning. But we cannot use drugs for the revealing of spiritual truths. Here the method is discipline. And it is quite a different process altogether. All the phenomena produced by any drug whatsoever are related to the release of chemical energy. This release of energy produces activation of the subconscious, and the subconscious is brought out. We come in direct encounter with the subconscious mind's view of the cosmos. The name and form that we ordinarily perceive with our physical eyes is not a real view of the nature of the universe. With these drugs we can get another unreal perception of name and form. We get a view into the world of energy. This will not help us spiritually, and we should know that what we are seeing is not reality. But the value of the drugs is that we can realize that what we have been seeing is only a limited and very partial view. Drugs will help those people who believe that the sensory organs are the only instruments of experience and knowledge. At least we will know there are psychic perceptions also, not only the material world and the sense world. LSD could help the people of Russia. If LSD could somehow be used in Russia, people could come to see that the philosophy developed by Karl Marx is not truth, but was only something conceived of outward appearances, something based on the perceptions of his physical senses. And LSD could be useful to Americans who are attached to the worship of material attractions. These people could begin to see life with a different view. So drugs can open doors for those with very limited and narrow perceptions.

"But on the other hand, drugs are not helpful or interesting to those people who have got some understanding of the real values of the real world. For such people drugs are very unnecessary and mechanical methods. Such people can have the same experiences without the use of drugs and therefore without the harm of drugs. Those who repeatedly use drugs of any kind are not consistent in their thoughts; they become victims of their moods. They disturb the equilibrium of nature within them. And they have acquired double attachments. They are attached to the physical world and they are attached to the psychic world also. So there is no way to get peace through drugs, but only a temporary alternative insight. And there is no way to get freedom through drugs, although I think many in your country may be using drugs in trying to get freedom from boredom. You cannot get any spiritual experience by taking drugs. Spiritual experience is not an effect, it is already there. To experience spiritual reality we have to remove all these effects, all these phenomena and various types of perceptions. We cannot produce a spiritual experience by any kind of medicine or concentration or mantra. We can only produce certain kinds of effects—they may be very pleasant, very subtle, very happy—but they are all only effects."

"Several times you have used this word discipline. And in talking about drugs now, you have mentioned discipline again. What is meant by discipline?"

"Here discipline is not practice, such as doing asanas or pranayama, or following some habits. Discipline means first dispassion, then discrimination, and then self-control. Your attitude toward the world is this, that the body and the world are two realities, and you give value to the external things. You are born and brought up in this belief and attitude. And this attitude, which involves you in phenomena, must be given up. You must develop a definite dispassionate attitude toward the material things. There is no harm in living in the world and enjoying the world, but we should live like free men. We should enjoy things with independence and not live in the world like slaves. Our attachments in this world are not grounded upon reality. This we should know, and we should change our attitude toward this life and develop a dispassionate attitude. This is the first step of discipline. Then discrimination. You have to discriminate between the unreal and the real. Behind this changing world there is a changeless truth. With discrimination we know what to give value and what not to give value. We know what we have to leave behind in order to move toward something closer to the truth. True nonattachment is born of discrimination. Then comes self-control. Control of the mind and control of the senses. Through this, we get the power to achieve a certain calmness and quietness of the mind. We get the power of endurance, the power of confidence and courage, and the power to control desire. Once we have fully achieved this discipline we have acquired these powers. When an aspirant is fully attuned with these disciplines, and with this control of mind, he becomes a qualified disciple. Then a true teacher, a real guru, can return him to the higher realization very easily and within a moment. These disciplines are the qualifications. 'Empty thyself and I shall fill thee.' Discipline is a kind of emptying. The moment you have emptied yourself the real self is revealed in you—the master in you is able to come forward. I have given you this in a nutshell."

"I can feel in the things you say about drugs and discipline and everything you talk about that you believe people should continually rely upon their intellects."

"This is extremely important—reasoning. Let us take the tea before it cools completely."

Hridaya, who had been sitting quietly on the edge of the bed poured tea into four cups. The swami immediately lifted his cup and took a long, noisy sip.

"In my country," I went on, "people are now saying that the rational mind is not capable of any real valuable function but is only in the way. They are saying that the intellect is not capable of dealing with that which is above it, and therefore we would do well to disconnect or turn off this intellect. This is what many people are doing with drugs. They are trying to kick their rational minds out of the way."

"Rationalism is one of the criteria of Vedanta. Three criteria are there: authority, reason, and intuition. The point is not to be antireason but to know that reason has its limitations. The point is not to rely on reason exclusively. Reason is an essential instrument, and though intuition may be higher than reason, one need not abandon reason to make use of intuition. Simultaneously they must operate. One must maintain reason to the fullest possible extent. One must make the best possible utilization of the rational mind. The right use of reason is part of the discipline. Reason, used properly, is the sharp weapon. It is the saber that destroys all ignorance—it cuts through the entangling jungle of ignorance. When ignorance is destroyed, the weapon is also destroyed, because then, only then, there is no more need for that weapon. Suppose we cut a cucumber in half. The moment the cucumber is cut into two parts, the act of cutting also comes to an end. We should not remove or impair reason with drugs or any other means. In order to remove reason we should use it to remove ignorance. Reason leads us to the door of truth, and there we leave it on the step when we enter. In the dawn of spiritual illumination, reason automatically vanishes."

By now the sun had gone down behind the hills. Hridaya and Uma had noticed that it was cooler outside than in and suggested we carry the chairs back into the yard. The swami and Uma and I sat in the three chairs, and Hridaya sat on the doorstep and played his wooden flute. "He is just like Krishna," Uma said.

For a moment we listened to the playing of the flute, which blended with the many songs of the various birds. All of India was alive with birds. They sang in the trees, hopped across the ground, and darted through the sky in a rainbow of colors. There was such a variety of bird songs I knew I had heard songs whose singers I had never seen.

This evening as I watched and listened to the birds, I wondered at the strange and unnatural manner in which human beings lived upon this planet. It was not unreasonable to think that humans were coming dangerously close to destroying this planet and everything else that was trying to live here. In all the talk about gurus, mantras, meditation, *sadhana*, and *samadhi*, there was something that remained unspoken—something serious and important: man's spiritual responsibility to the earth, to the condition of the world.

"There's one question that seems important and timely to me," I said to the swami, "and that's the question of man's relation to the earth, the question of man's spiritual responsibility for the human condition." I paused for a moment to try to construct a carefully worded question.

But Swami Kaivalyananda had heard enough from me to

have something to say about it. "When we see disease, when
we see disaster, when we see pain, we suffer. What do we
get? We get pain. But everybody does not get that. Everybody is not compassionate. Some people are very cruel; some
people get pleasure with other people's pain. Nero put his
whole city into fire, and he enjoyed it. But there are people
who are good in their hearts, and when they see the suffering of others they also get suffering. In the Gita it is said:
'How can you give me devotion? By considering the suffering
of others as your own suffering, this is how you give the
highest devotion to me.' You see, this is the way of devotion
to God. People confound these things, you see. They take
Krishna as a deity made of stone. But Krishna is not a stone,
Krishna is the absolute truth. And how can you get the absolute truth? By taking the pleasures and pain of others as your
own pleasures and pain. 'Then,' Krishna says, 'you achieve
that universal consciousness and you get real love for me.
You love me because you love humanity, you love the cosmos.
You love me because I am all this.' "

"I guess that answers what I was going to ask you," I said.
"I have a really precise concept about every human being's
obligation to the earth. I believe this obligation should be
realized in all its aspects, in all the relationships with nature,
people, and nations that one can possibly have in this world.
My feeling is that any spiritual path any human can possibly
walk on runs right through the middle of the world and all
the worldly conditions—not just the path of karma yoga but
every path. When a person is physically manifest, it seems to
me, his spiritual endeavor takes place in the spiritual condition that happens to be manifest on the earth and that he
happens to be a part of. So I think every physical human's
most immediate *sadhana* is directly related to the condition
of the world—the social condition and the international
condition."

Again the response was immediate. "As long as we live in
this physical body, not merely in this material body, but in
the conditions of the material world, all the universe be-

comes an expression of the highest consciousness that we are. We speak about one world. But if one does not have world consciousness—one-world consciousness—how can one realize it? People say, 'One world, one world,' but they do not have that one-world consciousness. Though they may like to talk about one world, one world government, one world brotherhood, one world life, they have got so many disparities and diversities within them. They have got caste systems, they have got racial discrimination, they have got exploitation systems and international profiteering, they have got opportunism and favoritism, they have got nationalistic feelings. They don't realize their own consciousness, their own unity consciousness. But when we have the absolute realization, the real view and vision, all these disparities and diversities will go away from us. We then are seen to be universal beings. This truth, the attainment of this truth, is not a product of evolution. This is an already self-existent truth. We have only to discover it. We have only to uncover it. We have only to realize this one-world consciousness and we will live in that reality."

"Then it's true, isn't it, that so long as a part of our being is in the world a part of our spiritual endeavor is of and for the world?"

"Yes."

"Can we not say that our work in the world is to develop this one-world consciousness?"

"No. It is existing even as we talk here. It is not a thing to be developed. It is a thing to be discovered."

twenty

On the following day we had to cross the river in the mid-afternoon heat because Swami Premvarni Balyogi wanted to meet us at four o'clock. It was about an hour's trip across the river, along the road toward Laxman Jhula, and up the long path to the ashram, which came into view when we reached to the top of the hill. There were a few small and simple buildings, and across the top of the main building were the words: "Lead me from Darkness to Light, Lead me from the Unreal to the Real, Lead me from Death to Immortality." It seemed a quiet place. There were no people to be seen, no sounds to be heard as we walked through the garden toward the main door. A young Western man came out to greet us and ushered us inside. There were but three people at the ashram that day, not counting the three of us who had just come to visit. They were Swami Premvarni and his two disciples, a young man from England and a young lady from New Zealand.

"Swami Premvarni Balyogi is a friend of mine," Uma had told us some days ago. "I want you to meet him. His students and disciples are mostly Westerners, and he is always asking me to stay at that ashram. He knows that I am familiar with Westerners and their ways and that Westerners are attracted to this devotional singing that I am always doing." His name was Swami Premvarni and he was called Balyogi, Uma had explained, meaning that he had been a child yogi or one who had come into his present life already possessing the assets of a yogi.

We found the swami in his lotus posture, looking as

though he had been sitting in that manner—and in that place—as long as there had been an ashram here. He seemed to be a very young swami, and he seemed to look even younger than he was. He had thick, shoulder-length hair and a soft, youthful face with wide, round eyes. He sat on a thick mat against the wall of this long, narrow room and we sat on straw mats against the opposite wall, only a few feet in front of him. His legs, locked in a lotus, were completely hidden under his long robes and remained so motionless that I could almost wonder whether he had legs at all. He kept his hands folded loosely in his lap and seldom moved more than his lips, but he looked totally at ease. He had a benevolent manner and a gentle way of speaking, and his voice was so soft I had to actively listen in order to hear him.

"Will you try some mint tea?" Swami Premvarni asked.

The tea was served by the disciple from New Zealand.

After tea, I began with my questions. Swami Premvarni did not talk like Swami Kaivalyananda. This swami spoke hardly at all. His voice was so soft and his answers were so brief that I, who was asking the questions, felt as though I was the talkative one. This swami really had nothing to say, I realized as we talked, he was simply allowing himself to serve my need to ask questions of swamis. In any case, I assumed he had no objection to this interview because he and Uma had arranged it between themselves. He was just being the way he was.

I began by asking him the meaning of the word "swami."

"You can make it any way you want," he replied. "You can say the word means master. So you can use it for master. You can use it for one who is having that consciousness. You can use it for God, for the consciousness of the universe. You can make it 'so am I.' So am I one who is having that consciousness, that master within me. You put together *so*, s, o, and *am*, a, m, and *I*. It becomes 'soami.' And if you are a servant and serving a master, you may call him swami. Swami so-and-so."

Uma began suggesting the names of some of the swamis we knew.

"Oh, that is another word," he told Uma. "Here is a different meaning of swami. That swami means something separate. That swami means *sanyasi*. So we can make many words having the same sound."

I wanted to ask this swami some of the question I had asked Swami Kaivalyananda. The questions I had asked Swami Kaivalyananda yesterday—my last day with him—and the way he had responded to those questions had been specific and precise enough that I thought it would be useful to hear this swami's words on the same subject. I wasn't looking for discrepancies, I was hoping for agreement. Even if the answers were the same, a different approach to the wording of the answers would add to my understanding. And this swami was brief enough that it would be a quick and easy matter to cover most of the same ground. I asked him first about the meaning of guru.

"You call me swami," he said, "You cannot call me guru. Guru is a close and intimate one. There are different relationships. Speakers and seekers. Spiritual teachers and aspirants. Gurus and chelas. These are different relationships."

I told him about how the word "guru" had come into popular usage in the West, how Westerners were using the word for all kinds of individuals who were starting ashrams, founding systems, giving lessons, and gathering crowds.

Swami Premvarni dismissed the subject, saying simply, "It is a Sanskrit word, not in your dictionaries. Some people there have changed the meaning in their own interest. Now it is a different word having the same sound."

That was all that was said about the word "guru." He was equally brief on the subject of drugs, and he answered my question in not many more words than I had asked it. I had constructed a complicated question about advantages versus disadvantages and whether the use of mind-altering drugs might have different implications for different people.

"Drugs are never useful on the spiritual path. The spiritual path is the path of purification. Drugs are poison. The process is clear consciousness, and drugs pollute the consciousness. It is a difficult process to be less confused, and if you take drugs you will be more confused. But you may feel it as a new and interesting experience."

For my next question I decided I too would be brief. "What is the meaning of spiritual discipline?"

"Spiritual discipline is the ground—grounding. This is the very beginning. This grounding comes first, which is very important, because reality begins on the ground. On the ground you attain *samadhi*. Unless you are on the ground when you attain *samadhi*, you cannot use it properly. You can attain it. You can be a magician. You can attain any power, any psychic power or any psychic energy without being on the ground but it is of no good and too risky. And you may become only a destroyer."

"But in the West," I said, "at least in America, there is almost no distinction between psychic phenomena and spiritual attainment. Almost all the people, maybe ninety percent of the people, who talk about concentration, meditation, yoga, consciousness—or what they call altered states of consciousness—think of all this as the pursuit of psychic phenomena and psychic experience. I don't believe they make any distinction between psychic phenomena and spirituality."

"Astral trip," he said. "This is astral trip—in the West it is called astral trip. But for this astral trip nothing is needed. For it there is no necessity of any understanding or concentration. Purity is not necessary. This is a mechanical development, and easily you can achieve it, experience it. But without that purity you become only a destroyer—a devil. This is the original meaning of devil."

I tried to talk a little more about drugs from Swami Kaivalyananda's view that they might at least provide a first inspiration to otherwise materialistically oriented and narrow-minded people. But Swami Premvarni believed, as he had several times indicated, that all the astral trips and experiences and all the psychic powers with which "modern Western scientists" were so enamored were easily attained. Such phenomena as we Westerners were studying in our laboratories and discussing in conventions were simple mechanical developments that in his view were neither important nor impressive. I felt then that his views on drugs were based on his belief that they were not needed. But this was not the case. There are things that are not required that are at the same time not harmful. Drugs, he believed, were both needless and damaging. He seemed to be aware of a number of means, which he did not describe, by which one can easily achieve astral experiences and psychic powers, and he felt sure that in the United States this phenomena was about to become commonplace through the "science" of "brain mechanics" and "brain electricity."

"Then all these things are quite different from the spiritual trip? Is that what you are saying?"

"Absolutely not. Absolutely not a different trip. This is all the same trip. This is all on the way."

His main point, he said, was still the importance of the spiritual discipline in the beginning. The ground. Getting on the right track in the beginning. This means having a road, a supply of power, and a direct connection to the source. When one is riding on the train, on the tracks, as he put it, the trip becomes safe and controllable. You go at your intended pace. You go or you stop. You may get off in certain places, or you may simply "look out the window as you go by." Or you may choose not to look. If you are a scientist by nature you may get off on the astral level, because here is the source of the creation that the scientist is interested in. But if you become intrigued with the perception of creation that you will get on that level, you may spend thousands of lifetimes involved in the countless and complicated scientific details of planets, forces, arrangements, energies, and forms. At least, if you are there by natural means and without the use of drugs, you will be there with your intellect and you can make sense of what you see. Swami Premvarni made it clear that he considered it harmful for one to have an experience beyond his intellect's capacity to interpret. He believed it wrong for experienced people to induce others to have experiences which they then need to interpret for them.

The physical and astral planes, he said, were the gross planes, and our preoccupation with the phenomena of either of these planes must ultimately be defined as gross desire.

So we arrived at the question of renunciation and *moksha*. In a series of questions I tried to ask whether with the right combination of renunciation of the this-worldly and devotion to the other-worldly, one could travel from wherever one is to the point of absolute truth in one lifetime. It was the same question that was always with me: whether one could—or should if one could—jump from here to there without doing the steps in between.

"The fact that we have this body means that we have gross desire. Gross desire produces the body, and if we eliminate all gross desire during this physical lifetime, this body will not stay. Within twenty days it can disappear. If your gross desire is completely satisfied or overcome, then you will lose this body within twenty days. The energy will leave that holds this body, and within twenty days the physical matter will disperse. Your body will evaporate and disappear."

I had never seen anything like that happen. I could not say that it never happens, but I could guess that it does not happen very often. In any case, if it ever did happen, it would be a spectacular demonstration of *moksha*. I asked him about the hundreds of robed sanyasis who walked along the roads and the riverbanks in Hardwar and Rishikesh and the literal millions of pilgrims who came to the *ghats* and the temples. I wondered whether these people were aiming for *moksha* with their renunciation and worship, and particularly whether they believed they could expect to achieve it by their methods within their present lifetimes.

"This is not propaganda," he answered. "This is not a matter for propaganda."

I had to dwell on that for a moment, but when I believed I understood his answer I supposed he meant that what these people practice is not the result of any advertising campaign. Unlike the many instances of commercialized spirituality in the West, there were no posters here, no high-powered inducements to join up with a particular ashram or guru, no promises of serenity, success, or salvation. These millions of people, he was saying, simply believed in a higher existence, a higher state of being, and they were reaching for it—in their variety of ways—as best they knew how. Yet Swami Sivanandapuri had talked about the competing loudspeakers at the *ghats* and "exploiting the people in the name of religion." Very likely this was a recent thing, influenced in part by these people's ideas of Western ways and doing things.

"But can it be achieved in one lifetime?"

"It takes many, many lifetimes."

Swami Premvarni Balyogi had to stand up then, because the discussion was over and we were all going outside to take some photographs. It was a pleasure to see him stand up. I had almost suspected he would be bowlegged from sitting so long as he did. At least he should have hobbled painfully for a few steps, as I would have done, until the blood began to circulate. He simply rose to his feet, keeping his hands gently folded in front of him, and moved out through the door.

That night in my room I spent a few minutes trying to stand up as Swami Premvarni Balyogi had stood up. I could do it, after a fashion, but my ankles thumped against the floor when I unlocked my feet from the lotus posture without using my hands, and when I stood up with my hands folded it made my elbows stick out.

"Well, I guess it's no big deal," I said to Hridaya. "I guess I could do it with enough practice. I've never really tried it before. One thing I've been thinking, though. Most of the popular athletics and gymnastics in the West can't hold a candle to yoga in terms of physical beauty and physical development. In less than six months of watching yogis in India I've seen as much physical strength, grace, precision, and control as I've seen in all the rest of my life. And, as Swami Kaivalyananda says, the physical part is hardly even the beginning of what yoga is all about."

twenty one

Hridaya and I pulled up to the front of Kanpur's New Valerios Hotel in a bicycle rickshaw. Mr. Dudeja and his friend Mr. Shukla were both standing out in front. Hridaya would be going home from here, and I would be going to the Dudeja residence for at least a day or two. But Mr. Dudeja had one of the hotel employees take us to a room so that we could wash up and change clothes. We were dusty and sweaty from the long train ride and we had dirt in our hair and mouths. Bipan came to the room with cold drinks and ice in tall glasses and turned on the air conditioner. It was like being back in the big city.

I stayed four days in Kanpur enjoying the Dudejas' air-conditioned guest room, delicious meals in their home and their new restaurant, and other comforts of the material world. They wanted to hear about all the swamis I had talked with and all the sadhus in their caves in the hills and their little shacks along the river. They were not so much interested in what all these people had said to me as in what I had thought of them.

Hridaya came to the house one morning to help me with my accounts. He was the one who had handled all the rupees during our expedition, pointing out that many prices, fees, and tips would be way out of reason if the money came from my hands. I had tried to keep a daily record of expenditures, but the figures for our last two busy days of travel were in his head, not in my book. Hridaya balanced my books and identified all the receipts that were labeled in Hindi. "We have spent so many days together in Hardwar and Rishikesh," he said. "Now let us spend one full day together in my Kanpur." He wanted to show me around his city and have me meet all the friends and acquaintances whom he had already told me about and promised to introduce me to. His friends and neighbors had worried about him while he was gone because he had left too suddenly to tell anyone where he was going. One day someone had called the office where he worked, and finally the word had gotten around to all his friends that he was off on a venture with some American seeker. Now everyone he knew wanted to have a look at me.

"But you have never yet met a saint," said one of Hridaya's neighbors, as we sat in his livingroom drinking tea. "The next time you come to India, I shall take you myself in search of a saint." He looked at Hridaya. "Of course Hridaya will be along also."

"Thank you," I responded.

"No, no. It is not a thing to be thanked. We shall find a true saint. And having seen him, there is also nothing to be said. Because anything said is inadequate. We cannot say, 'Oh, I have seen a saint today.' And suppose there is a saint among ten people taking tea in this room, we shall know it. He will not say, 'For your information, I happen to be a saint.' He will not even say, 'I am a swami, I am a yogi, I have renounced all these things to which you are attached.' He may wear a necktie and take tea and biscuits. But if he is a saint, we shall feel it in our hearts."

Hridaya knew a beautiful family within walking distance from his apartment. They were two brothers and a sister, all college age, who were bright and energetic and had warm and cheerful parents. Hridaya and I spent a few hours with them in the evening. We talked, laughed, sang songs, and played records, and the father told a couple of swami stories of his own.

"My father," he began, "the grandfather of these three friends here, had a colleague who was very close to him over a number of years. They were both practical men, good men,

I suppose—diligent, knowing their business, doing their work. Well, as circumstances developed they went their separate ways, for some reason or other, to pursue their own business. My father heard from time to time that his former colleague was doing fine, busy and sufficiently successful. Then he heard no more news, but he gave it no care, thinking only how busy everyone was getting. One day, in his travels, my father stopped in Meerut, and in Meerut he saw a holy man on a street corner. It was not the crowd that attracted my father. Such sights are commonplace here in India. It was something about the old sadhu's voice that intrigued him. But just as my father joined the crowd, the sadhu turned and walked away. Some of the people followed after and my father also followed, because by that voice, and that familiar step, my father knew that under those sadhu's robes and that long hair and beard was his former colleague. Was he happy to see him? There was no question of happy. He could not believe what he knew to be true! This was like one of those dreams where your friends turn into other characters and yet you know they are still the same friends. So he had to see him, to talk to him. Father was running to catch up, and the old sadhu was hurrying along in his robes with his faithful followers close behind. They dashed into a crowded restaurant and sat down at some tables. Father rushed in behind them, puffing for breath, and the moment he was inside he clearly saw the face of his friend in business. In the peak of his surprise he loudly called his real name saying, 'What are you doing dressed up like a *sanyasi*?'

"His friend was horrified and nearly lost his holy bearing. 'Shut up!' he shouted. But when he regained his composure he said, 'Come, sit here beside me. Do you not see that I have renounced all the things of the world?' So my father sat down at the table beside him, and his former colleague whispered that he should not use his name or speak of past associations. My father learned all about his friend's new situation. Such a beautiful place he had for his own use with gardens and fountains and people to serve him. And he had donations for his livelihood. All this had come to pass in a relatively short time as though the old colleague had a special calling for this particular role.

"So my father said, 'Then I should not let it be known that we were once in business together, isn't it?' And his old friend said, 'Yes, you should forget how you have known me.' My father asked, 'Is it that you are hiding your past from these people?' And he answered, 'No, you see, I myself have actually forgotten it. I have renounced everything.' And it was true. He had become a sanyasi and he had renounced everything from his past. And he was having much, much more as a renunciate than he had ever had as a successful businessman."

One of the sons took some bottles and ice cubes from the refrigerator on the other side of the living room and poured out soft drinks into cocktail glasses. "So you could actually do this yourself," the father said to me. "Now, I am telling you, and this is my point, you could grow your hair and your beard, put on some nice robes fitting for a swami—not the old rags and ashes, because then you don't get much—and you could simply walk about and tell some stories and you could have fame and fortune in a few years' time. Definitely you could do it!"

His other story was about the saint and the lioness, and though I had never heard the story, it sounded familiar. It sounded like one of those tales that probably gets repeated thousands of times all over India. "There was an old sage, an old saint, way in the south someplace—I can't recall now just what place it was, but anyway, it makes no matter—and he used to sit by a frequented path . . ." He interrupted himself and turned to his wife. "Where was that place? It was somewhere in the south."

"What place?"

"This is what I am just asking. Where was that old saint who had a lioness for a wife?" He turned to me again. "Well, now, I have just told the story—he had a lioness for a wife. Anyway, the place makes no matter. He was for a long time just an ordinary saint with an ordinary saint's wife for a wife. And then one day, they say, he had a lioness for a wife, which made him peculiar even among saints. A curiosity, you see. The fact was, or was supposed to be, that she was one and the same woman, sometimes in human form and sometimes in lioness form. Every day he sat beside this frequented path with his wife, always in lioness form, at his feet, and he was showered with rupees and gifts of all descriptions. Then he would confer blessing upon the people. The curiosity was kept alive, you see, by the stories some told that on certain occasions, only in the night time, the wife was with him in her human form.

"Now just see how he was worshiped—and this is the point of the story—for sitting on that path with a lioness at his feet. There were those who worshiped him as a true renunciate for giving up his truly beloved while at the same time going on providing for and looking after her. There were those who worshiped him as the highest form of lover for proving that he cared for the soul and presence of his wife and not her physical form. And there were those who worshiped him as a man of power for being able to transform a woman into a lioness. Then, of course, there were those who worshiped and gave their gifts to the lioness because she had renounced her beauty and her vanity to lie humbly at her husband's feet as a dumb animal, and still others who gave her gifts because they feared she might be truly a wild beast. And now suppose the old saint was a mere charlatan with a pet lion? Those who believed this appeased him with their gifts, thinking him a dangerous man. For either he had tamed a dangerous animal or he was having a wild beast as a pet. And then there remained the question—if this creature was not his wife, what had he done with his wife?"

Seeing that my glass was empty, he interrupted himself

again. "Just hold out your empty glass and you will soon find it full again." I held out my glass and the son refilled it out of another bottle from the refrigerator.

The father continued: "But all those reasons I have suggested accounted for only half of the people in that place who either worshiped or respected the saint and the lioness or appeased them with their gifts. Half of the people worshiped them having no other reason than the fact that everyone else was doing it. You see? One who is worshiped is worshiped because he is worshiped."

When I left Kanpur this time I had no idea when I would be back—or if. In my two trips to India, I had been in and out of Kanpur five times and altogether had spent several weeks in this city. Now that I was beginning to get so familiar with this place, and getting to have so many friends here, I could not believe I would never return. "I'll be back," I told everyone.

Hridaya arranged to take another two or three days off from work, having already been absent for so many weeks, in order to accompany me on the train to New Delhi. He would not see me off at the airport, as I planned to stay in New Delhi for about a week, but he would see that I got safely to New Delhi and to my hotel and that I got my return-trip reservation without difficulty. I could have done all those things alone, but it was much easier with Hridaya's help and certainly more pleasant. I actually enjoy traveling alone, but I enjoy traveling with someone else even ten times more.

Hridaya and the Dudejas and I drove in two cars from their house to the station. The entire Dudeja family went to the railroad platform to say goodbye to me. They stood on the platform until we were on the train, and we waved to them through the window. "I'll be back," I told them.

In New Delhi, Hridaya and I parted. We walked around for a while, went slowly through a busy marketplace, and had a late lunch together. There was nothing more for Hridaya to do here, so he thought he might as well go to the train station and home to Kanpur. He said goodbye to me in my room.

"Wait a minute," I said, "I'll walk out to the circle with you." But when we were on the street I suggested that we have a last cup or glass of something together. We had espresso in a nearby coffee shop. "Maybe I'll never see you again," I said as we shook hands on the street.

"I don't know," he replied, with his usual serious sincerity and his staccato speech. "I can't say."

"Well, I'll be back."

"All right. I shall see you then."

It felt different here without Hridaya with me, and I realized that fact even before he disappeared out of sight as I was watching him walk away.

I was standing at the very center of New Delhi, on Connaught Circle, innermost of the city's concentric, circular streets. My new hotel room was in York Hotel on K Block, Connaught Circus. Since I had just spent many weeks in such a different part of India, I thought it reasonable, now that I was here and might never be back, to spend my last days in this country in the heart of the capital city. My interest was simply to walk around and look at all the people. "You can't get lost in New Delhi," Hridaya had explained. "Since the streets are circular, you will definitely arrive where you intend to go, even if you start out in the wrong direction."

On my way back to the York Hotel I got an immediate introduction to what life would be like for me in the center of New Delhi. It had taken Hridaya and me only a few minutes to walk from my room to the center street, but I spent a much longer time getting back to the hotel. The many people who wanted to get money from me blocked my way and tried to hold me. If I had not given up, if I had tried to save my money, it would have taken me a painful half-hour at least to reach the front door of the hotel. I believed

in giving money to beggars because it was a statement of
attitude, a recognizing of my relationship to the total human
condition, and an act toward overcoming the temptation of
disassociation. Also, beggars usually really need it. Nevertheless, I knew that to give money to a selected few among
a swarm of beggars could be dangerous. Here there were ten
or more people of various ages and sizes, walking in front
of me, trying to hold onto my arms and legs, tugging at my
clothing, cooperating to overcome me and yet competing for
what I had. It would be too great a struggle in this case to
try to avoid giving them anything. I decided what I believed
was the best strategy. I had to let them get it all, and I had
to let them get it by themselves so they would know when
there was no more. I stopped trying to move along the sidewalk, and I let them know that they were welcome to reach
into my pockets and get what they could find. I was carrying
a large amount of money in small bills; I assumed or hoped
that it got fairly evenly distributed.

I didn't give away that much money again for the rest of
my days in New Delhi simply because I did not carry that
much money again. But it was never possible for me to walk
on the street as I had planned to without great physical effort
and emotional discomfort. Each time I went out of my hotel
room I carried a dollar or two worth of rupees in small coins
and single rupee notes, and I always gave it all away, but the
greatest difficulty came when it was all gone and people
would not believe I was not carrying money. If I tried to
hold off a particularly aggressive beggar, he or she would cry
out in pretended pain. But I kept going out. Perhaps I
thought I could somehow overcome this particular problem
with the beggars or break through the aloof and impersonal
disposition of Indians toward foreigners in this city or maybe
even develop a friendship with someone. I had never before
in my life been any place where this turned out to be so
impossible. After four days of walking the streets of the hub
of New Delhi, I checked out of the York Hotel and went
back to the Lodhi. It was not to escape anything, it was be-

cause I felt more alone than I had ever felt before. P. Suresh was at the Woodlands Restaurant in the Lodhi Hotel, and it would be good to see him.

I had two days and two nights left before departure for New York's Kennedy Airport, and I spent a lot of that time with P. Suresh. He stayed with me most of the time when he was not working, and sometimes when he was working I sat in the Woodlands. P. Suresh and I agreed that my experience with the beggars had been far beyond the normal fare for foreigners. For one thing, foreigners almost never walk alone where I walked alone. They travel in groups or at least in pairs. Another point was that most foreigners are in town for souvenirs and artifacts. They have little interest or concern for the people on the streets, and they maintain an emotional distance which makes them less approachable. I was only slightly interested in India's sights and Indian merchandise, and I was really here to be with people. I had been a good target.

I was willing to talk openly about the beggars and about other thoughts and impressions because I did not feel that such talk was either condescending or degrading. Nor did I feel that I was discussing other people's affairs. A combination of international economic influences was pushing a gigantic mass of the people of India under the poverty line, below the life-and-death borderline. That was *my* problem, and I was inclined to think about it. I knew from history that India was not solely to blame for her contemporary situation. Anyway, blame was not the point. The point was that all of us now had to accept responsibility for all of us—because all of us *are* responsible, because all of us are part of the total cause and effect.

On my last day in New Delhi, I spent the entire afternoon going over my thoughts. The one thing I had wanted to do during this last week in India, besides being with people, was to go over my mental storage of events and conversations of the past weeks and begin to make some notes. I had not done that either. Although I had used my recorder on a few occasions, I had never tried to take notes while listening to people. Taking notes would have detracted from my effort to listen completely, to be fully and purely attentive. And in all the days in Hardwar and Rishikesh there had never been time enough between conversations and observations to try to write anything down. Even if there had been time, I would not have wanted to obstruct the flow of input by beginning to make summations and digests then. I had planned to do that in New Delhi just before leaving India. This last afternoon at the Lodhi Hotel was my final chance to do it. I did not write anything down, but I did go over my thoughts. I sat at the desk, I paced the floor, I lay on my back on the bed and watched the ceiling fan spin, I walked back and forth on the balcony outside my door, and I talked to myself:

The hills are full of sadhus and sanyasis, and even saints and sages, without most of us knowing how few or how many (though as Hridaya's friend had said, a true saint could be sitting in someone's living room somewhere having tea and biscuits). There probably really are great sages and saints secluded and sequestered in high and almost inaccessible peaks of the Himalayas. In every city, town, and village there are swamis to fit every meaning of the word.

All the sadhus, sanyasis, swamis, seers, saints, and sages are indeed living in the world and are indeed part of the world. They have their own work and their own will like all other humans, and as with all other humans, their thoughts and acts become part of the condition of the world. Swami Rama had said, "The rivers would not go on flowing, nor the moon go on circling but for those great ones whose powerful will on earth carries out the plans of the Masters of the universe! All the functions of the worlds are delegated and carried out in a practical manner!"

If this is true, then the highest human beings existing on this planet are themselves concerned with the workings of the world—are themselves focused upon what some have chosen to call illusion. We are all responsible for the circumstances in which we exist, and they are not illusion. Our spiritual work is in our world. Our spiritual work is with disease and hunger, war and peace. Our spiritual work is to cut away the ignorance that blocks the light in the world—the ignorance of living in monologue rather than in dialogue, the ignorance of separatism, of personal and national separatism. Our spiritual work is to discover one-world consciousness.

In all the outpouring of words from the spiritual teachers and swamis of the contemporary world, what is important now is talk about the condition of humanity and the earth, talk about the earth as a being, talk about the real responsibility of each so-called individual for the total human condition.

It may be possible to believe that from the point of view of the Absolute the condition of the world is unreal. But from the point of view of the Absolute, the spiritual path itself is equally unreal. To the extent that we can speak of the spiritual path we can speak of the human condition and of human evolution—of the movement of humanity along the spiritual path from the unreal to the real. The spiritual path leads right through this earthly realm, and those of us who find answers here together, in human form together, can but move on together—and to move on beyond this point will require cooperative group endeavor on an international level.

I walked back in from the balcony and sat in the chair at my desk, I turned my mind to some immediate practicalities such as planning my packing so that I could do it all quickly and in an organized manner when the time came. I would need to keep separate what I was to carry on the plane. I looked over my ticket, my immunization record, my rupee supply and my traveler's checks. Among my papers I found a newspaper clipping the Mahant had given me before I left Rishikesh. On my last day there I had gone with Uma to the guesthouse at Bharat Mandir to say goodbye to Mahantji. He had offered me his thoughts about all the sadhus and sanyasis who lived in the area and walked the streets and ate in the mess halls which he had established; and he had told about times when the human atmosphere was more tranquil and human vibrations more nearly pure and many true saints and rishis would move openly among the population. Before I left he had showed me, with some amusement, an item in the newspaper which he told Uma to cut out for me so that I could take it along. Now as I was going through my papers, the clipping fell from between the pages of a small notebook. The headline read: " 'Mantras' Cause Fire." The article reported that a Brahmin had on that day "unfolded mysterious power of mantras to produce a fire without any combustible aids." He had started a wood fire, the article said, by reciting navarnava mantra, and he had performed his demonstration in the presence of a "distinguished gathering." The article called it a "recital," however, rather than a demonstration. The last paragraph read: "The recital was preceded by three hours of singing of hymns in praise of the 'astra bhuga' deity." It is an interesting thing, I thought to myself, looking again at the article and thinking about Swami Rama, Rolling Thunder, and my experiences at the Menninger Foundation, how unwilling most American scientists are to consider ritual and faith as important variables in cause-and-effect relationships. There had apparently been scientists present at the Brahmin's "recital," however, because the article mentioned that thermocouples had been used to measure temperature variations and that there had been no indications of any increases in temperature until the wood actually caught fire. It was not difficult for me to suppose that the scientists present very likely participated in the "singing of the hymns" and the "praise of the deity" as a valid part of the event. Eastern scientists are more often able to do these things without embarrassment. Some Westerners might like to suggest that they are not true scientists, but that would be an erroneous hope. The fact remains that while Eastern scientists may be aware of higher truths beyond and in addition to the limits of biology, physics, and chemistry, they are equally informed in the facts of the physical sciences.

Both times I read that newspaper clipping I was reminded of an anecdote Swami Rama told in Topeka:

There was an aspirant with an unquenchable, burning desire for the *darsan* of a particular wise and powerful saint. In his youth he traveled a great distance to see the saint, but as he was not received, he returned to his village and spent thirty years of his life preparing to try again. For thirty years he worked perpetually and perseveringly to develop his faith and his concentration and he repeated his mantra so many times and developed such powerful concentration that he found he could produce fire from his mouth at will. Ecstatic with joy he journeyed to find the saint, to implore him to be his spiritual teacher and lead him to knowledge. Because the saint had been in the man's thoughts for thirty years, the saint gave the man audience.

The moment the man saw the saint, he prostrated himself at his feet. He could not help but say, "For thirty years I have dreamed of seeing you. Thirty years I have spent in constant work and devotion!"

The saint said, "So?"

"I have developed intense faith," the man declared, "and intense powers of concentration."

Again the saint said, "So?"

"I can produce fire from my mouth."

"Go and begin doing something useful," the saint said calmly. "When we are all having matches, why have you wasted your time?"

Again I left the business of planning and packing and returned to my thoughts and again I began to pace about and verbalize to myself:

"Work on yourself," people are saying. Anyone can work on oneself. In fact one cannot but work on oneself—that is

all that one can do. The saints and the swamis and the tonga drivers are all working on themselves. Whether a man meditates, produces fire from his mouth, or helps to clean the streets of Rishikesh, he is working on himself.

"Work on yourself" has been more often repeated than understood. More often than not, it has been used in a sense directly opposed to its true meaning. It has been used as a spiritual justification for avoiding what Buddha called right action. It has been used as an excuse to withdraw into preoccupation with the personal self. It has been used by people who feel self-conscious about their own sense of compassion.

"All you can do is work on yourself," people have been repeating, as if to say, "Every man for himself." That's not what it means. "All you can do is work on yourself" means "All that you do, you do unto the Self." It means "To be selfless, to work selflessly, is to discover the true Self." It means "Your work is to be selfless and to do selflessly because to work selflessly is to discover the Self."

There may be saints in those hills, but the true saints known to the current population are Mahatma Gandhi of India and Martin Luther King of the United States. They were the true spiritual teachers of contemporary history. They worked on "themselves" in the total sense. They may not have said much about exercises and asanas, they may not have said much about mantras, mentations, and meditations—though they understood and used those tools as they were needed. What they talked about and lived about went far beyond those limits. They taught selflessness. They taught communication and social work. Harmony. They taught the spiritual business of breaking down the obstacles of separation—of person, caste, race, and nation. So they were living examples of man's spiritual business on this planet, living examples of the meaning of the words "work on yourself."

I was still walking back and forth on the carpet in my room. It occurred to me that I could go sit in the Woodlands. I looked at the travel clock on the desk. No, it was just the wrong time. Seven-thirty. This was the height of the suppertime rush hour. I would eat later, and then wait in the restaurant until P. Suresh got off work. I would not leave the hotel for the airport until one A.M., and I could pack in thirty minutes. So I had a lot of time. Obviously I was not going to be making any notes today. I could sit down and practice producing fire from my mouth. Or I could go buy a magazine and read it. I chose the magazine.

An American newsmagazine might help prepare me for reentry into New York City. Besides, I should know what's going on in the world. I walked through the lobby and past the various souvenir shops to the book stall and newsstand and paid the lady seven and a half rupees for the June 3 issue of *Newsweek* magazine. I flipped through the pages as I went back through the lobby, glancing up occasionally to see where I was going. I would read the cover story later, I decided, maybe on the airplane. At least not now. I did not want to be pacing the floor again at least until after supper. On the cover of this weeks *Newsweek* was the serious face of Prime Minister Indira Gandhi, and the banner read: *India Goes Nuclear.*

When P. Suresh got off work that night he went to my room with me and watched me pack my things in my two suitcases and my carry-on bag. "Now, I'll leave these things right here by the door." I said. "But let's not just sit in here until the final hour. When the time comes, I can easily rush up here and grab my bags."

He looked at me in surprise. "Not you!" he exclaimed. "The bellman. Just you give word, and the bellman comes."

P. Suresh waited with me until I left for the airport. I told him about Hardwar and Rishikesh and about the people we had met. We sat in lawn chairs out on the grass and a room-service waiter brought us ice cream and coffee floats. It was a pleasant evening. The grass had just been watered and there was a mild breeze, so the air was fragrant and cool. And it was quiet except for the birds—there were always the birds.

I supposed all my swami friends were sleeping now—Swami Kaivalyananda in Room 12 at the Sivananda Ashram, Swami Premvarni in his own small ashram on his hill, the outspoken swami and the others at the Sanyas Ashram in Hardwar, and Swami Sivanandapuri at the institute, or in some room somewhere, hopefully. I had no idea when I would see them again, but their faces and voices would stay vivid in my memory for a long, long time. The lives of these swamis were different from the lives of all the people I would be seeing again in New York and San Francisco. Aside from their various austerities, however, and behind their cultural habits and their orange robes and their darker faces, they were not really different from any of the rest of us. I could believe that many of my American friends were now on their way to becoming more like them. I was thankful for the thousands of words I had gotten from Swami Kaivalyananda—they were just the words that my people needed to hear. They had not been new ideas for me and would not be new to many of my friends. But he had put them eloquently enough and clearly enough that everyone I knew could enjoy them and benefit from them. What Swami Premvarni said about *grounding* had made a strong impression on me. Those words were important for many of my peers who had now become so intrigued with psychic and psychedelic activities and phenomena—important to the point of being urgent. Swami Sivanandapuri I had simply liked—he was that kind of a swami, the kind you like—and what made him seem to me such a valuable swami was not so much what he said as what he did. I felt sure he would continue to roam about through the holy cities along the Ganges and meet Westerners. And only to meet them would be enough—to meet them, to rouse their interest, and to take them to people like Tat Walla Baba. Tat Walla Baba. Somehow I could not picture him lying asleep in his cave. Maybe he was sitting in meditation or talking to some of the babas on the mountain. But it was past midnight, and most likely he would be asleep now. Then he could awaken about the time my plane took off to bathe in his quiet mountain stream and do his early morning *puja*.

There was a time, many years ago, when people like Tat Walla Baba in their mountain forests and caves could live undisturbed and unaffected by the rest of the world. As renunciates they were not only free from such things as anxiety, pride, greed, and hate, but safe from those things in others and from the destruction they created. Now there is no such safety on the planet. Now the safety of the earth is in question. Now the question is whether energy and nature can endure the machinations of contemporary humans, whether the earth can continue to support life, whether the earth itself can survive. The question now is whether we wish to maintain this earth as one of the arenas of spiritual activity and spiritual evolution or to allow the earth to perish. It is possible that the spiritual path will not move through this earthly realm much longer, that this entity will have to be discarded as a vehicle for spiritual evolution, that the earth will die. But if it is to be otherwise, it will have to be a unanimous decision and a collective endeavor—a joint effort of swamis, scientists, babas, and beggars. To me it seemed almost fortunate, almost a blessing, that survival will now require communication and cooperation across all the boundaries of cultures, customs, races, and nations. Eventually there will be no escape through riches or renunciation because neither riches nor renunciation will remain as options in the future.

There is no real ashram where people can withdraw from the cares of the world. There is no real temple where people can live in some sort of holy isolation. The only real ashram where people can live and work is the world itself. The earth is our temple, the temple where through work, humility, and devotion, we acquire the knowledge to live not in withdrawal and isolation but in harmony with all of life.

"Now you should give your key to the bellman," P. Suresh warned me at a quarter to one. "He will go straightaway for your luggage. And you should have him fetch the taxi just now."

Earlier I had felt I had nothing but time and nothing to do but wait. Now it seemed that my last hours in India had sped by too fast.

P. Suresh stood in the driveway as I stepped into the taxi. "It's been nice talking to you," I said. "I'll look you up when I come back."

The taxi ride to the airport took an hour, and all the red tape of money exchange, immunization and passport check, inspections, customs inspection, and checking baggage took another three. It was all the waiting in line that made everything take so long. As I sat on board our waiting 747 and peered out the little window into the darkness, trying to make out my last view of India, I complimented myself for having allowed plenty of time for details. Where did all these people come from? Where had all these Westerners been and what had they been doing? In my travels throughout India I had seen only a few Westerners. I supposed most of them had been in the large international tourist hotels and had stayed mostly inside. I remembered Swami Sivanandapuri saying, when I had first met him, that "the only thing that will save us is for Indians and Americans to become very good friends." It seemed to me that this important project had yet to begin. I hoped it would now begin on all the levels of relationship between America and India.

Now, in spite of all the "gurus" and "ashrams" and sitar music, it is a rare American, it seems, who really knows or perhaps even cares what is happening between India and America. Thousands of Americans now like Indian clothes and spices, thousands listen to Indian music, thousands repeat Sanskrit words and phrases. But I could not remember hearing any of these people talk about more meaningful relationships with India—with India's humanity.

"This is the age of group endeavor," it has been said. There may be too many who take it to mean "This is the age of group meditation." Perhaps what we should be saying is "this is the age of international endeavor and one-world con-

sciousness." In the age of group endeavor we should at last be able to begin our real sadhana, *our real spiritual business, and we should at last begin to perform our race-and-nation karma tasks. What we can do in the way of spiritual* sadhana *can go beyond the adopting of external forms, beyond the burning of incense and the repeating of Sanskrit phrases. What we can do in the way of spiritual* sadhana *is to attend to the principle of right relations, to see, for one thing, that our actions toward India are honest and just.*

I noticed that our plane was beginning to move and we were taxiing slowly toward the runway. External to the thoughts that went on in my head as I stared out at the buildings and runways was the constant monologue of the public address system inside the airplane. They had to talk about fastening seat belts and not smoking and to say that breakfast would soon be served, that passengers could later change seats if they wished to see a different movie from the one being shown in their sections, that headsets would be a dollar-fifty and we could buy them now from the stewardess coming through the aisle, and they had to repeat all this in several languages. We taxied for a long time before we finally turned, sped down the runway, and lifted into the air. I always marveled that these gigantic things could manage to get off the ground. Anyway, I thought, I'll be back.

I wanted to look down and see India one last time from the air. But it was too dark below and too light above. The dawn broke as we climbed into the air, and the ground faded out of sight immediately. From India to New York we would be chasing the sun. It would be a twenty-six-hour journey, with all the stops. Twenty-six hours from sunrise over New Delhi to sunset over Manhattan, and daylight all the way. Sunset in New York at a time when my body will be expecting sunrise. I could go to sleep at midnight in New York, pretending I was taking one of my afternoon naps at the Tourist Bungalow on the hill at Muni Ki Reti.

The real Light is omnipresent, and no one can travel to or away from the omnipresent Light. No one need withdraw or turn inward to the omnipresent Light. One has only to discover it, as the swamis say. It can be discovered everywhere. The possibility ahead is that we may discover the Light on the Earth—in every city and every nation and every corner of the world.

ABOUT THE AUTHOR

DOUG BOYD has spent his life seeking the common denominator between the "science" of the West and the "wisdom" of the East. He joined the Menninger Foundation in 1968 after ten years of work and study in Korea, and, under the direction of Dr. Elmer Green, became Swami Rama's assistant twenty-four hours a day. He subsequently traveled with the Greens to India, and then again, alone. In 1971, he met the American Indian medicine man Rolling Thunder, who became the subject of Boyd's first book, *Rolling Thunder*; since then, Doug Boyd has become deeply involved in American Indian religion and in the struggle for Indian rights.